Sue & Tai-chan

Konami Kanata

Contents

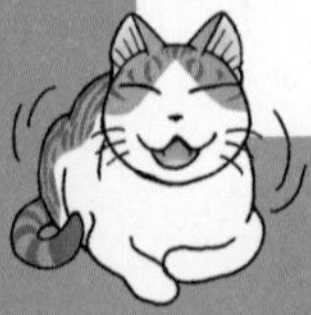

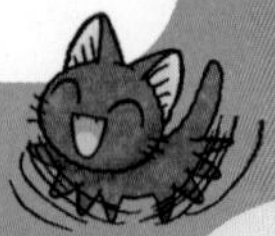

CHAPTER 34 Stairs Are That Simple?!

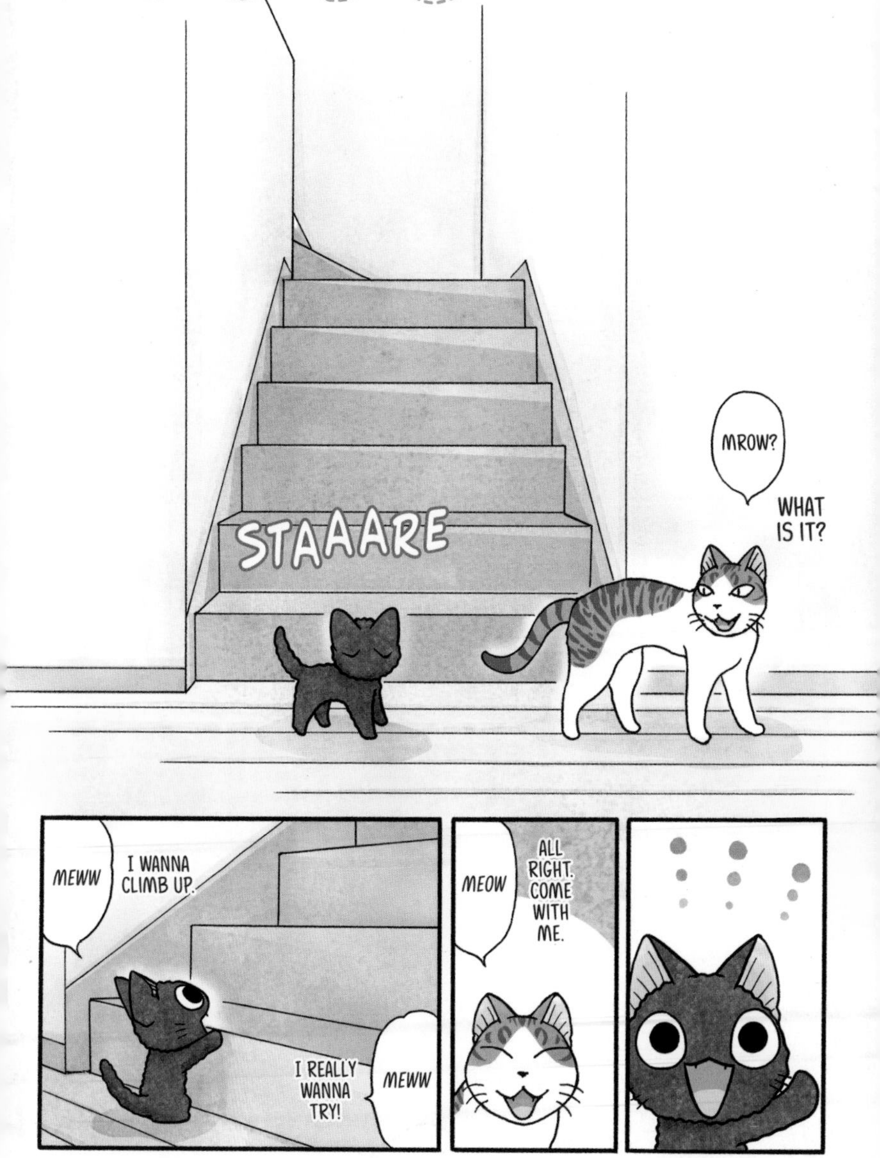
STAAARE
MROW?
WHAT IS IT?
MEWW
I WANNA CLIMB UP.
I REALLY WANNA TRY!
MEWW
MEOW
ALL RIGHT. COME WITH ME.

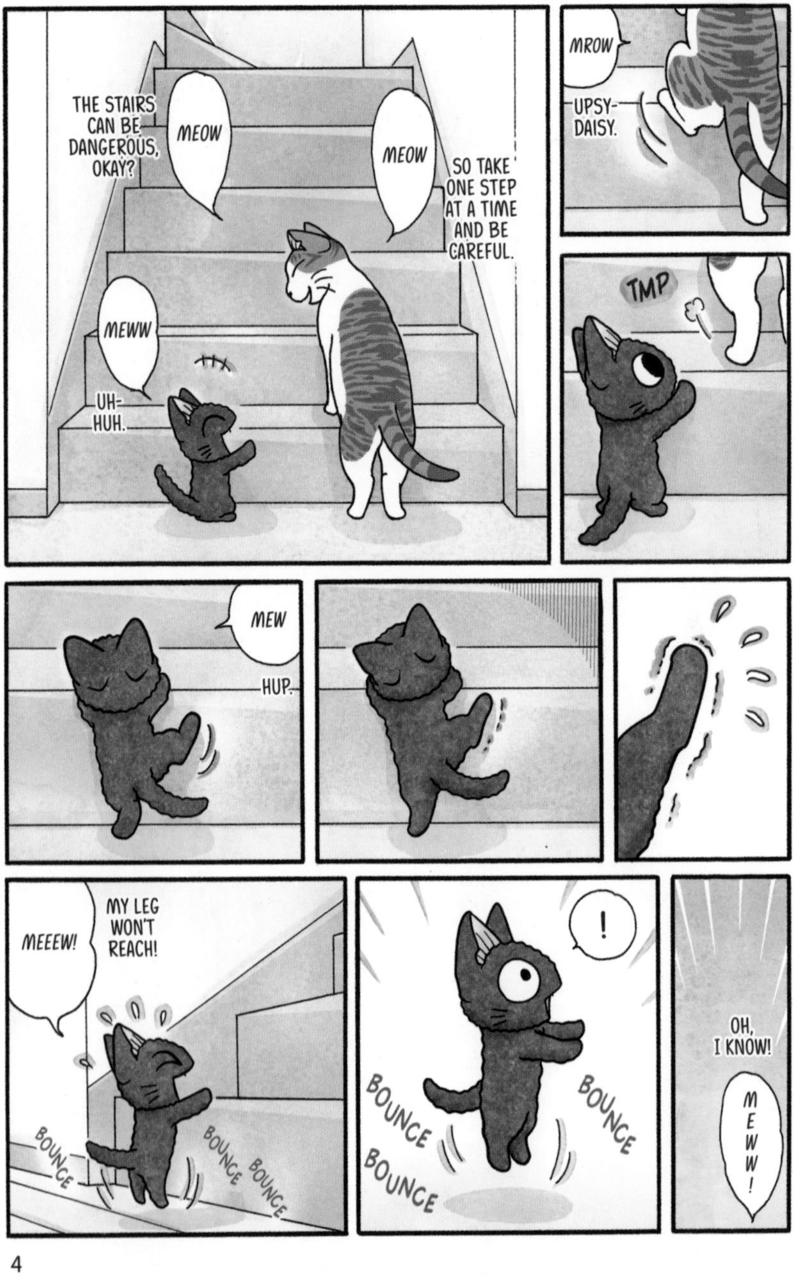
THE STAIRS CAN BE DANGEROUS, OKAY?
MEOW
MEOW
SO TAKE ONE STEP AT A TIME AND BE CAREFUL.
MEWW
UH-HUH.
MROW
UPSY-DAISY.
TMP
MEW
HUP.
MEEEW!
MY LEG WON'T REACH!
BOUNCE
BOUNCE
BOUNCE
!
BOUNCE
BOUNCE
BOUNCE
OH, I KNOW!
MEWW!

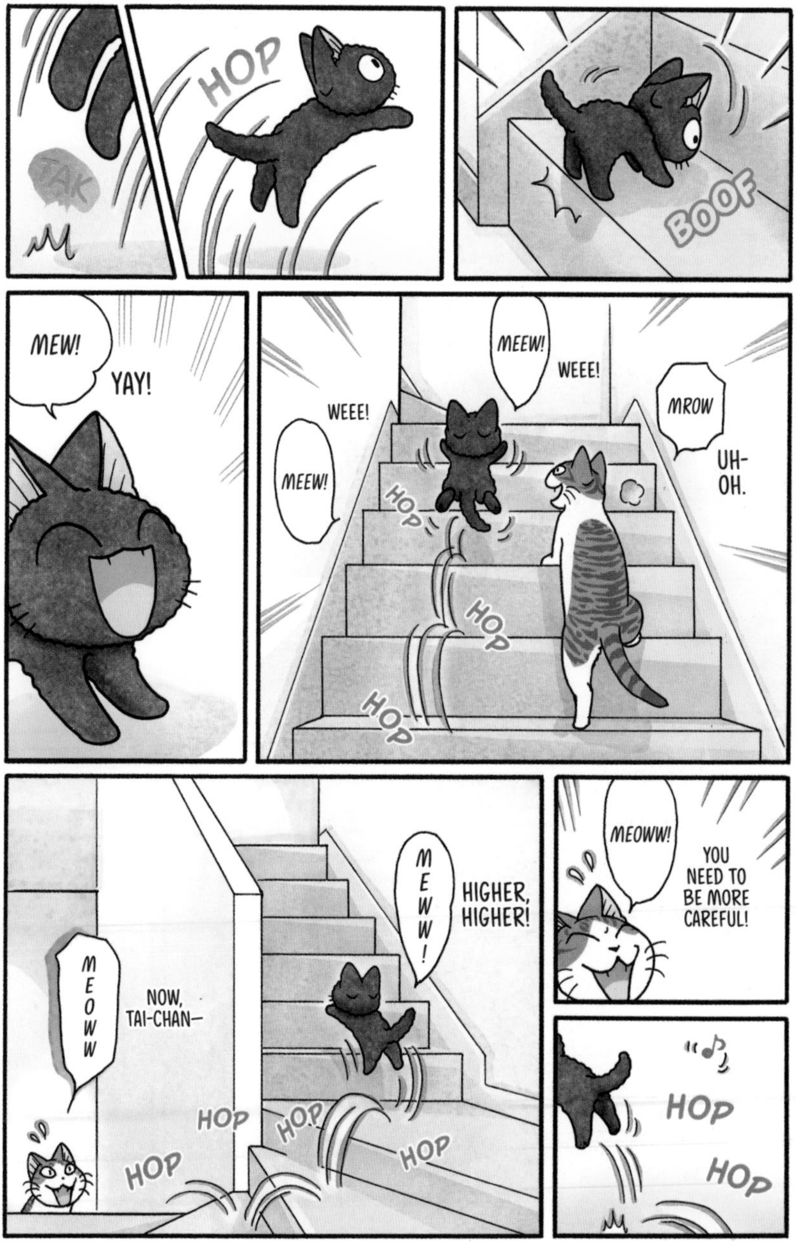
TAK
HOP
BOOF
MEW!
YAY!
WEEE!
MEEW!
MEEW!
WEEE!
HOP
HOP
HOP
MROW
UH-OH.
MEOWW
NOW, TAI-CHAN—
MEWW!
HIGHER, HIGHER!
HOP
HOP
HOP
HOP
MEOWW!
YOU NEED TO BE MORE CAREFUL!
HOP
HOP

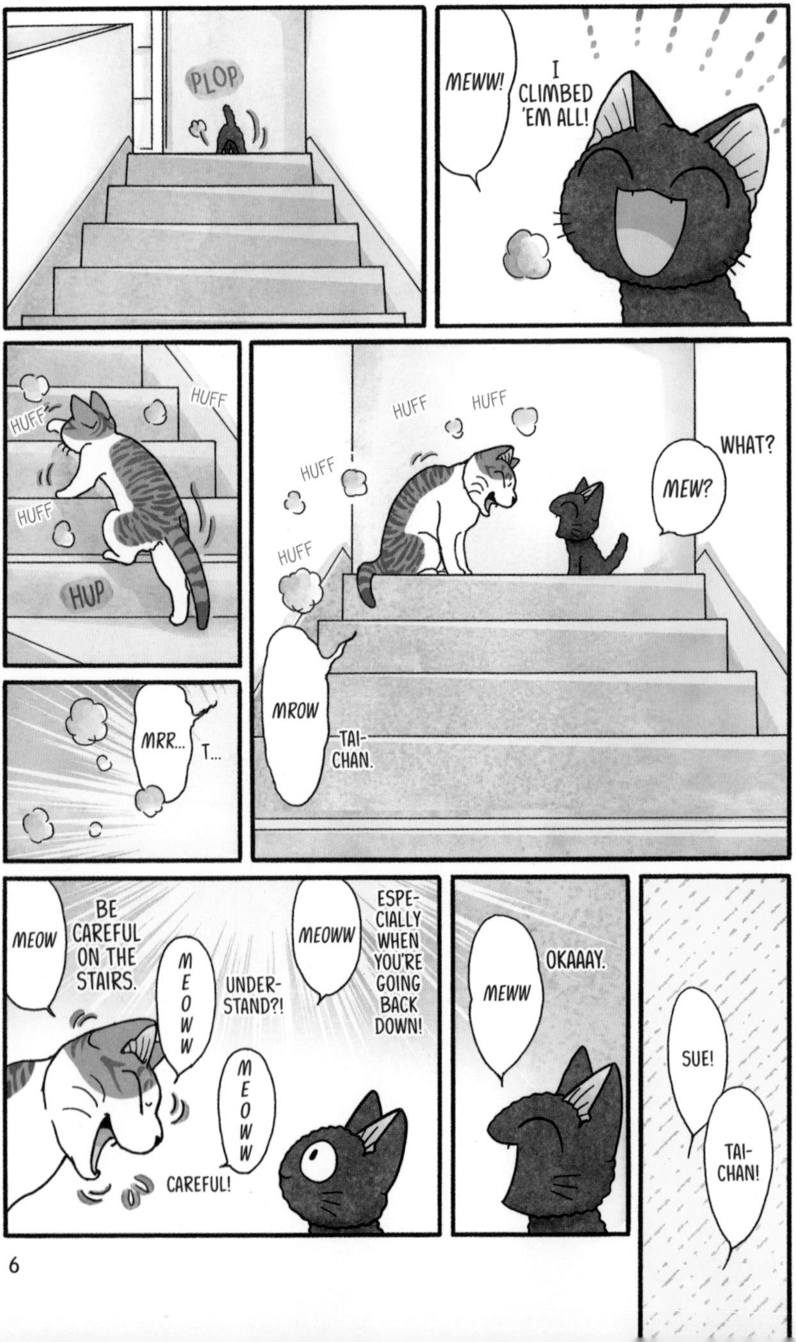

PLOP
MEWW!
I CLIMBED 'EM ALL!
HUFF
HUFF
HUFF
HUP
MRR...
T...
HUFF
HUFF
HUFF
HUFF
MEW?
WHAT?
MROW
TAI-CHAN.
MEOW
BE CAREFUL ON THE STAIRS.
MEOWW
UNDERSTAND?!
MEOWW
CAREFUL!
MEOWW
ESPECIALLY WHEN YOU'RE GOING BACK DOWN!
MEWW
OKAAAY.
SUE!
TAI-CHAN!

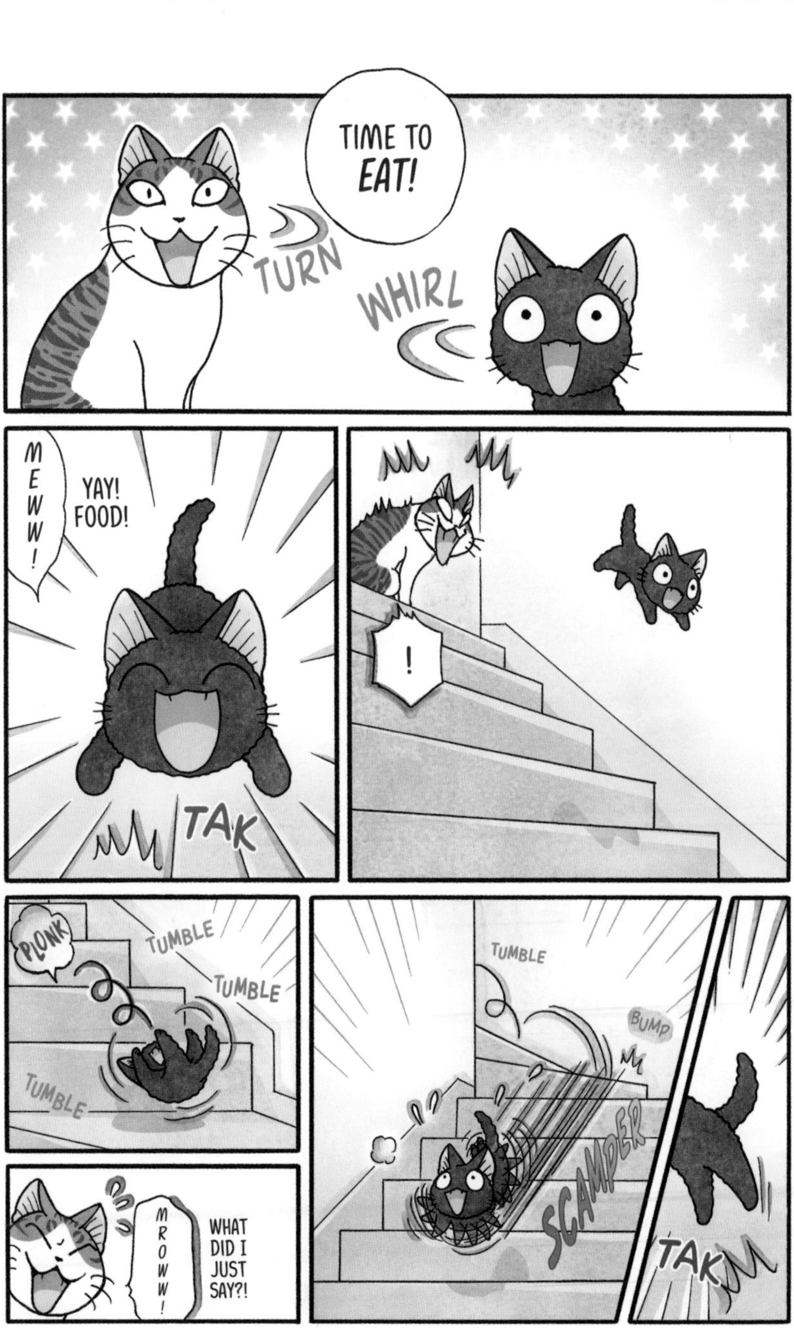
TIME TO EAT!
TURN
WHIRL
MEWWW!
YAY! FOOD!
TAK
!
PLONK
TUMBLE
TUMBLE
TUMBLE
WHAT DID I JUST SAY?!
MROWW!
TUMBLE
BUMP
SCAMPER
TAK

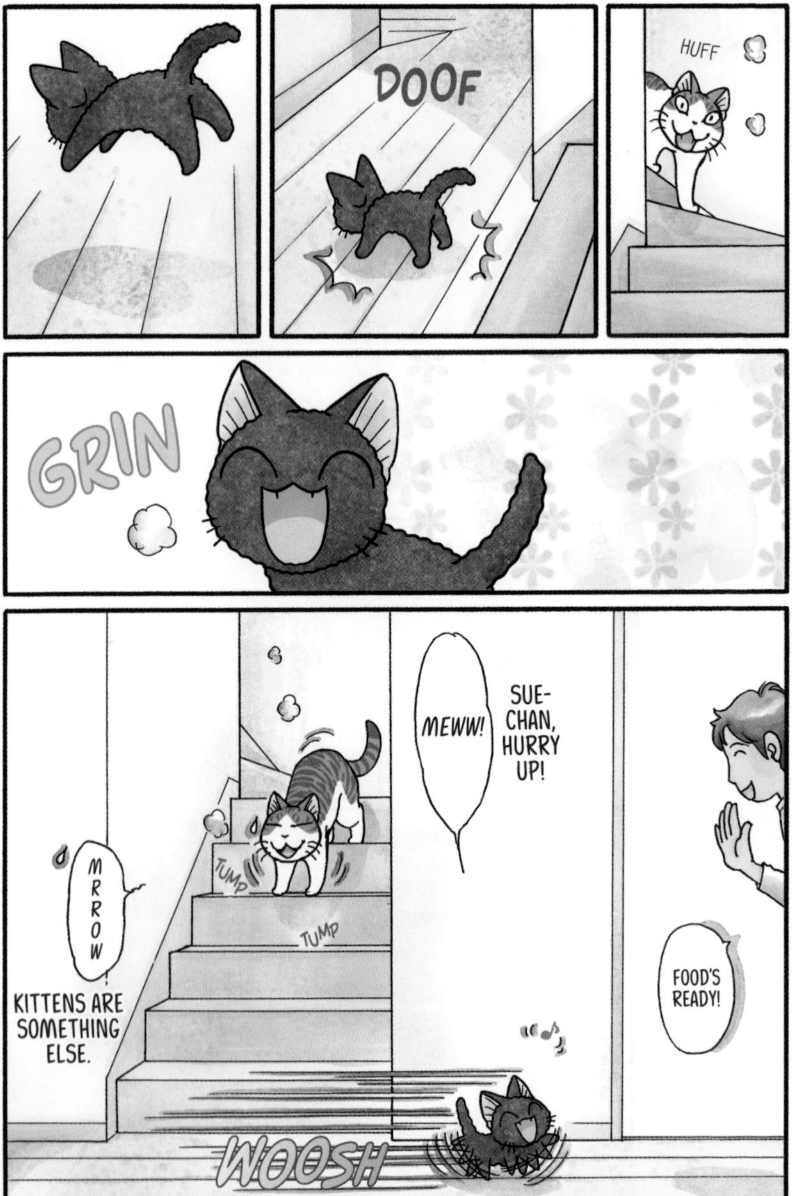
DOOF
HUFF
GRIN
MEWW!
SUE-CHAN, HURRY UP!
MRROW
TUMP
TUMP
KITTENS ARE SOMETHING ELSE.
FOOD'S READY!
WOOSH

CHAPTER 35 The Meow-sterious Bag

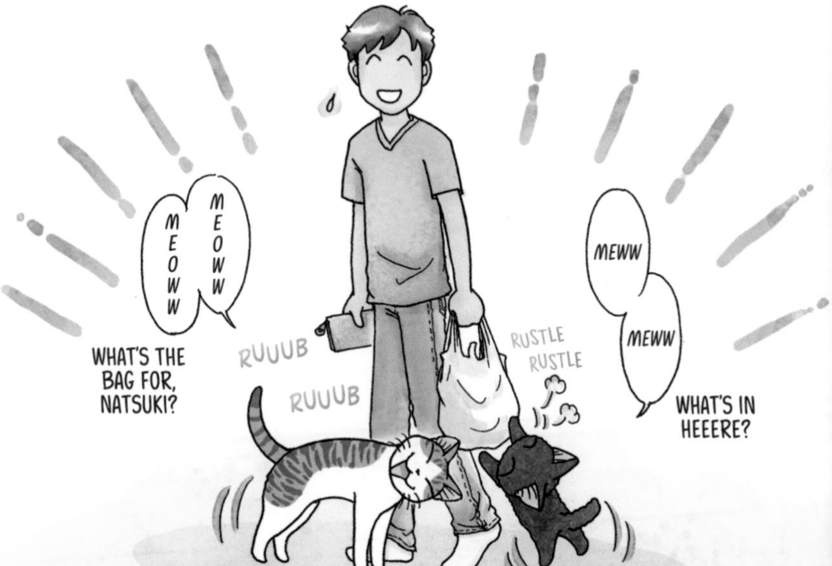
MEOWW
MEOWW
WHAT'S THE BAG FOR, NATSUKI?
RUUUB
RUUUB
RUSTLE RUSTLE
MEWW
MEWW
WHAT'S IN HEEERE?

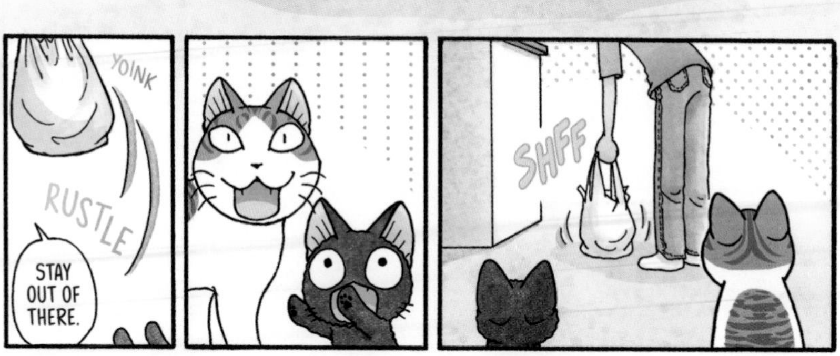
YOINK
RUSTLE
STAY OUT OF THERE.
SHFF

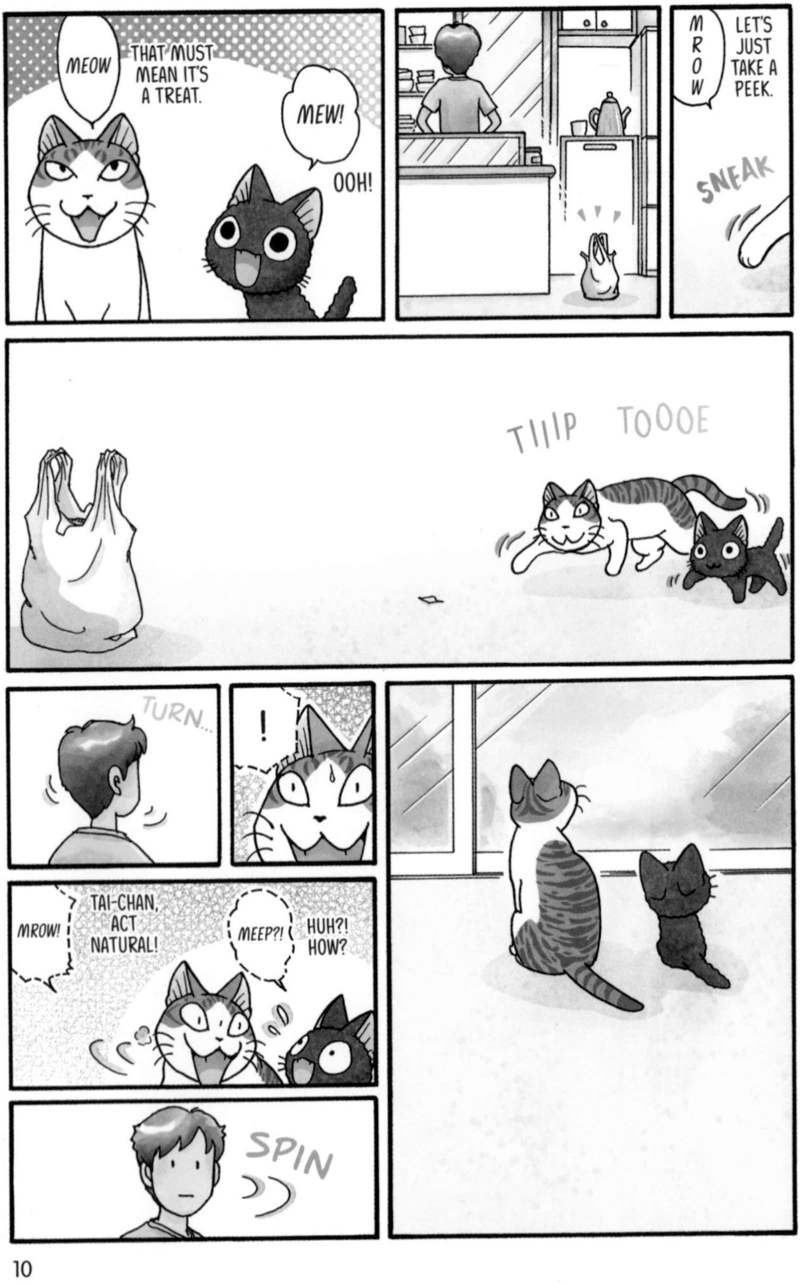
MEOW
THAT MUST MEAN IT'S A TREAT.
MEW!
OOH!
MROW
LET'S JUST TAKE A PEEK.
SNEAK
TIIIP TOOOE
TURN...
!
MROW!
TAI-CHAN, ACT NATURAL!
MEEP?!
HUH?! HOW?
SPIN

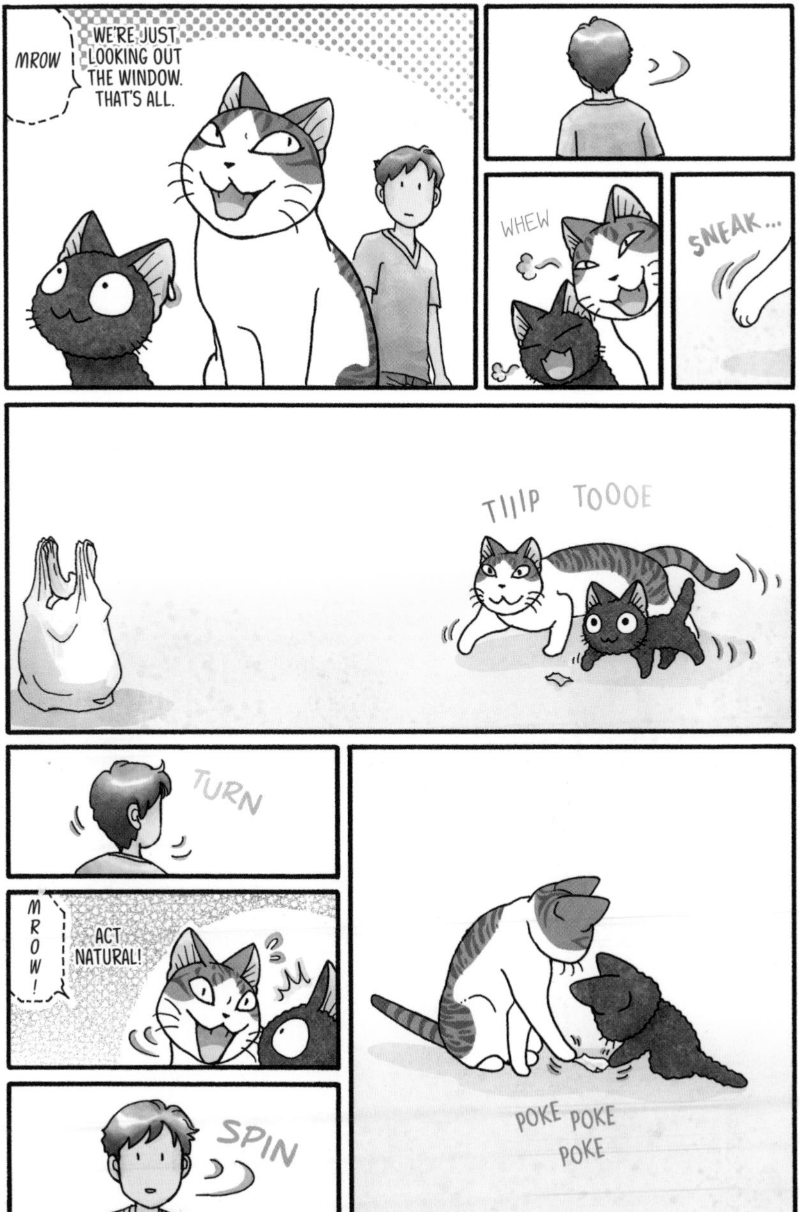
MROW
WE'RE JUST LOOKING OUT THE WINDOW. THAT'S ALL.
WHEW
SNEAK...
TIIIP TOOOE
TURN
MROW!
ACT NATURAL!
SPIN
POKE POKE
POKE

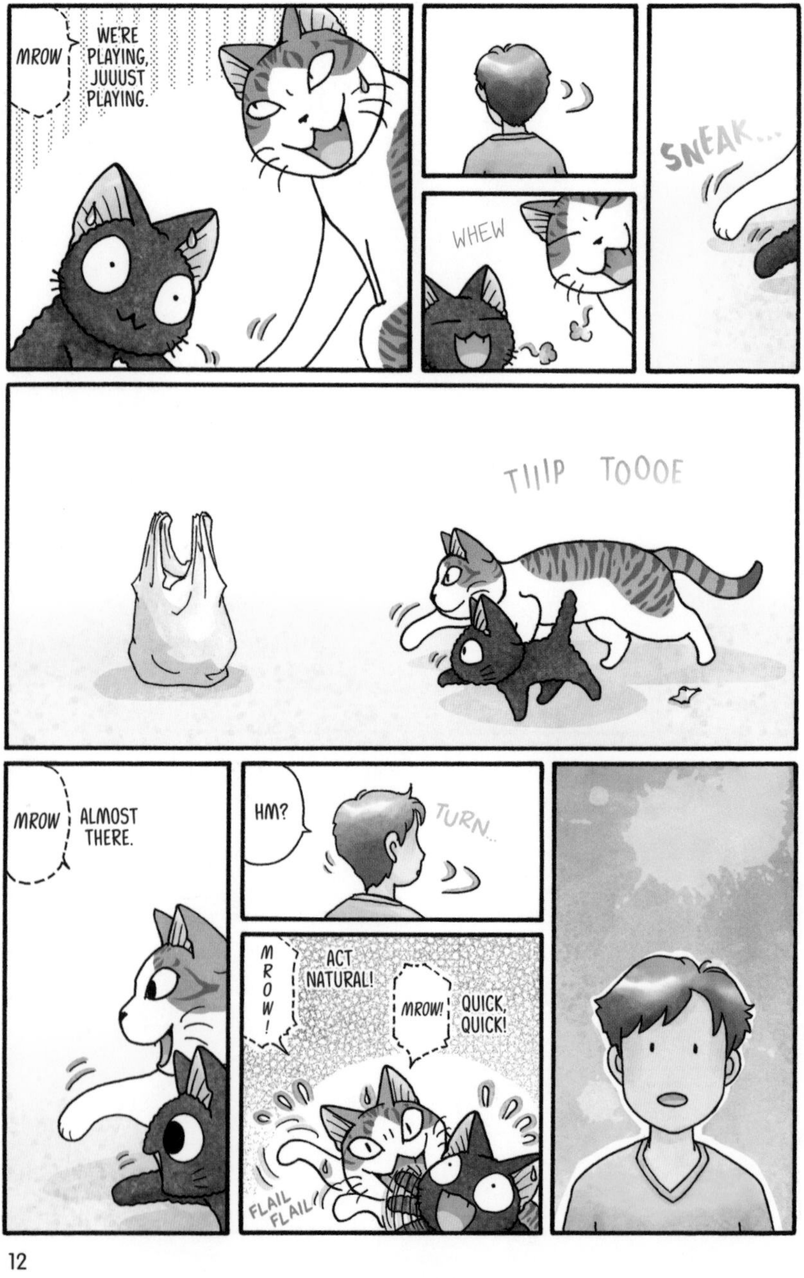
MROW
WE'RE PLAYING, JUUUST PLAYING.
WHEW
SNEAK...
TIIIP TOOOE
MROW
ALMOST THERE.
HM?
TURN...
MROW!
ACT NATURAL!
MROW!
QUICK, QUICK!
FLAIL FLAIL

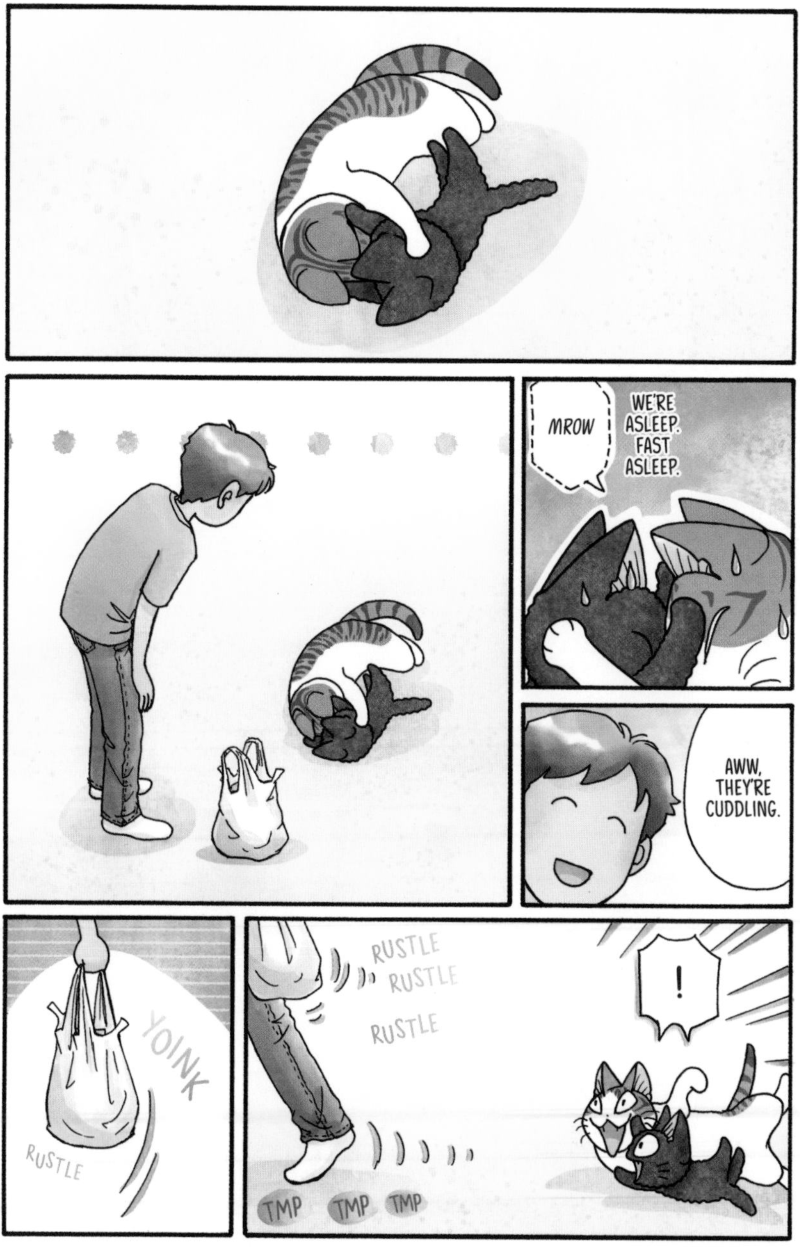
MROW
WE'RE ASLEEP. FAST ASLEEP.
AWW, THEY'RE CUDDLING.
YOINK
RUSTLE
RUSTLE
RUSTLE
RUSTLE
TMP TMP TMP
!

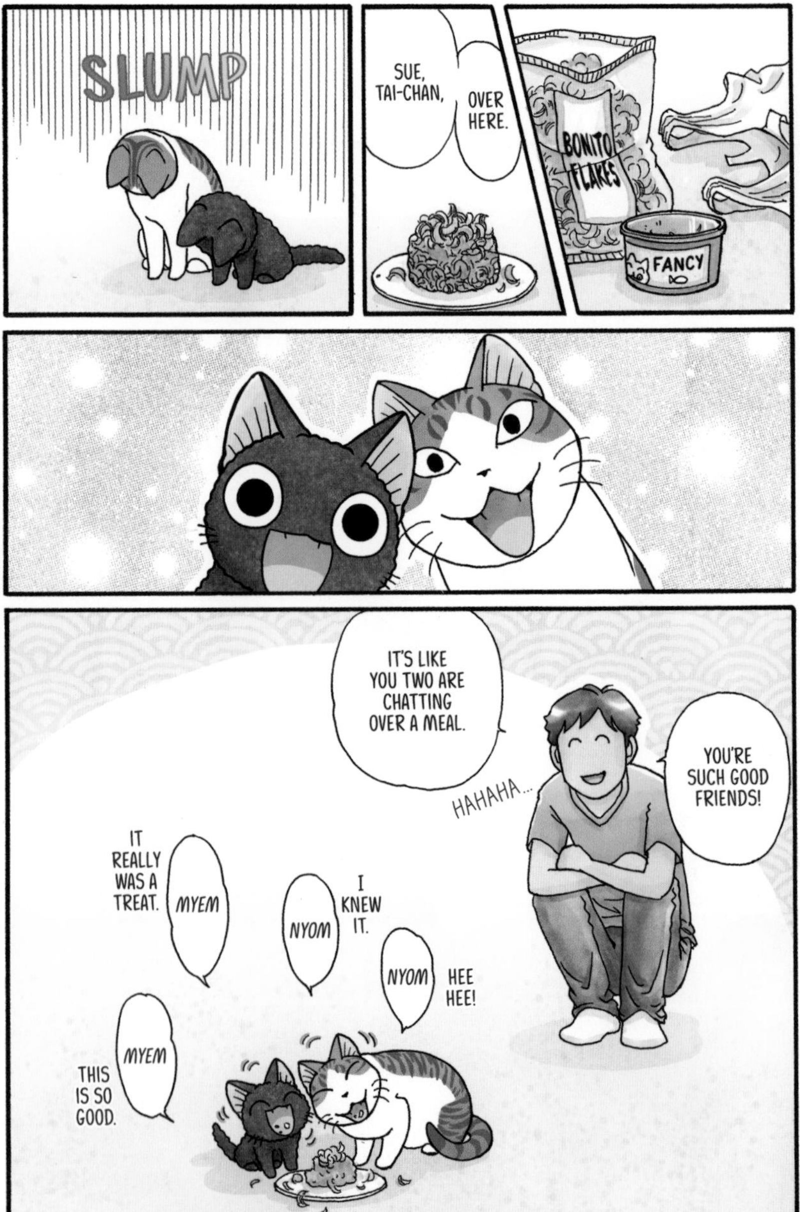
SLUMP
SUE, TAI-CHAN,
OVER HERE.
BONITO FLAKES
FANCY
IT'S LIKE YOU TWO ARE CHATTING OVER A MEAL.
HAHAHA...
YOU'RE SUCH GOOD FRIENDS!
IT REALLY WAS A TREAT.
MYEM
NYOM
I KNEW IT.
NYOM
HEE HEE!
MYEM
THIS IS SO GOOD.

CHAPTER 36 Someone You Missed?!

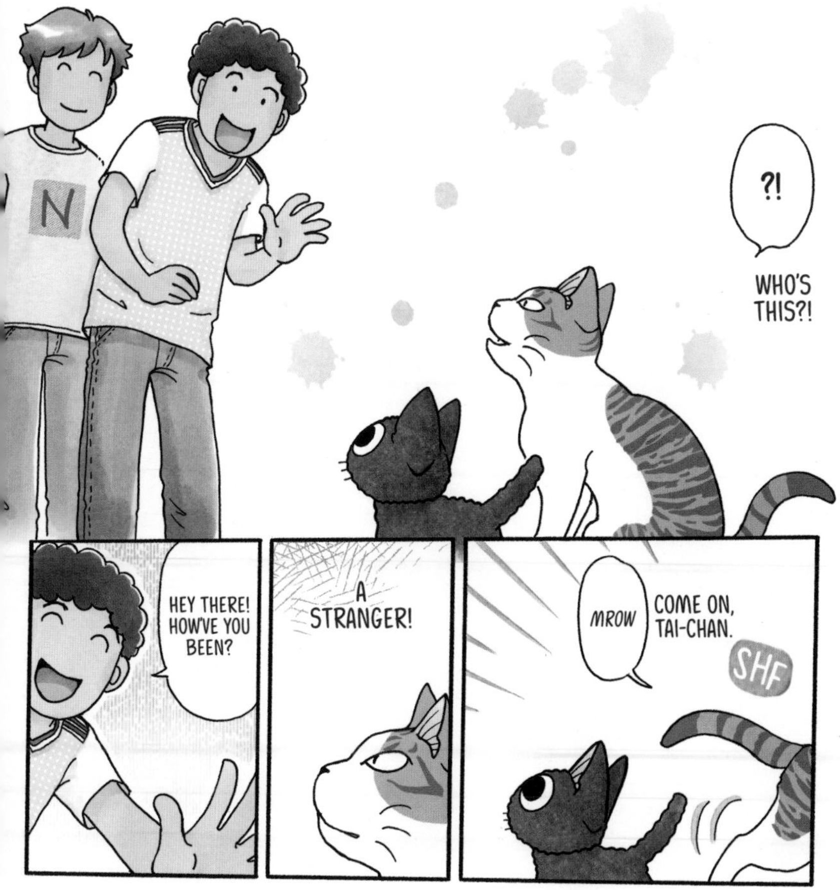
?!
WHO'S THIS?!
HEY THERE! HOW'VE YOU BEEN?
A STRANGER!
MROW
COME ON, TAI-CHAN.
SHF

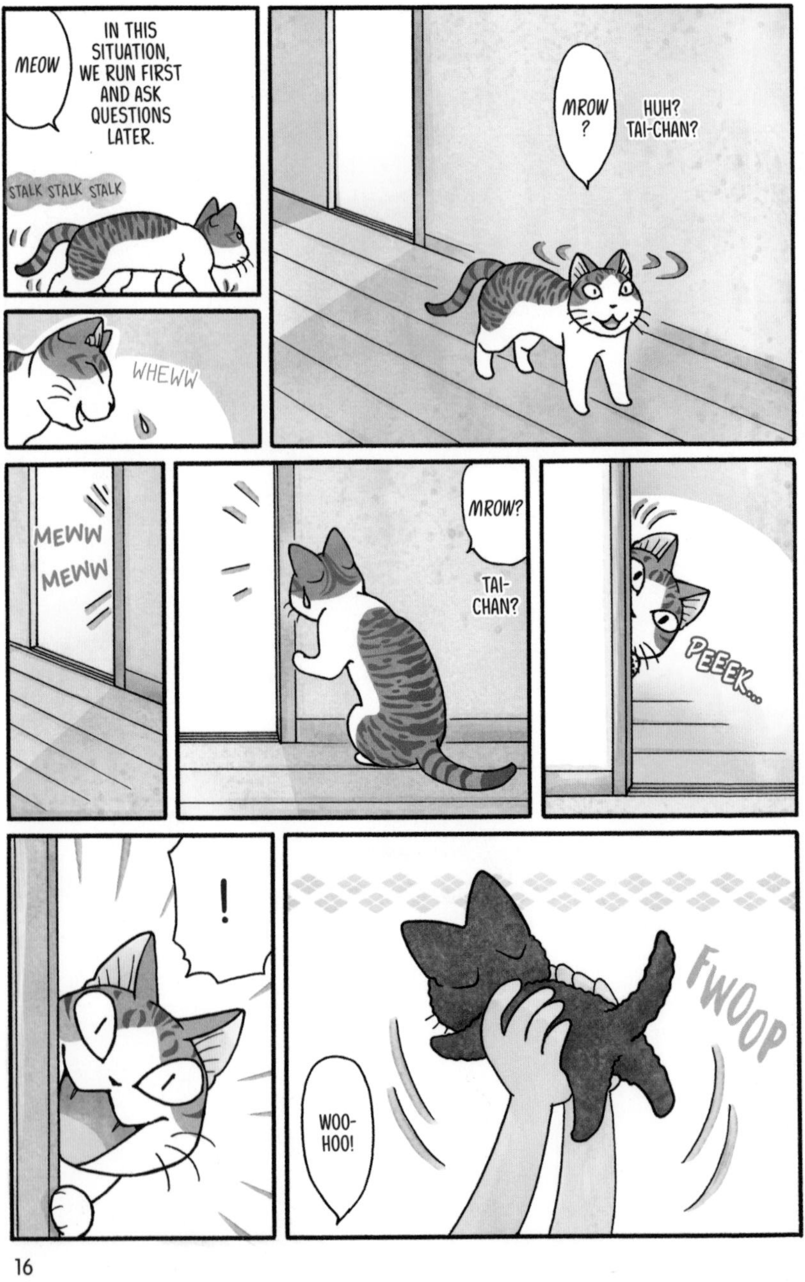
MEOW
IN THIS SITUATION, WE RUN FIRST AND ASK QUESTIONS LATER.
STALK STALK STALK
WHEWW
MROW ?
HUH? TAI-CHAN?
MEWW MEWW
MROW?
TAI-CHAN?
PEEEK...
!
FWOOP
WOO-HOO!

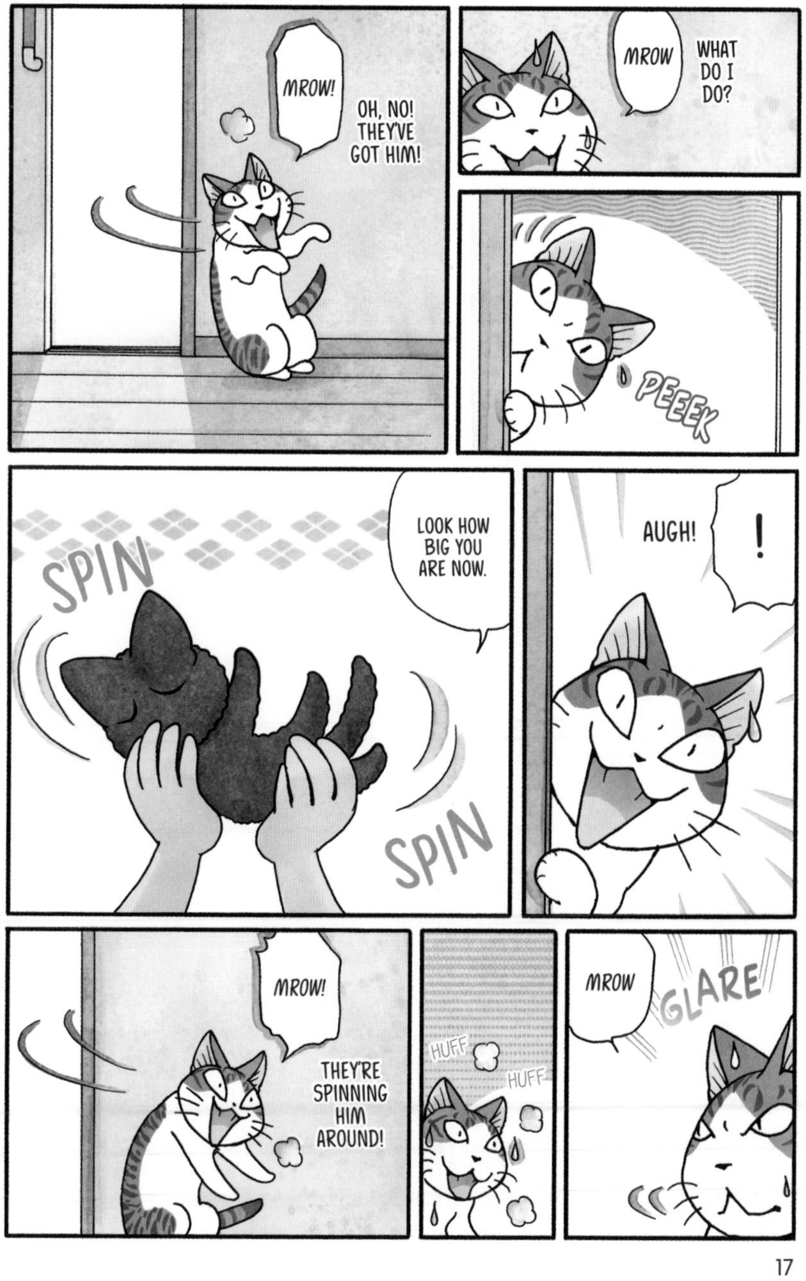
MROW!
OH, NO! THEY'VE GOT HIM!
MROW
WHAT DO I DO?
PEEEK
SPIN
LOOK HOW BIG YOU ARE NOW.
SPIN
AUGH!
!
MROW!
THEY'RE SPINNING HIM AROUND!
HUFF
HUFF
MROW
GLARE

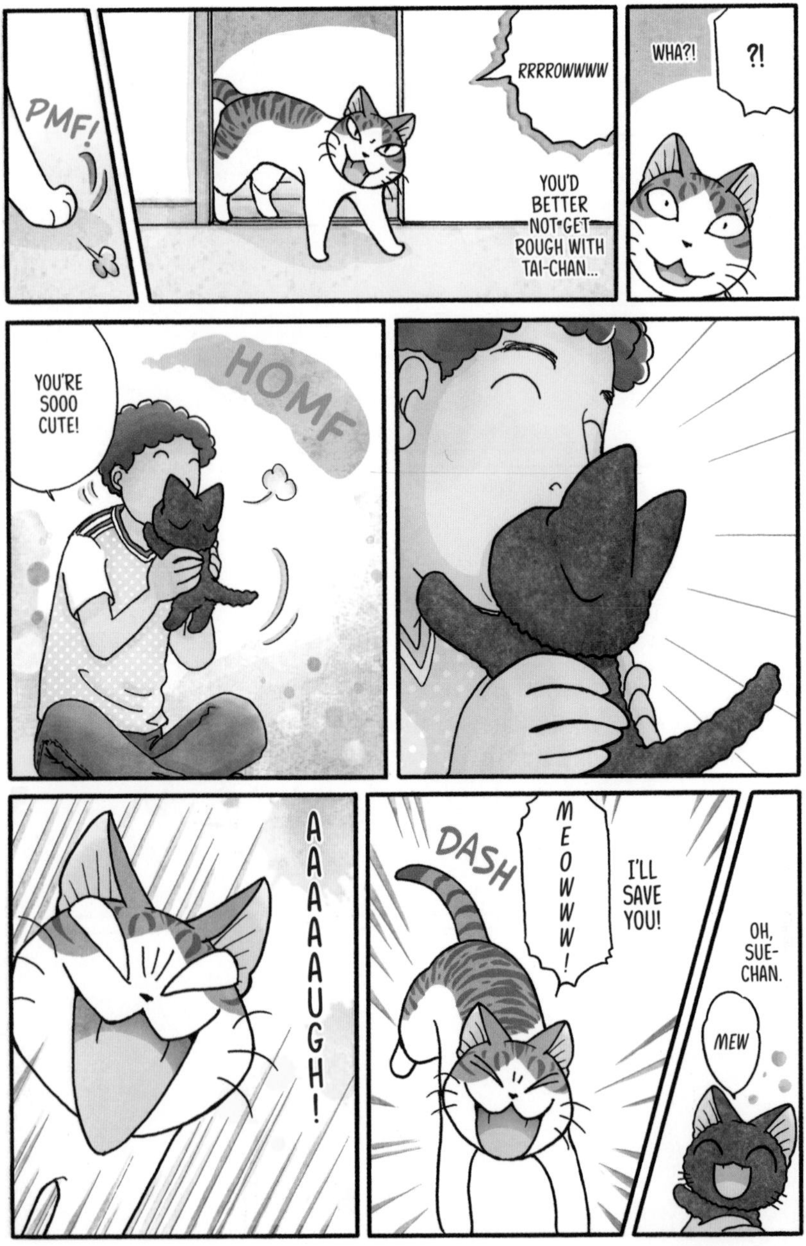
PMF!
RRRROWWWW
YOU'D BETTER NOT GET ROUGH WITH TAI-CHAN...
WHA?!
?!
YOU'RE SOOO CUTE!
HOMF
AAAAAAUGH!
DASH
MEOWWWW!
I'LL SAVE YOU!
OH, SUE-CHAN.
MEW

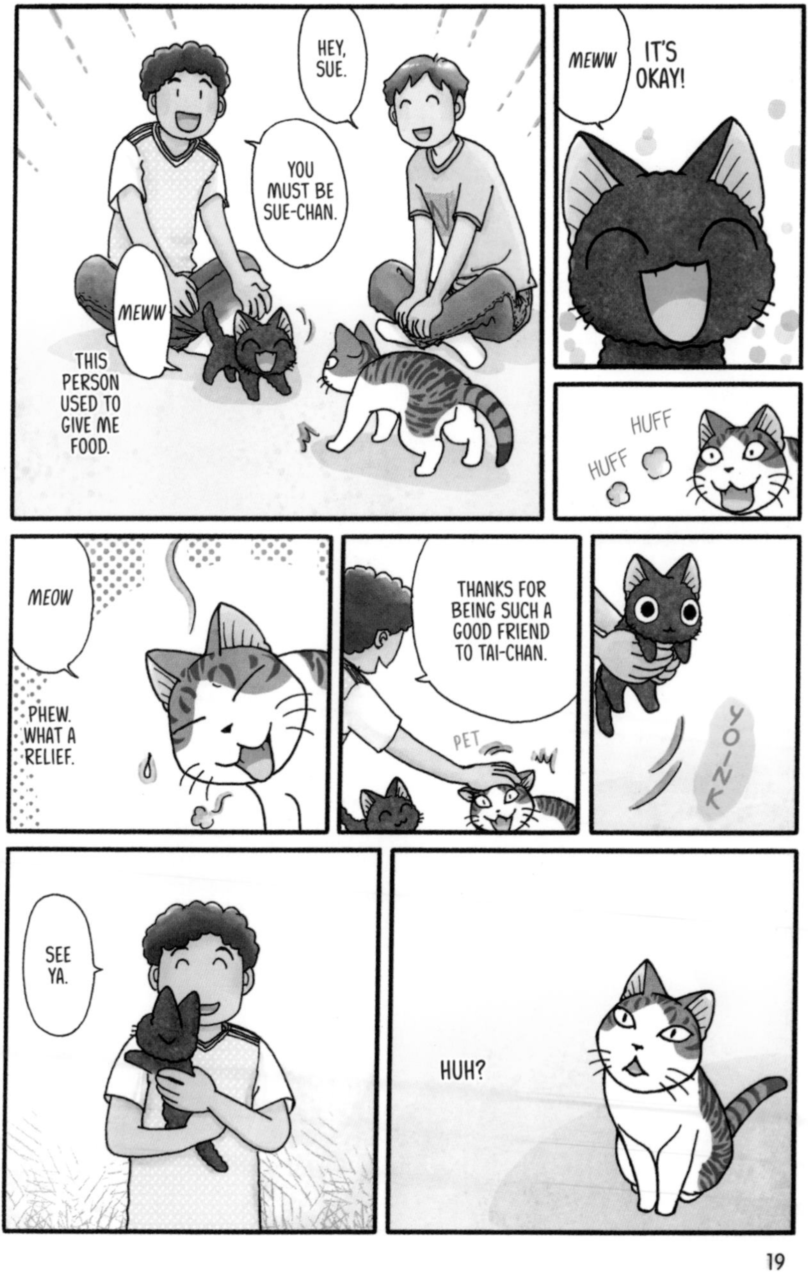
HEY, SUE.
YOU MUST BE SUE-CHAN.
MEWW
THIS PERSON USED TO GIVE ME FOOD.
MEWW
IT'S OKAY!
HUFF
HUFF
MEOW
PHEW. WHAT A RELIEF.
THANKS FOR BEING SUCH A GOOD FRIEND TO TAI-CHAN.
PET
YOINK
SEE YA.
HUH?

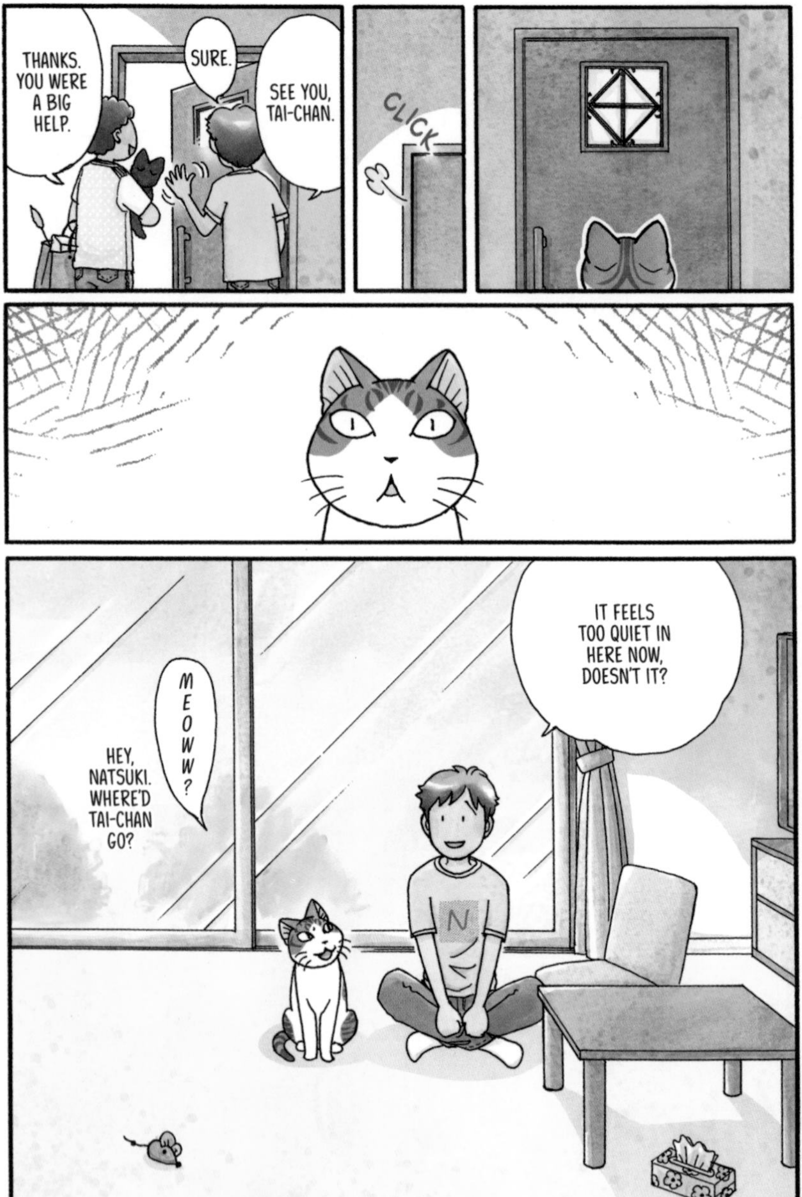
THANKS. YOU WERE A BIG HELP.
SURE.
SEE YOU, TAI-CHAN.
CLICK
HEY, NATSUKI. WHERE'D TAI-CHAN GO?
MEOWW?
IT FEELS TOO QUIET IN HERE NOW, DOESN'T IT?

Sue & Tai-chan

CHAPTER 37 Tai-chan is Gone

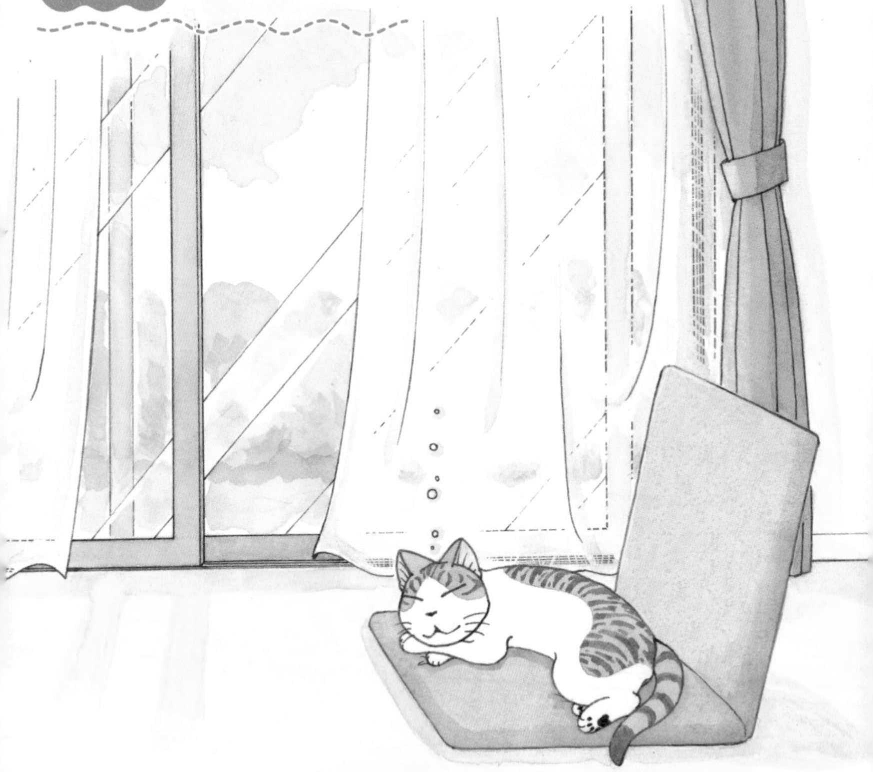

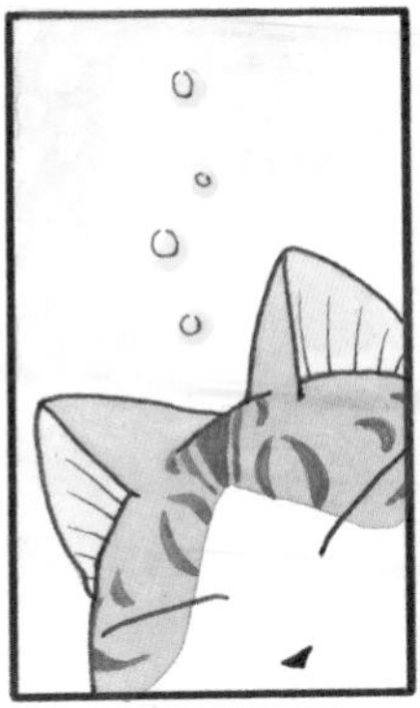

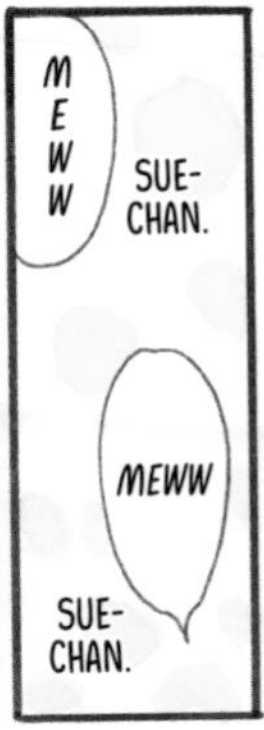
MEWW
SUE-CHAN.
MEWW
SUE-CHAN.

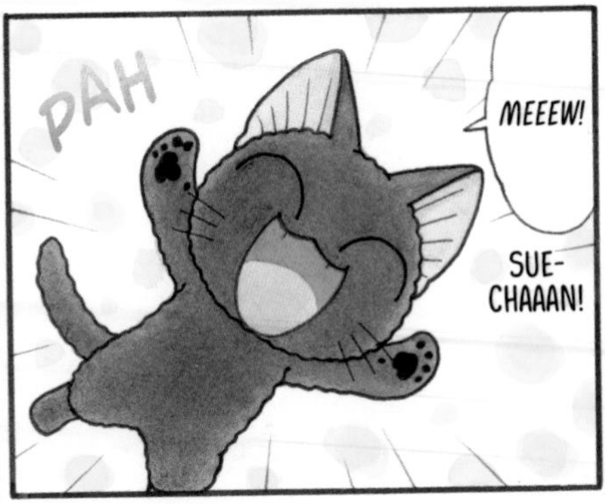
PAH
MEEEW!
SUE-CHAAAN!

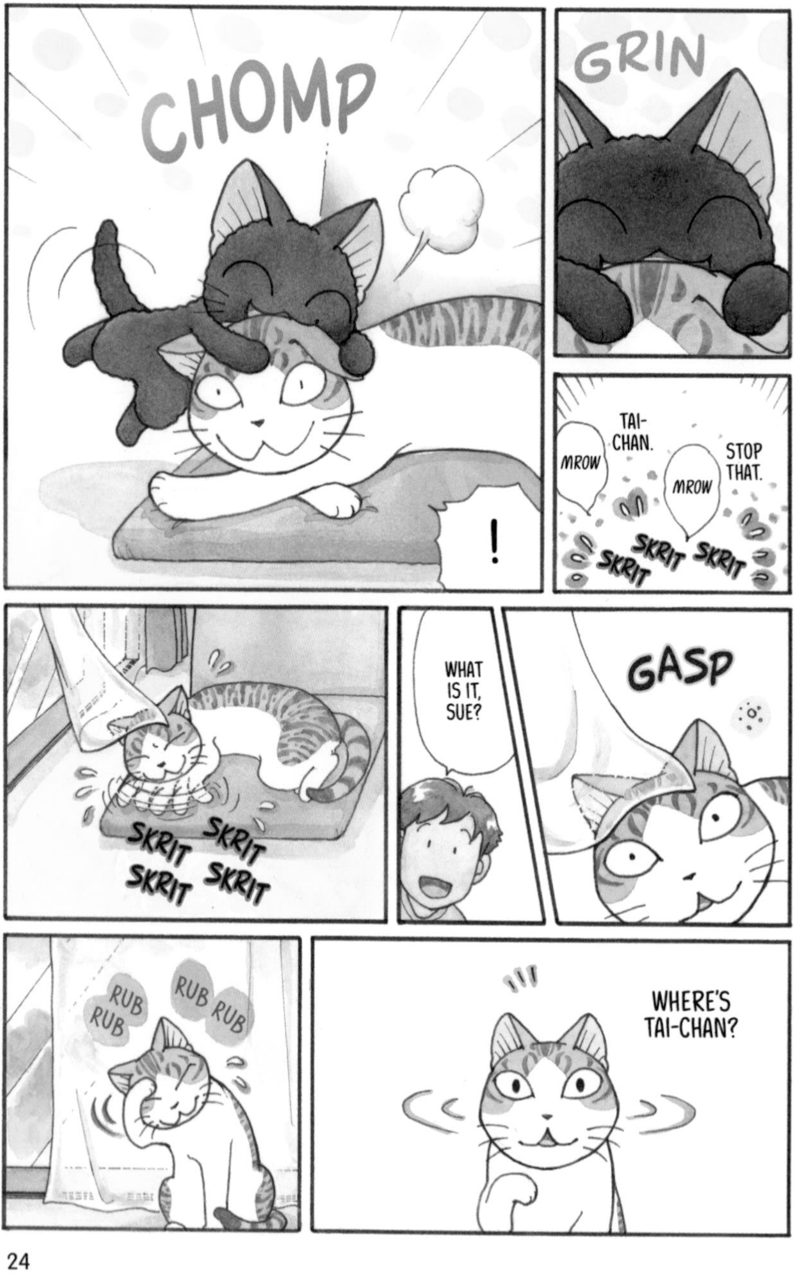
CHOMP
!
GRIN
MROW
TAI-CHAN.
MROW
STOP THAT.
SKRIT SKRIT SKRIT SKRIT
SKRIT SKRIT SKRIT SKRIT
WHAT IS IT, SUE?
GASP
RUB RUB RUB RUB
WHERE'S TAI-CHAN?

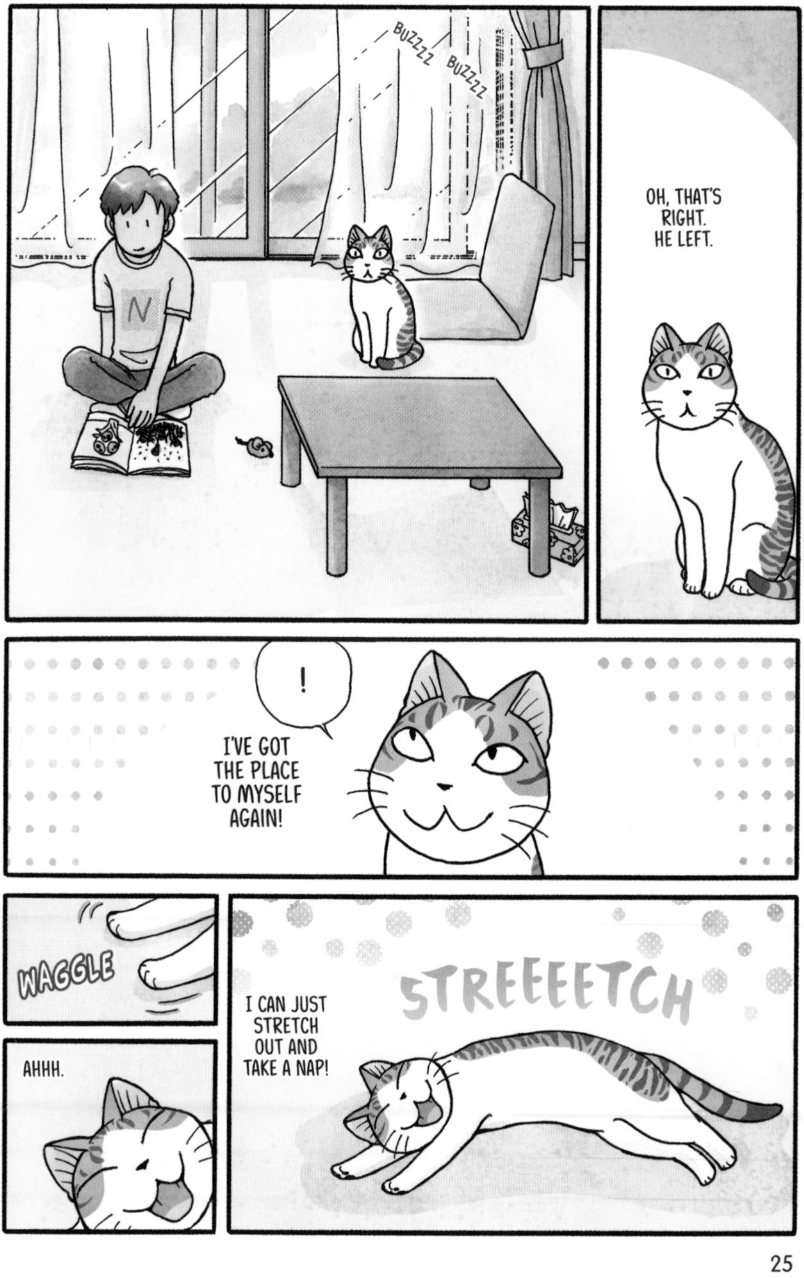

BUZZZZ
BUZZZZ
OH, THAT'S RIGHT. HE LEFT.
!
I'VE GOT THE PLACE TO MYSELF AGAIN!
WAGGLE
AHHH.
I CAN JUST STRETCH OUT AND TAKE A NAP!
STREEEETCH

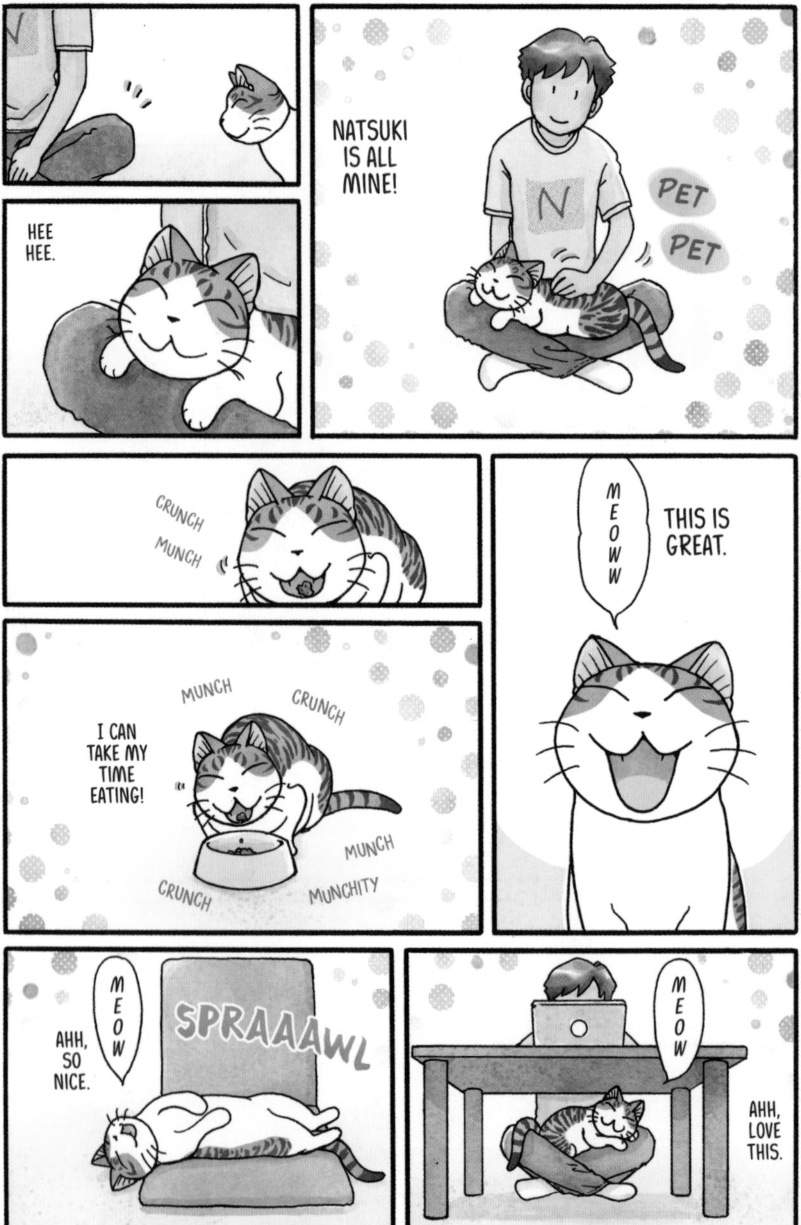
HEE HEE.
NATSUKI IS ALL MINE!
PET
PET
CRUNCH
MUNCH
I CAN TAKE MY TIME EATING!
MUNCH
CRUNCH
MUNCH
CRUNCH
MUNCHITY
MEOWW
THIS IS GREAT.
MEOW
AHH, SO NICE.
SPRAAAWL
MEOW
AHH, LOVE THIS.

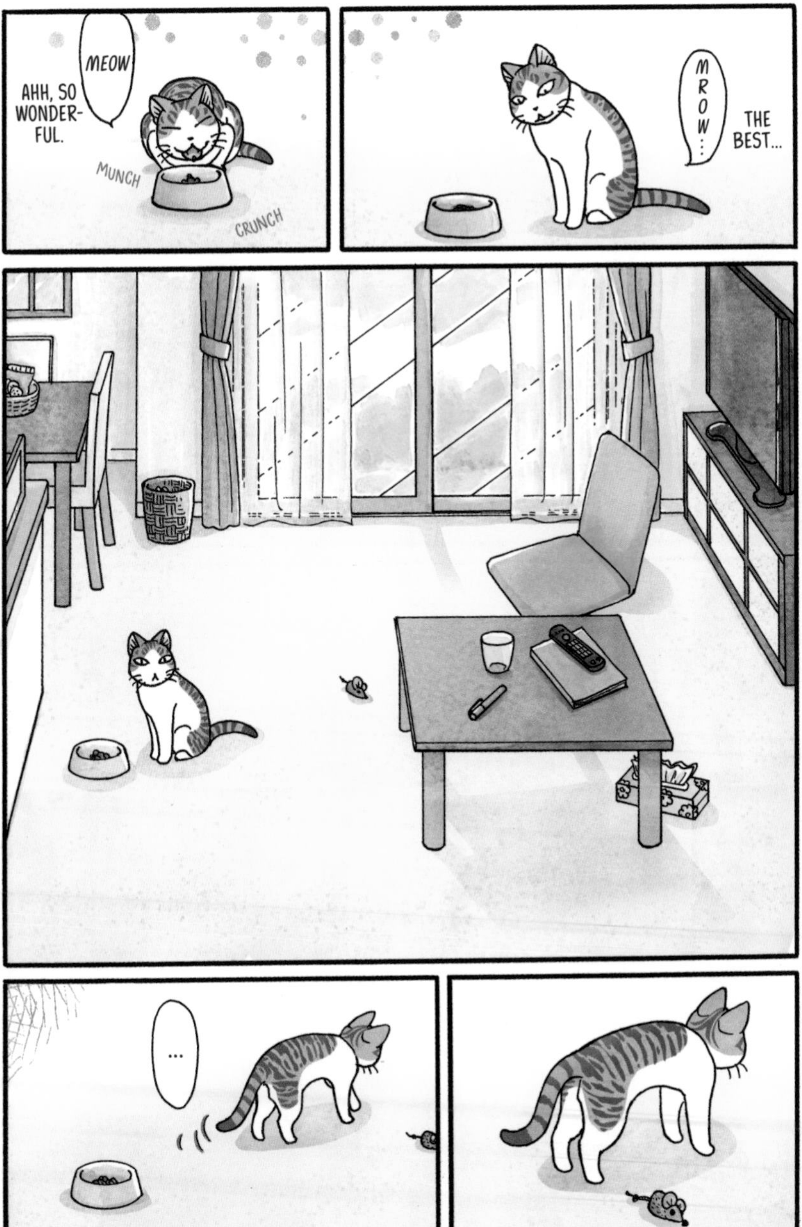
MEOW
AHH, SO WONDERFUL.
MUNCH
CRUNCH
MROW...
THE BEST...
...

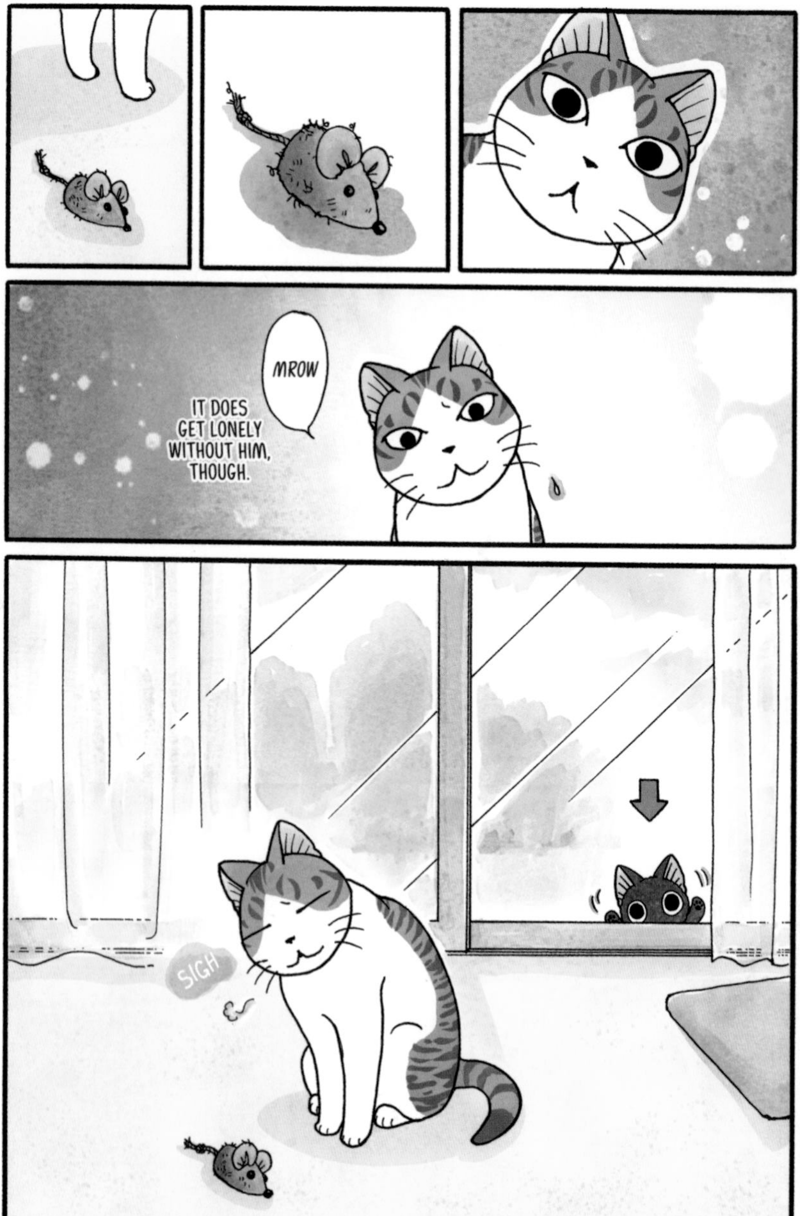
MROW
IT DOES GET LONELY WITHOUT HIM, THOUGH.
SIGH

CHAPTER 38 A Visit from Tai-chan ♥

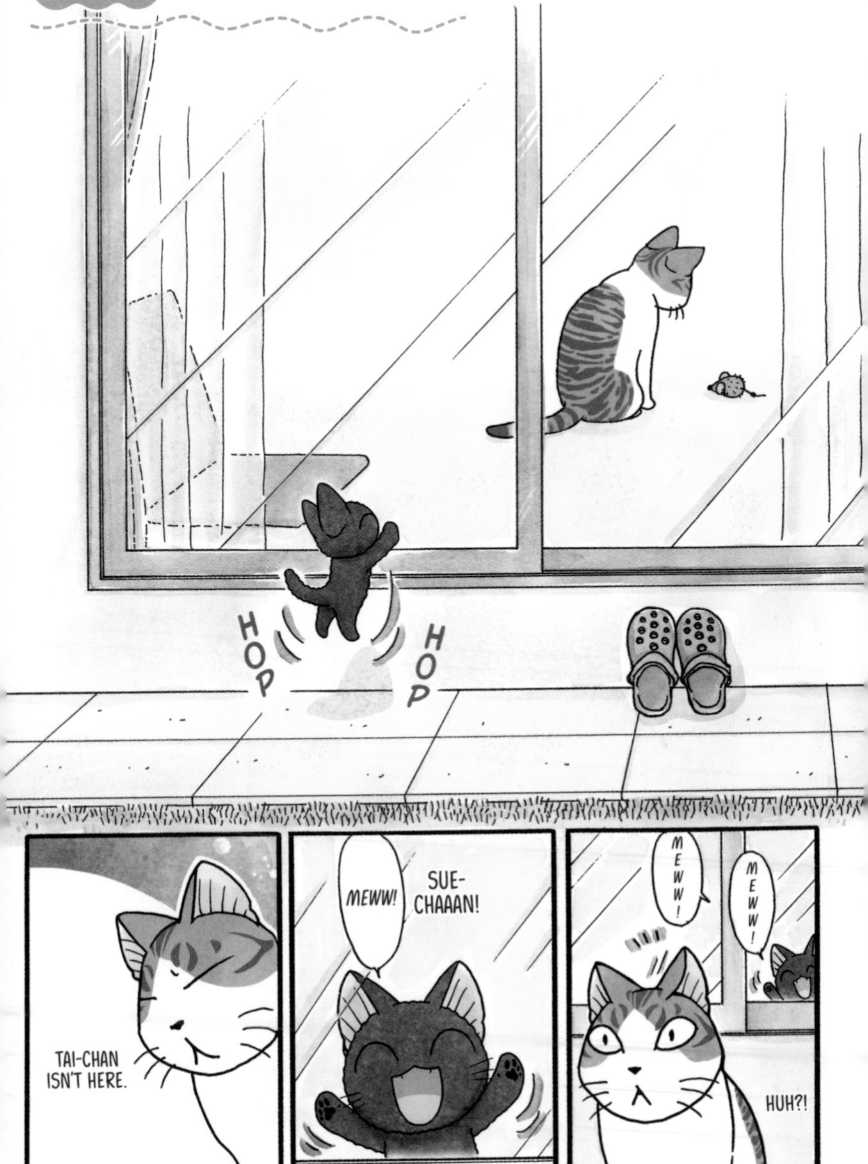

HOP
HOP
TAI-CHAN ISN'T HERE.
MEWW!
SUE-CHAAAN!
MEWW!
MEWW!
HUH?!

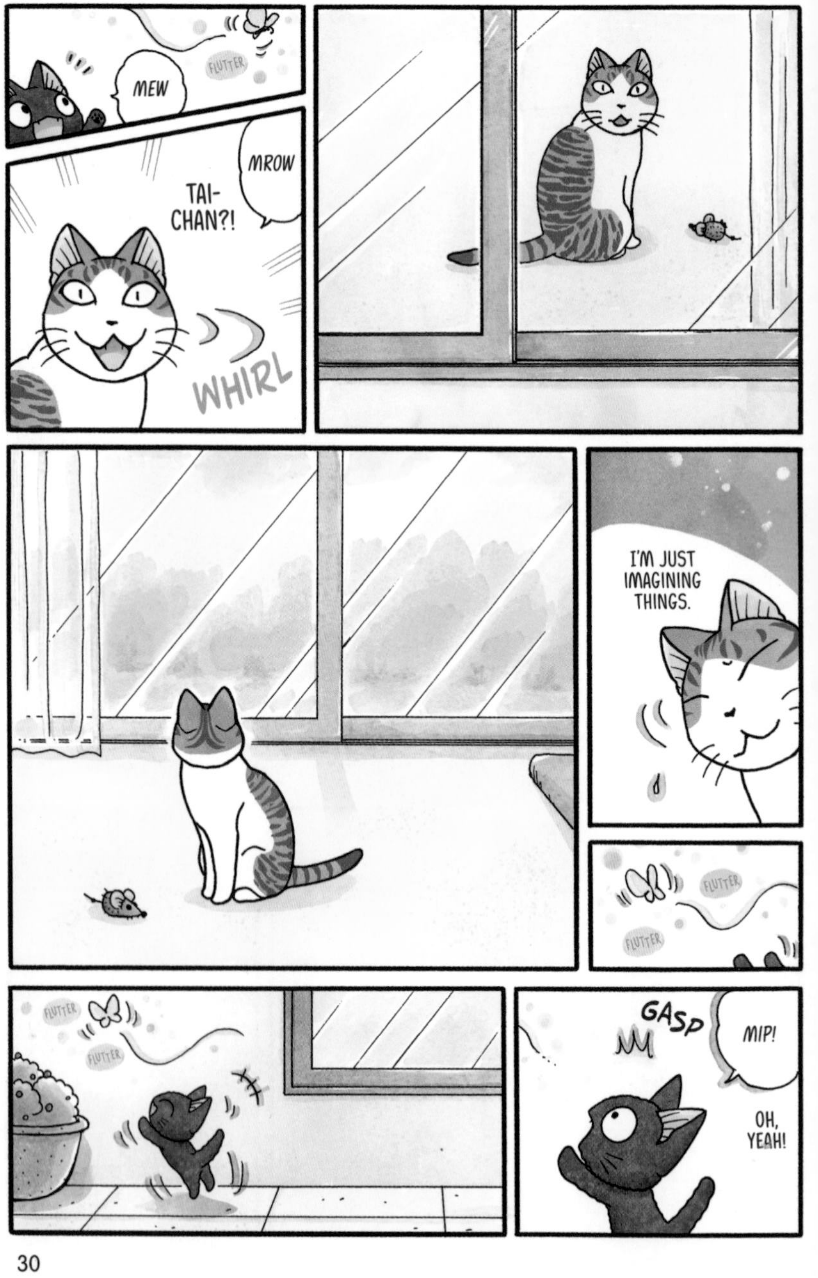
FLUTTER
MEW
TAI-CHAN?!
MROW
WHIRL
I'M JUST IMAGINING THINGS.
FLUTTER
FLUTTER
FLUTTER
FLUTTER
GASP
MIP!
OH, YEAH!

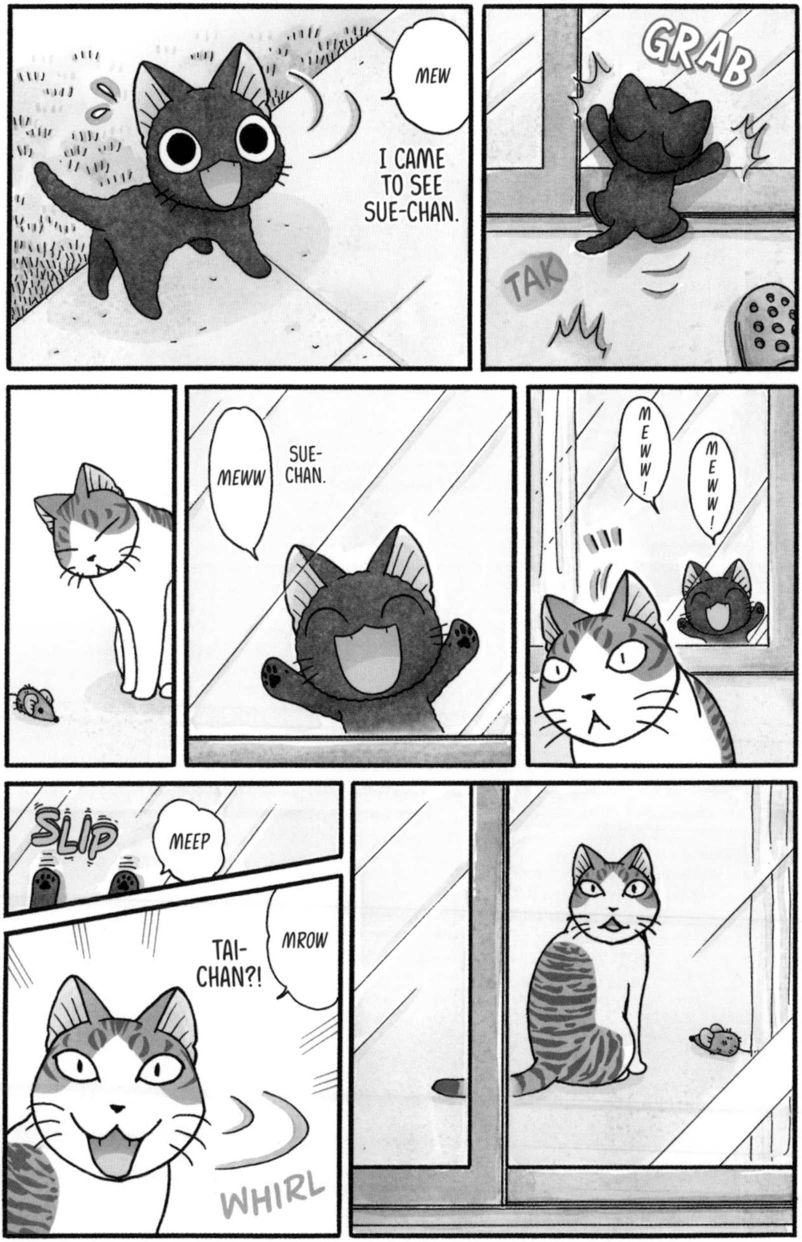
MEW
I CAME TO SEE SUE-CHAN.
GRAB
TAK
SUE-CHAN.
MEWW
MEWW!
MEWW!
SLIP
MEEP
TAI-CHAN?!
MROW
WHIRL

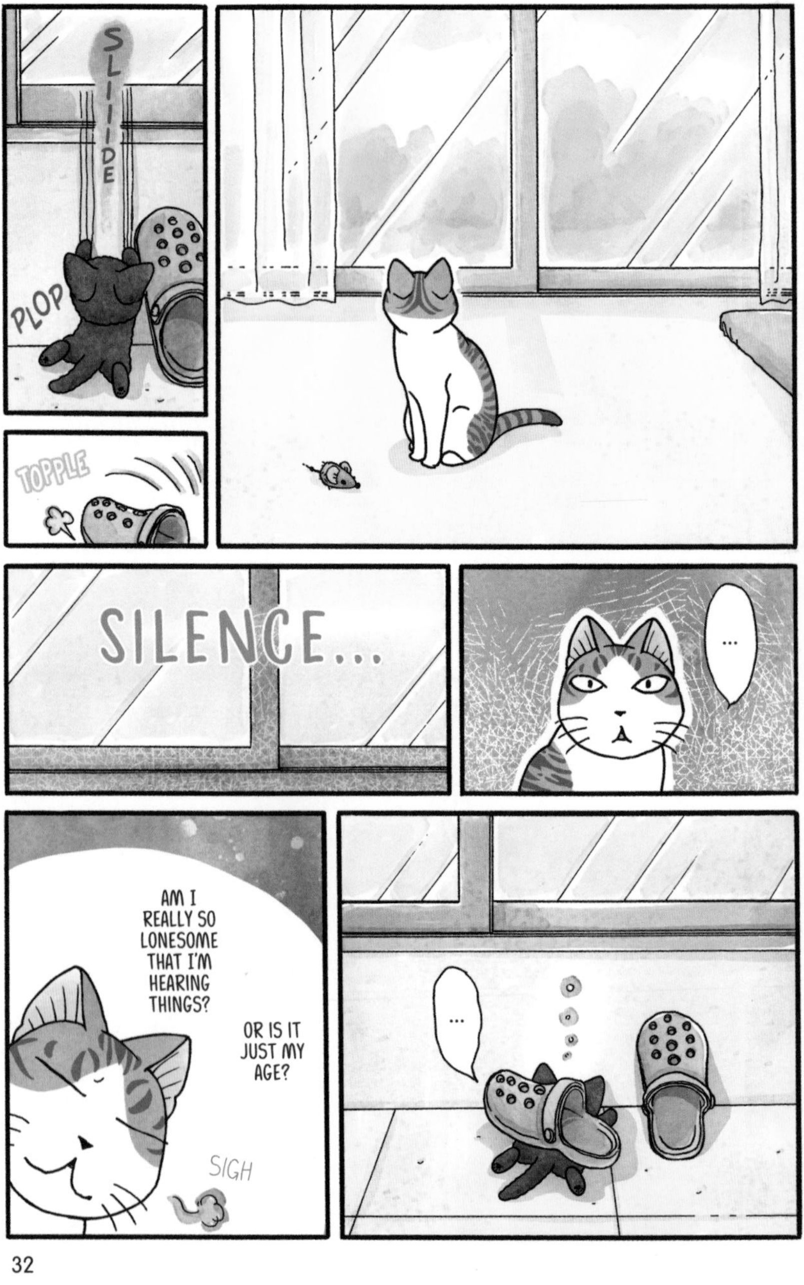
SLIIIDE
PLOP
TOPPLE
SILENCE...
...
AM I REALLY SO LONESOME THAT I'M HEARING THINGS?
OR IS IT JUST MY AGE?
SIGH
...

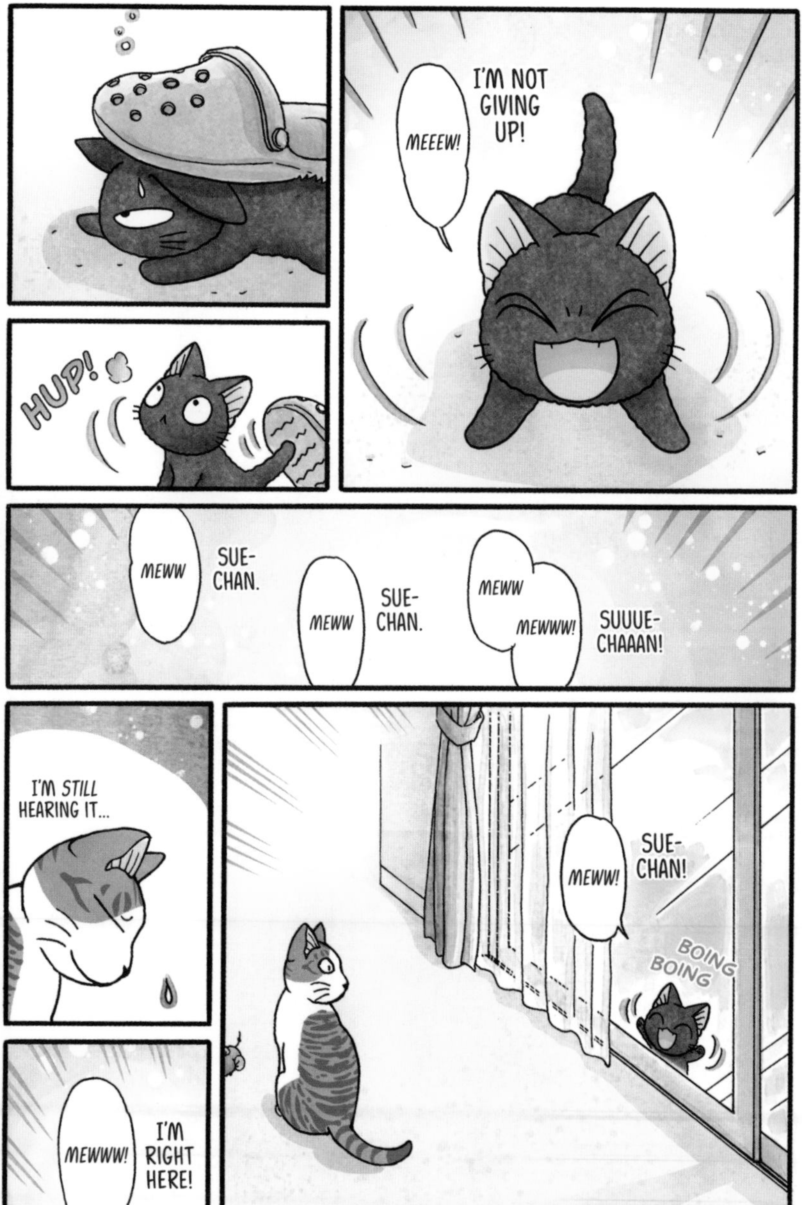

HUP!
MEEEW!
I'M NOT GIVING UP!
MEWW
SUE-CHAN.
MEWW
SUE-CHAN.
MEWW
MEWWW!
SUUUE-CHAAAN!
I'M STILL HEARING IT...
MEWWW!
I'M RIGHT HERE!
MEWW!
SUE-CHAN!
BOING BOING

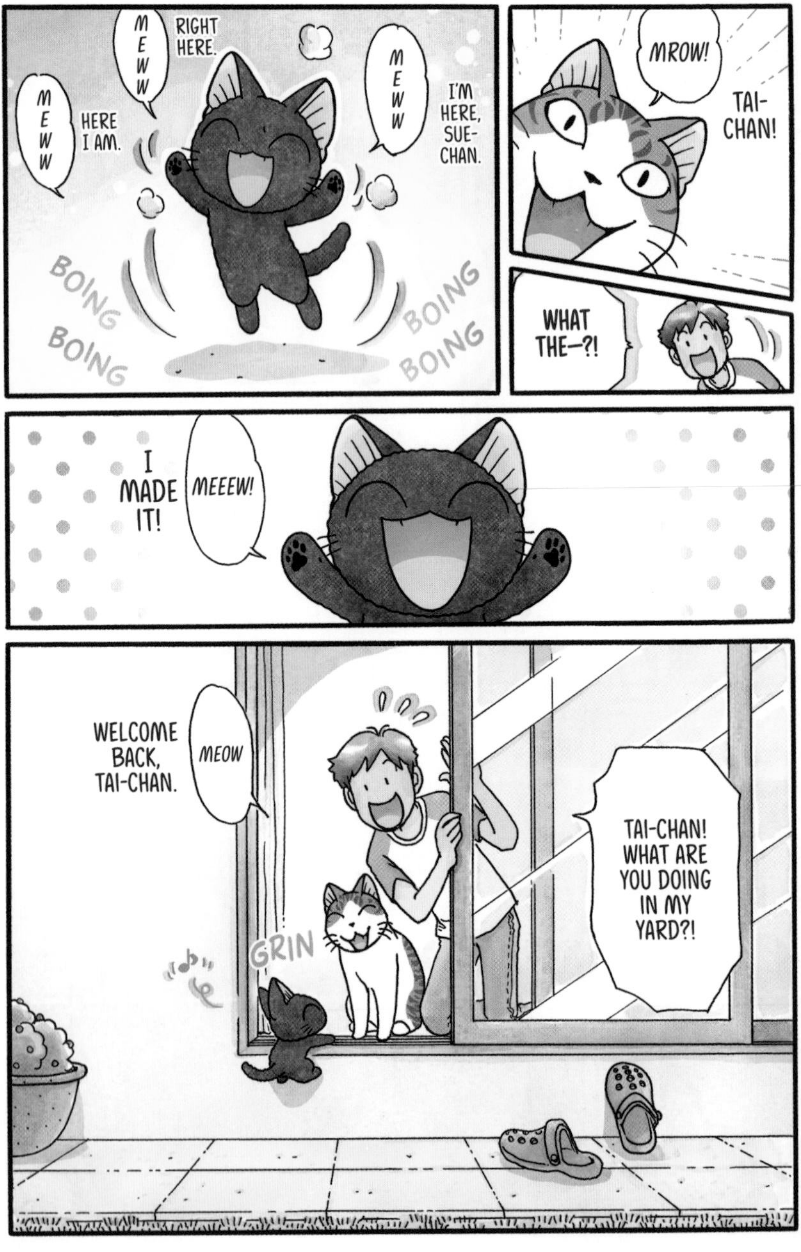
MEWW
HERE I AM.
MEWW
RIGHT HERE.
MEWW
I'M HERE, SUE-CHAN.
BOING BOING
BOING BOING
MROW!
TAI-CHAN!
WHAT THE—?!
I MADE IT!
MEEEW!
WELCOME BACK, TAI-CHAN.
MEOW
GRIN
TAI-CHAN! WHAT ARE YOU DOING IN MY YARD?!

CHAPTER 39 A Word from Sue

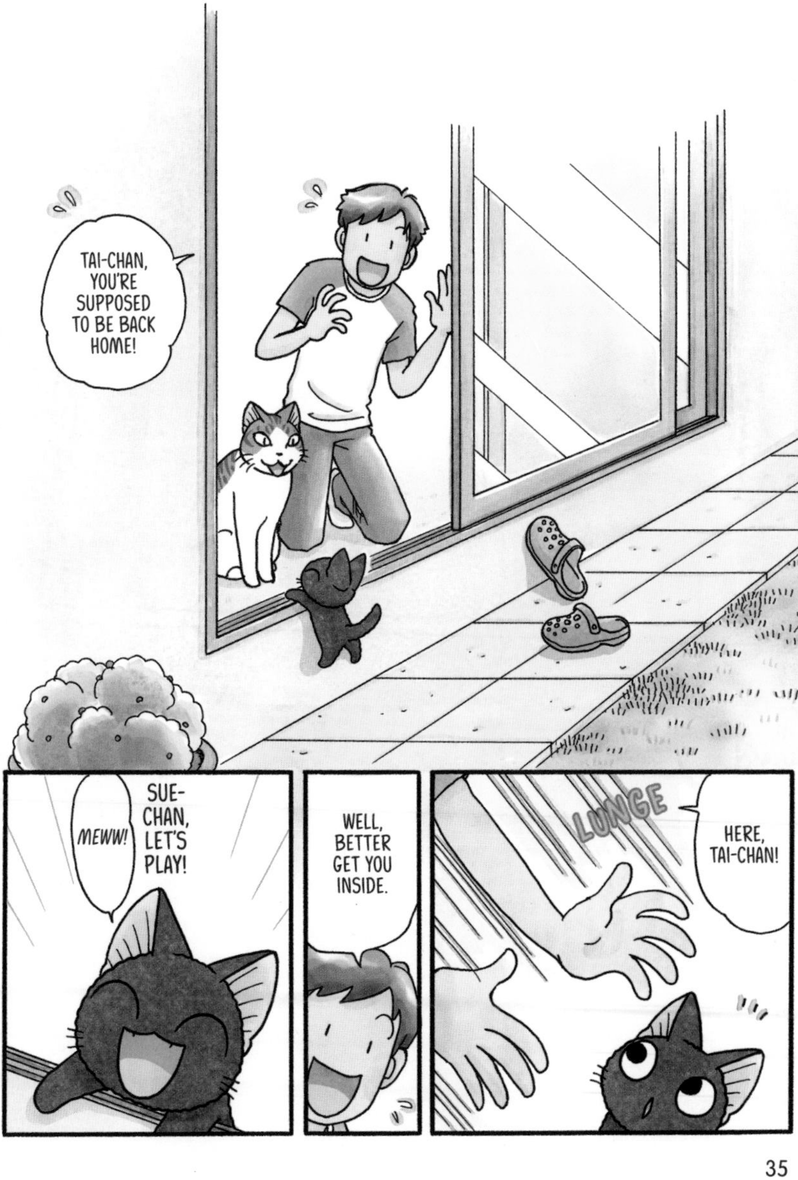
TAI-CHAN, YOU'RE SUPPOSED TO BE BACK HOME!
MEWW!
SUE-CHAN, LET'S PLAY!
WELL, BETTER GET YOU INSIDE.
LUNGE
HERE, TAI-CHAN!

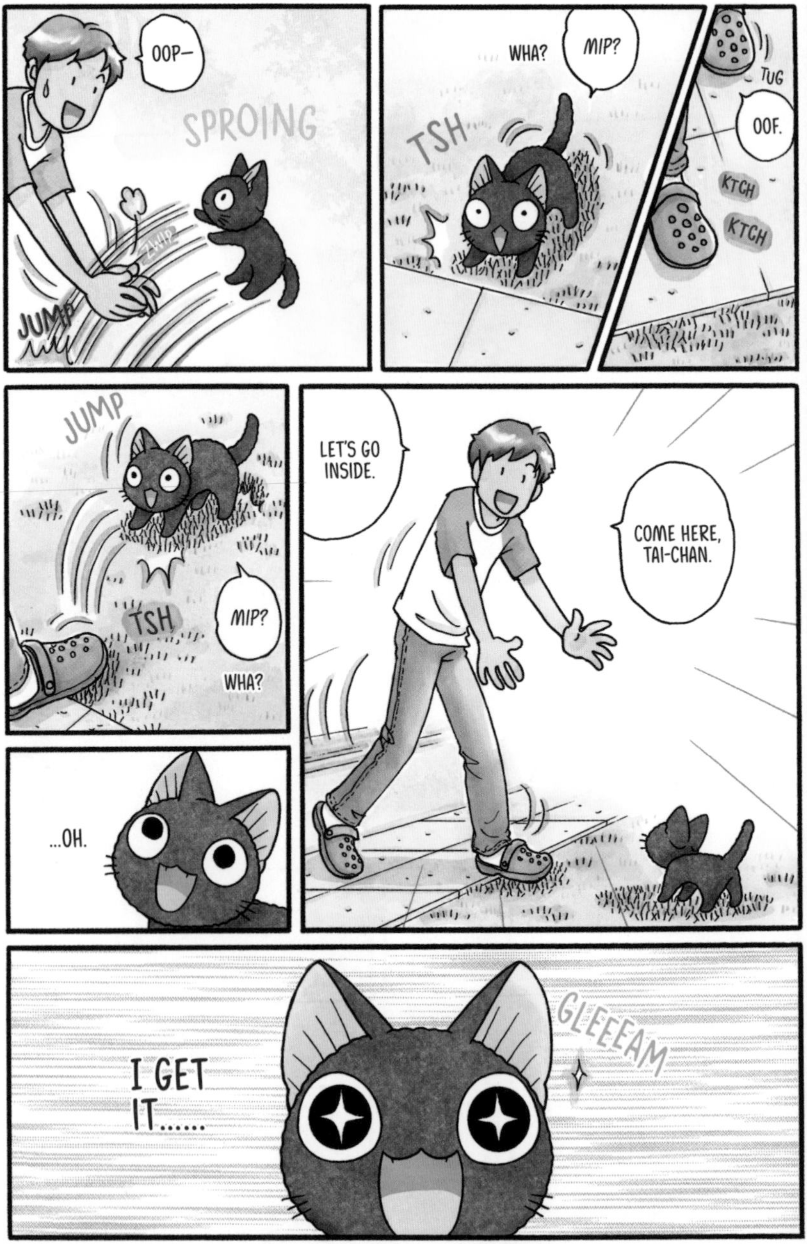
OOP—
SPROING
ZWIP
JUMP
WHA?
MIP?
TSH
TUG
OOF.
KTCH
KTCH
JUMP
TSH
MIP?
WHA?
LET'S GO INSIDE.
COME HERE, TAI-CHAN.
...OH.
I GET IT......
GLEEEAM

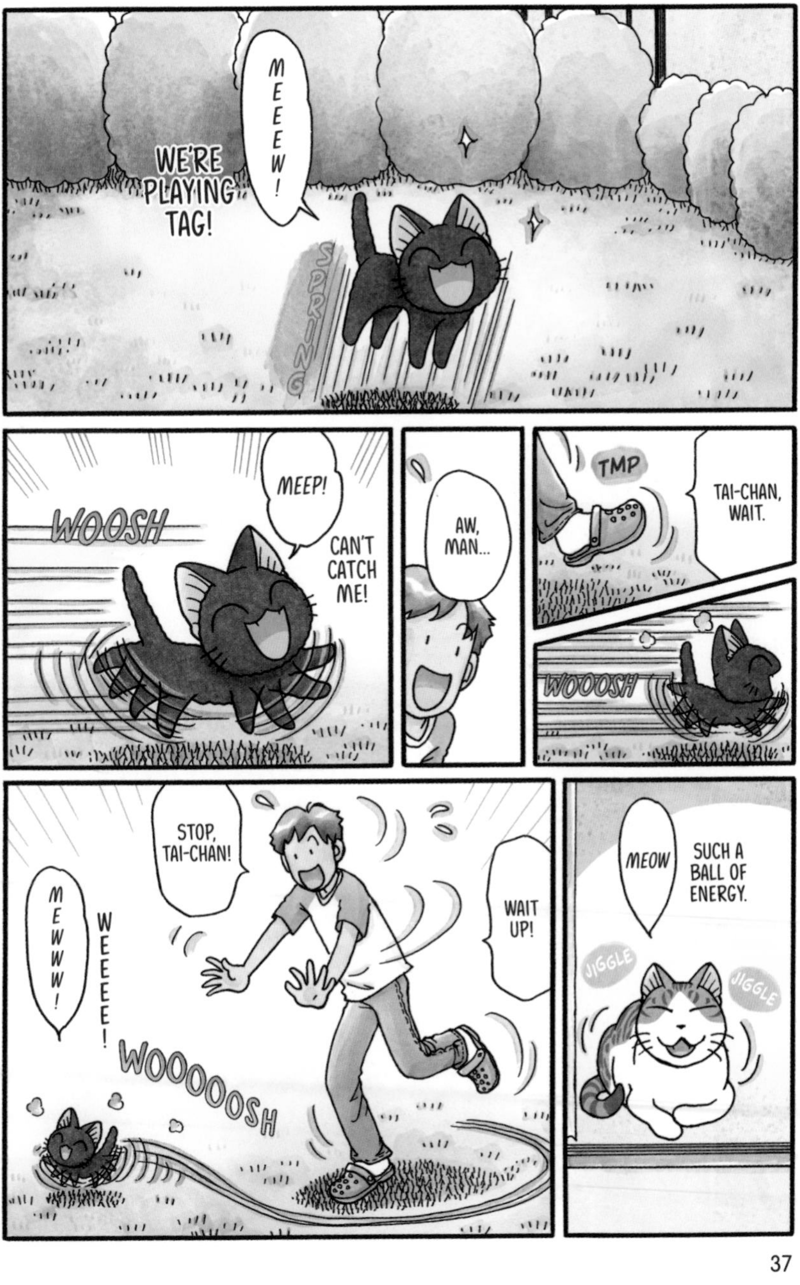
WE'RE PLAYING TAG!
MEEEEW!
SPRING
MEEP!
WOOSH
CAN'T CATCH ME!
AW, MAN...
TMP
TAI-CHAN, WAIT.
WOOOSH
STOP, TAI-CHAN!
MEWWW!
WEEEEE!
WAIT UP!
WOOOOOOSH
MEOW
SUCH A BALL OF ENERGY.
JIGGLE
JIGGLE

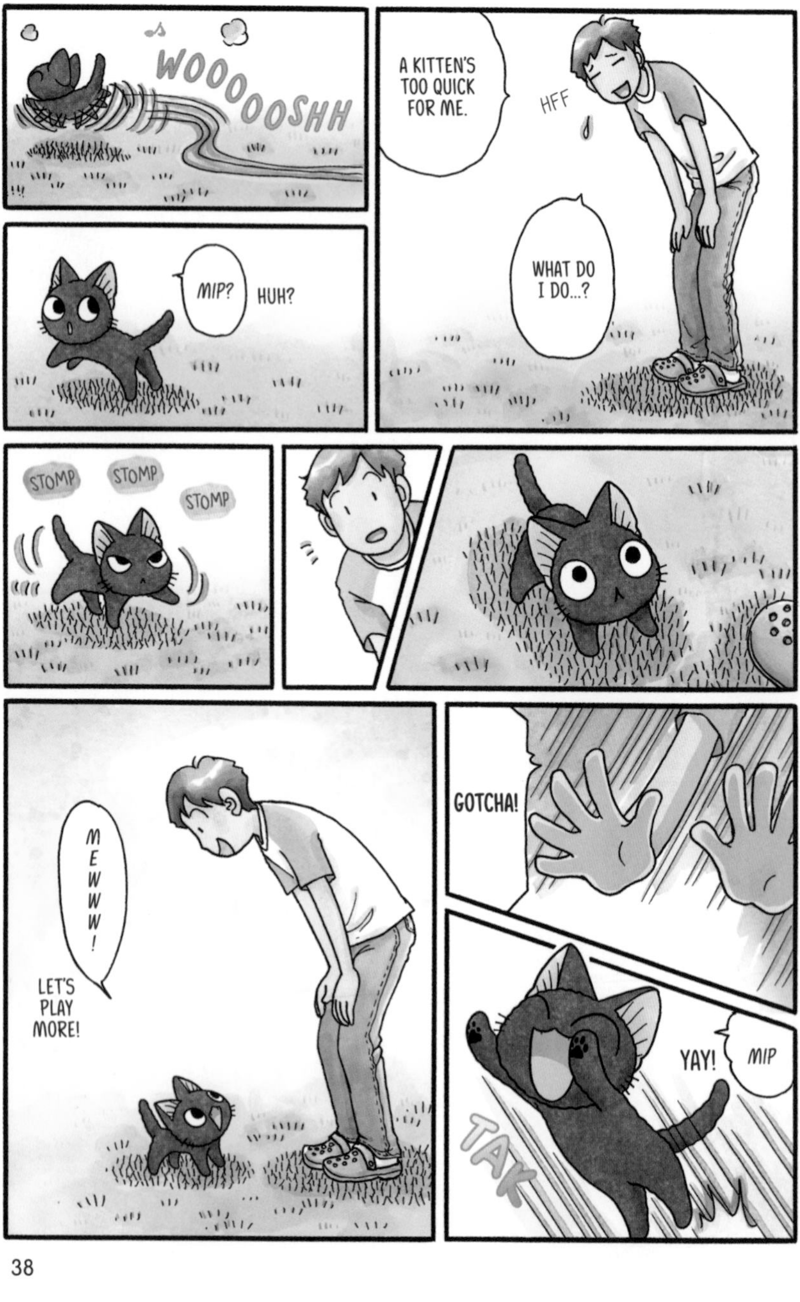
WOOOOOOSHH
A KITTEN'S TOO QUICK FOR ME.
HFF
WHAT DO I DO...?
MIP?
HUH?
STOMP
STOMP
STOMP
MEWWW!
LET'S PLAY MORE!
GOTCHA!
TAK
YAY!
MIP

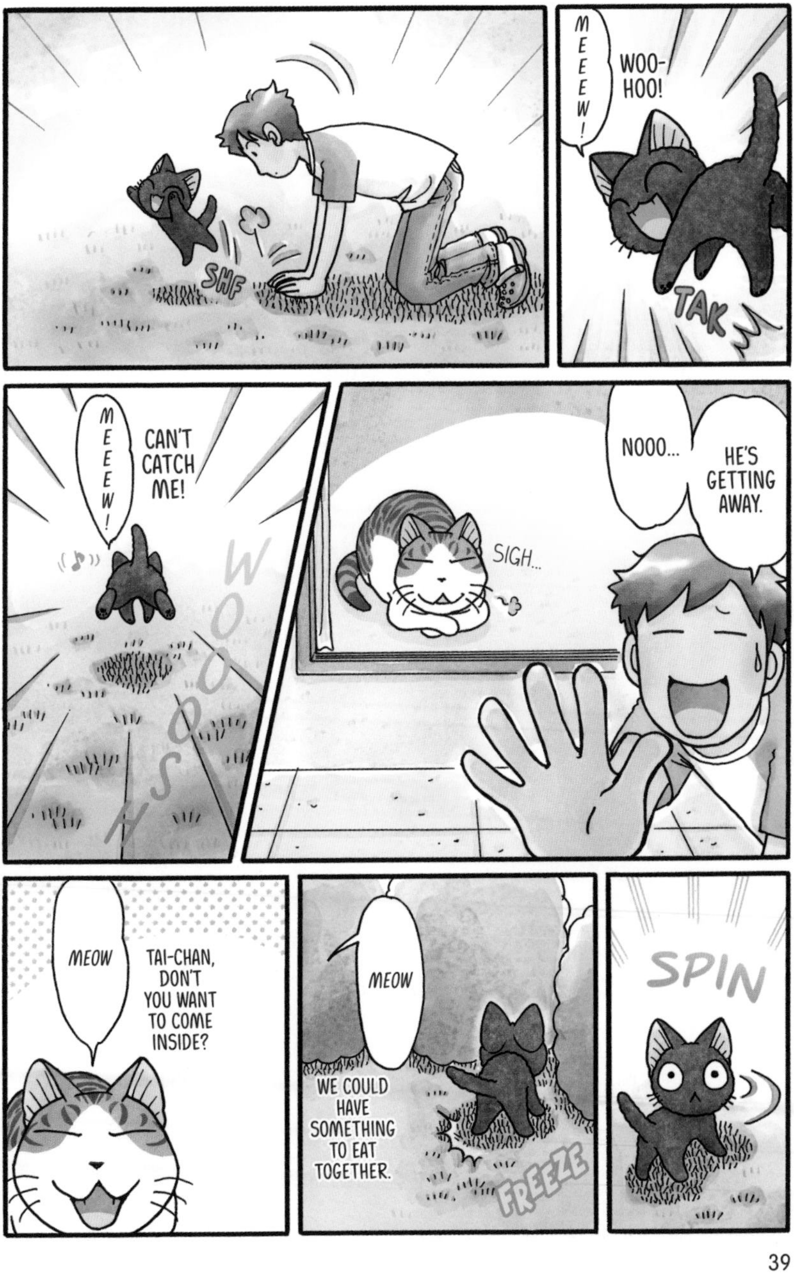
SHF
MEEEEW!
WOO-HOO!
TAK
MEEEEW!
CAN'T CATCH ME!
WOOOOSH
SIGH...
NOOO...
HE'S GETTING AWAY.
MEOW
TAI-CHAN, DON'T YOU WANT TO COME INSIDE?
MEOW
WE COULD HAVE SOMETHING TO EAT TOGETHER.
FREEZE
SPIN

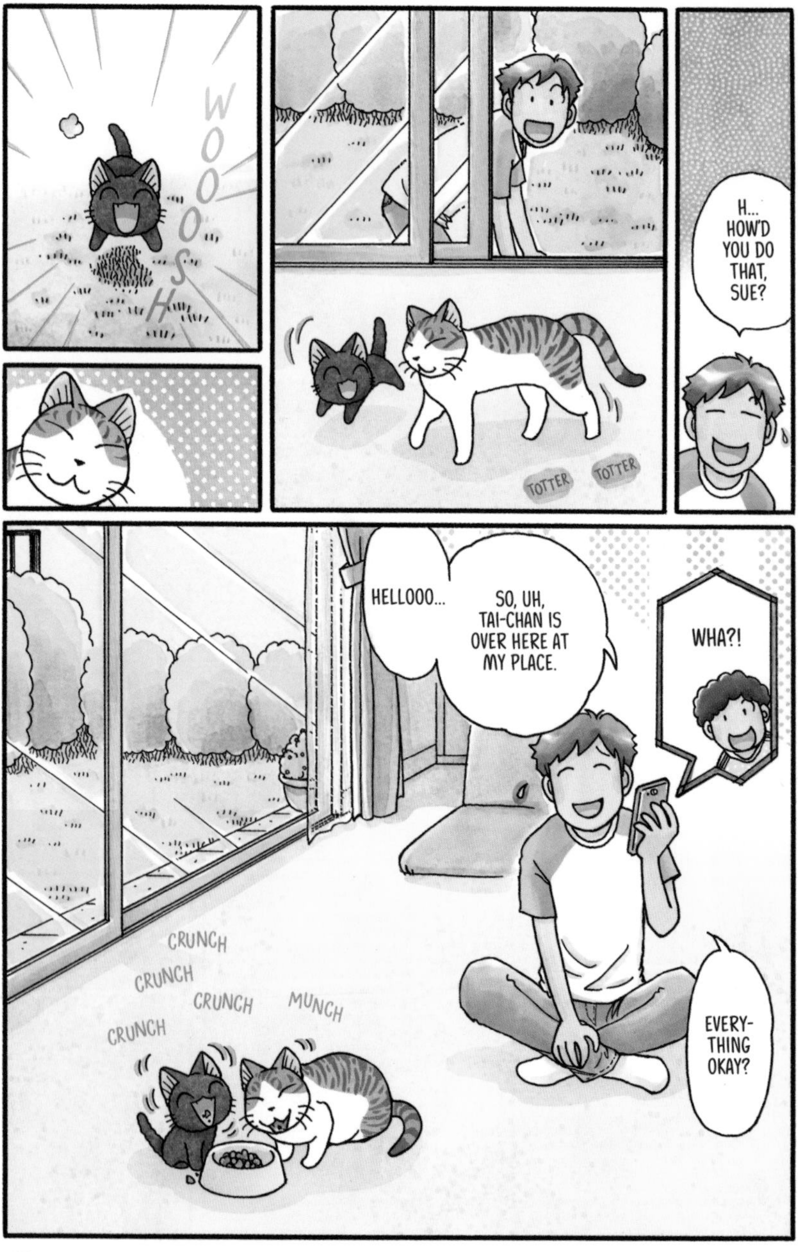
WOOOSH
TOTTER
TOTTER
H... HOW'D YOU DO THAT, SUE?
HELLOOO...
SO, UH, TAI-CHAN IS OVER HERE AT MY PLACE.
WHA?!
CRUNCH
CRUNCH
CRUNCH
MUNCH
CRUNCH
EVERY-THING OKAY?

SIGH...

Sue & Tai-chan

CHAPTER 40 The Bond Between Them

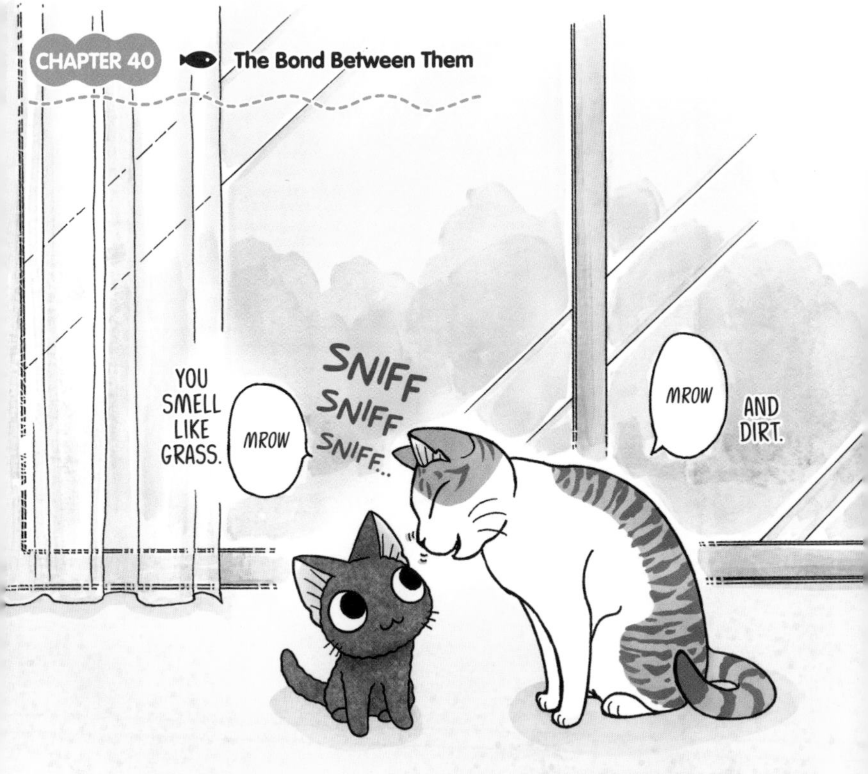
YOU SMELL LIKE GRASS.
MROW
SNIFF SNIFF SNIFF...
MROW
AND DIRT.

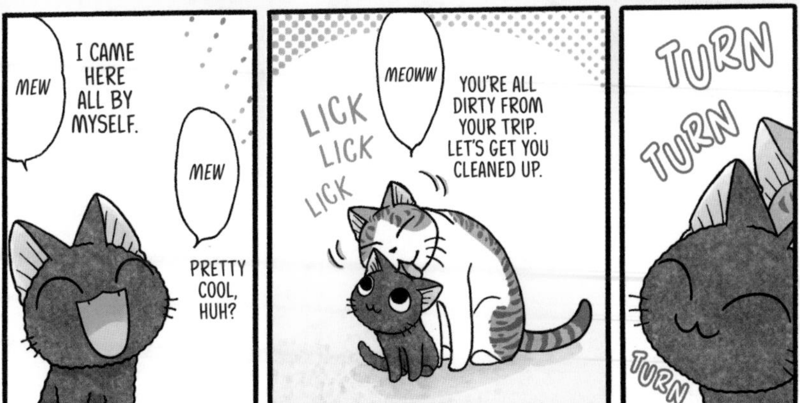
MEW
I CAME HERE ALL BY MYSELF.
MEW
PRETTY COOL, HUH?
LICK LICK LICK
MEOWW
YOU'RE ALL DIRTY FROM YOUR TRIP. LET'S GET YOU CLEANED UP.
TURN TURN
TURN

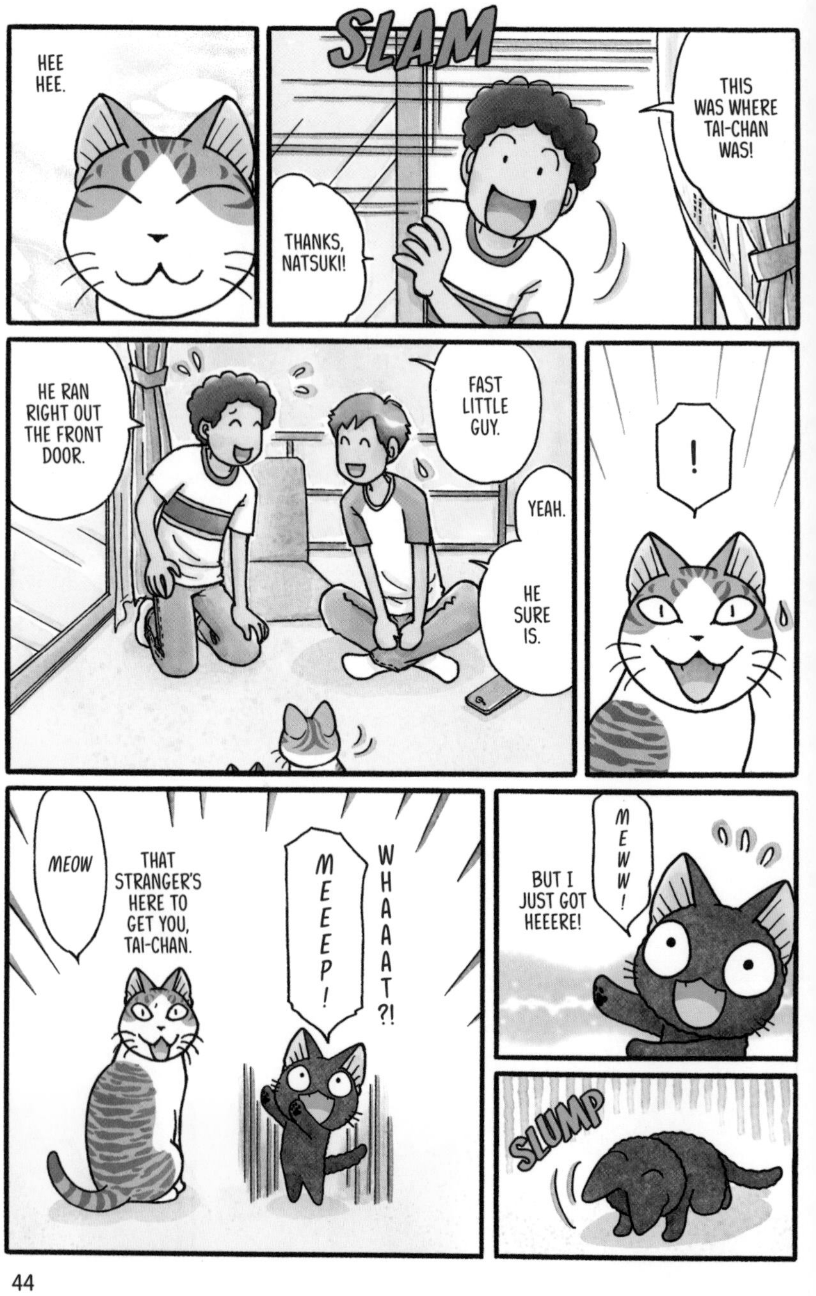
HEE HEE.
SLAM
THIS WAS WHERE TAI-CHAN WAS!
THANKS, NATSUKI!
HE RAN RIGHT OUT THE FRONT DOOR.
FAST LITTLE GUY.
YEAH.
HE SURE IS.
!
MEOW
THAT STRANGER'S HERE TO GET YOU, TAI-CHAN.
MEEEP!
WHAAAAT?!
MEWW!
BUT I JUST GOT HEEERE!
SLUMP

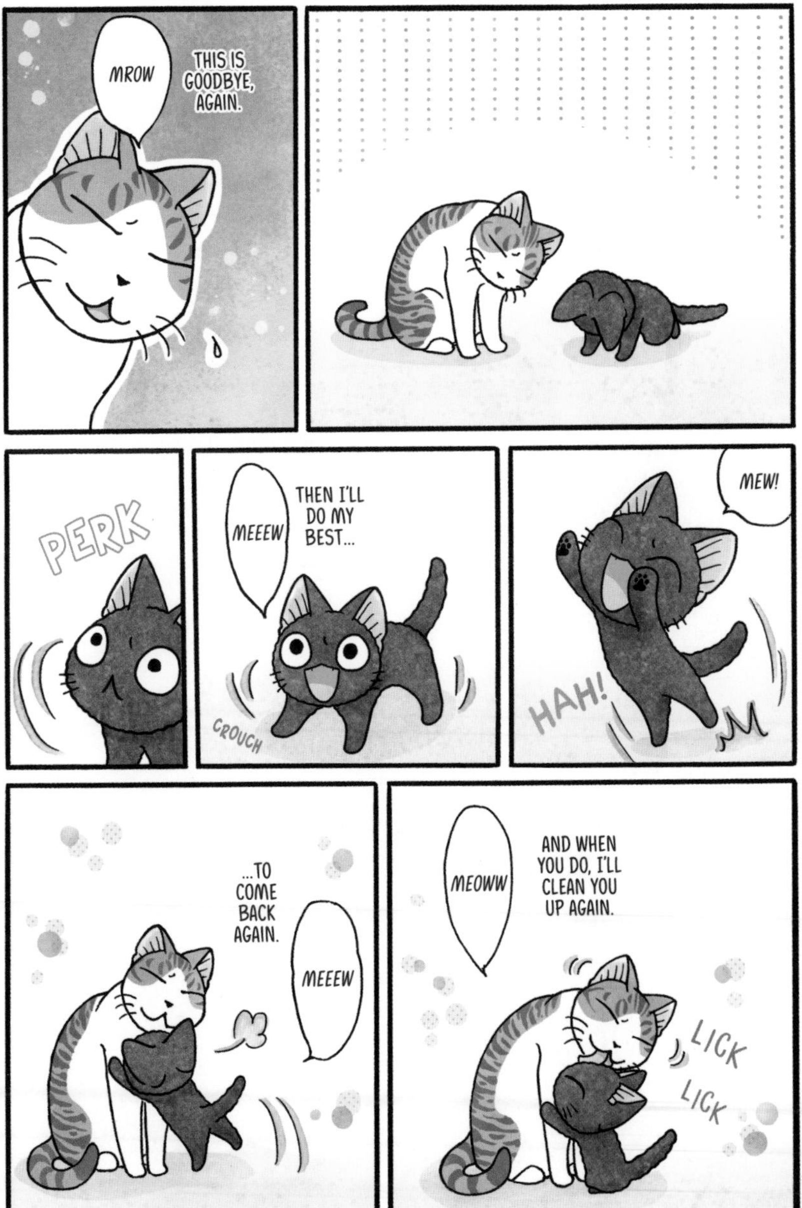
MROW
THIS IS GOODBYE, AGAIN.
PERK
MEEEW
THEN I'LL DO MY BEST...
CROUCH
MEW!
HAH!
...TO COME BACK AGAIN.
MEEEW
MEOWW
AND WHEN YOU DO, I'LL CLEAN YOU UP AGAIN.
LICK
LICK

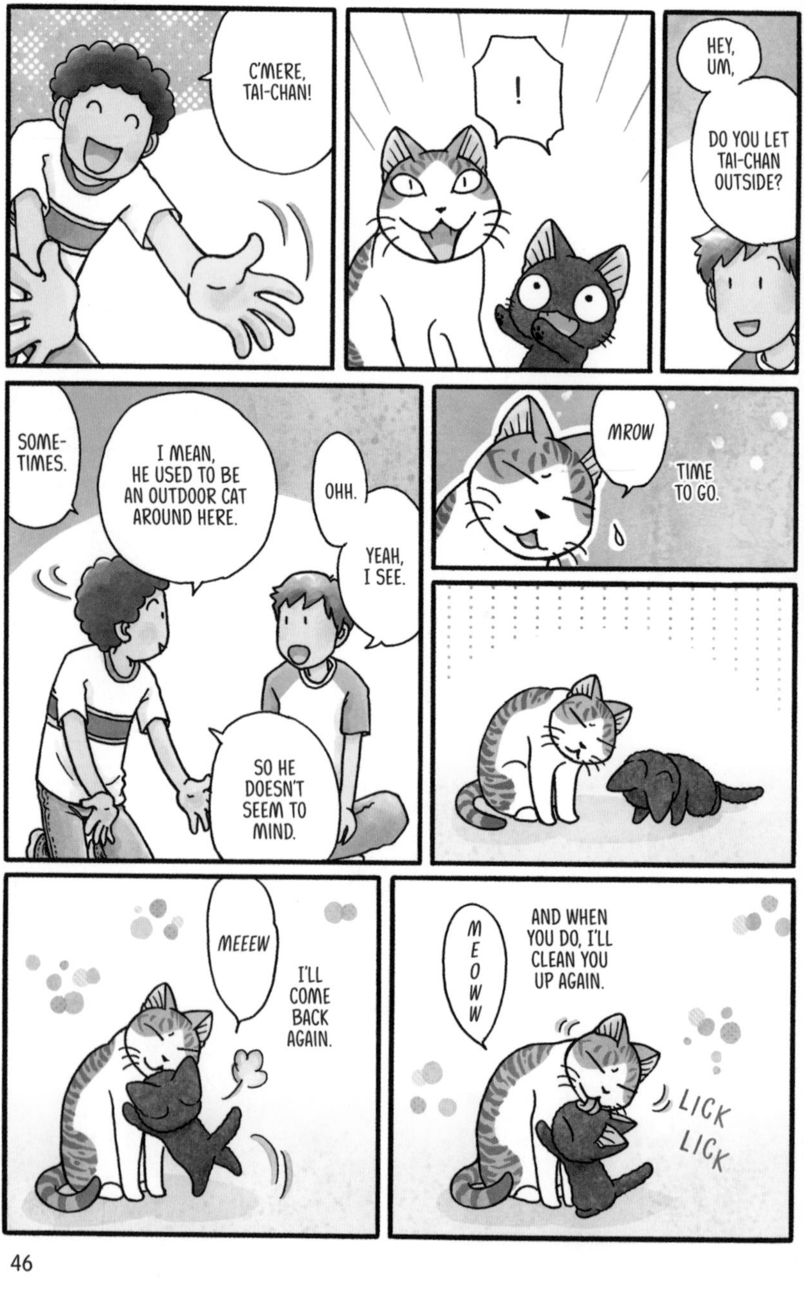
C'MERE, TAI-CHAN!
!
HEY, UM,
DO YOU LET TAI-CHAN OUTSIDE?
SOME-TIMES.
I MEAN, HE USED TO BE AN OUTDOOR CAT AROUND HERE.
OHH.
YEAH, I SEE.
SO HE DOESN'T SEEM TO MIND.
MROW
TIME TO GO.
MEEEW
I'LL COME BACK AGAIN.
MEOWW
AND WHEN YOU DO, I'LL CLEAN YOU UP AGAIN.
LICK LICK

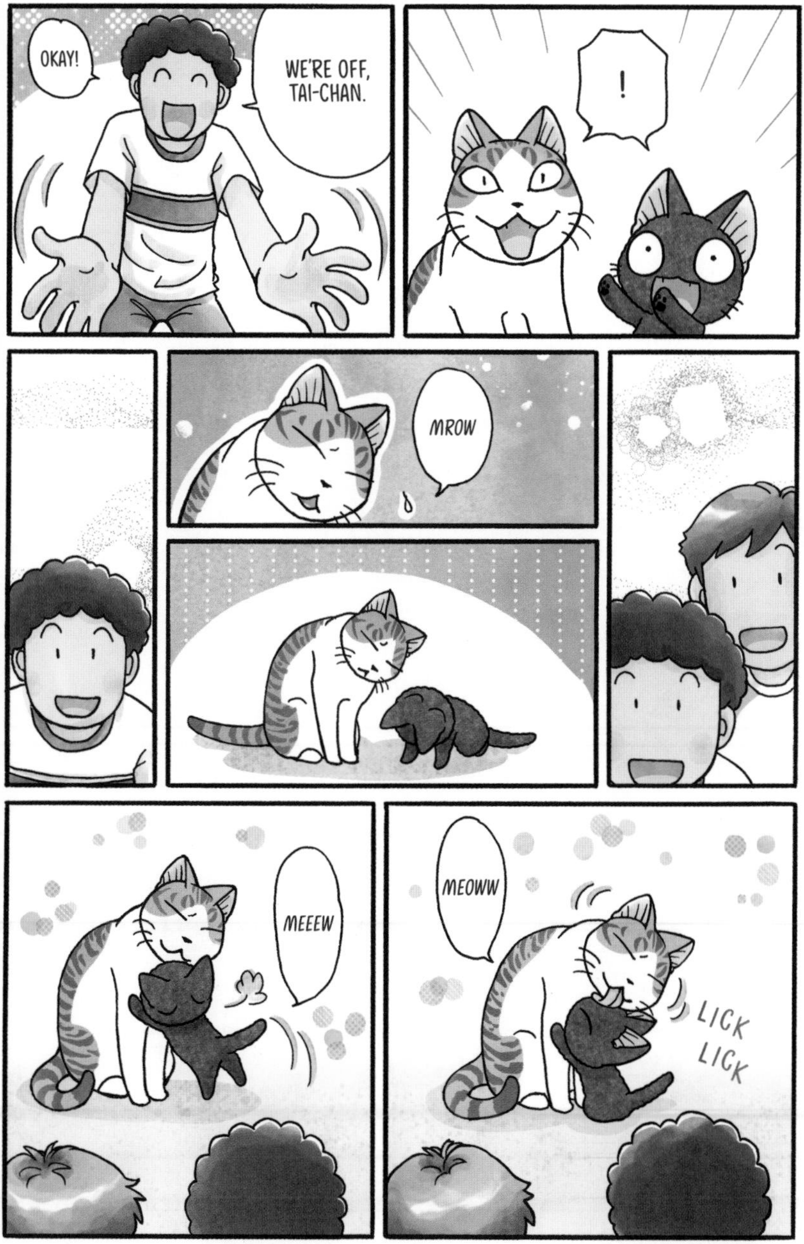
OKAY!
WE'RE OFF, TAI-CHAN.
!
MROW
MEEEW
MEOWW
LICK LICK

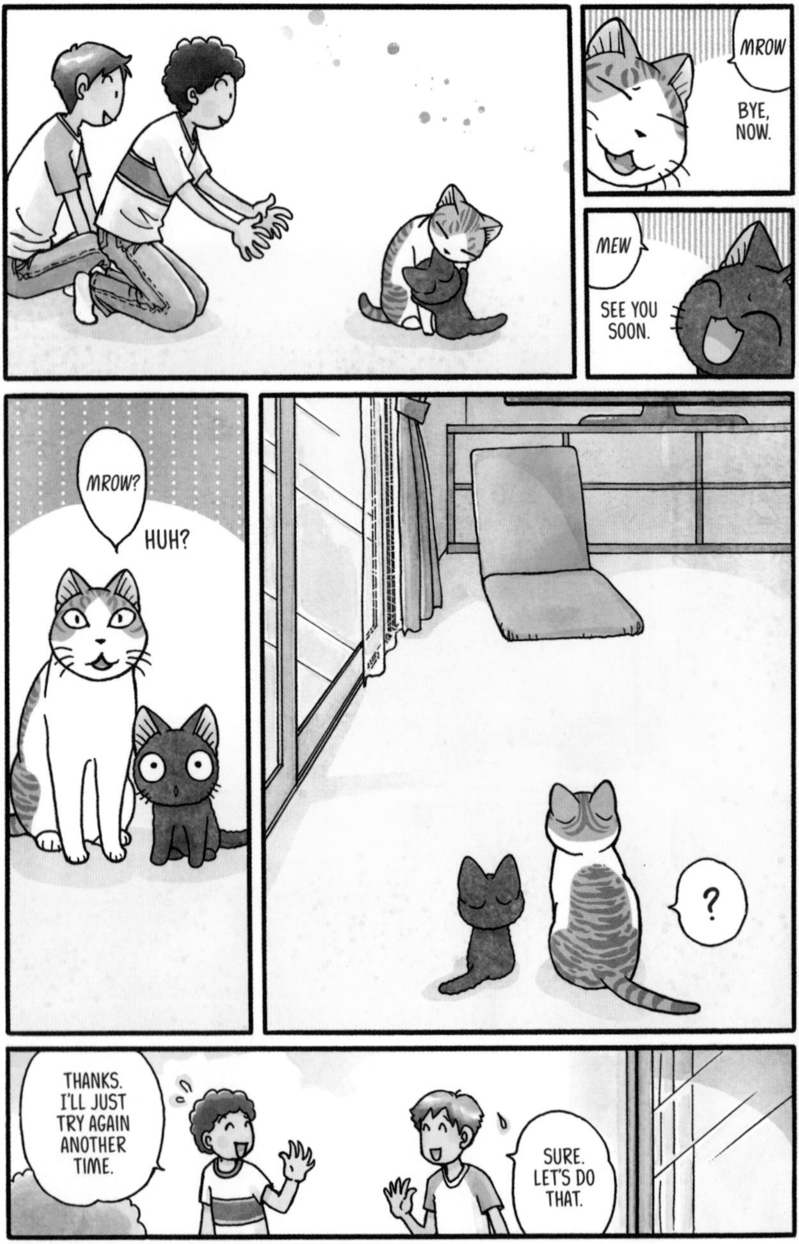
MROW
BYE, NOW.
MEW
SEE YOU SOON.
MROW?
HUH?
?
THANKS. I'LL JUST TRY AGAIN ANOTHER TIME.
SURE. LET'S DO THAT.

CHAPTER 41 Conflicted Kitten

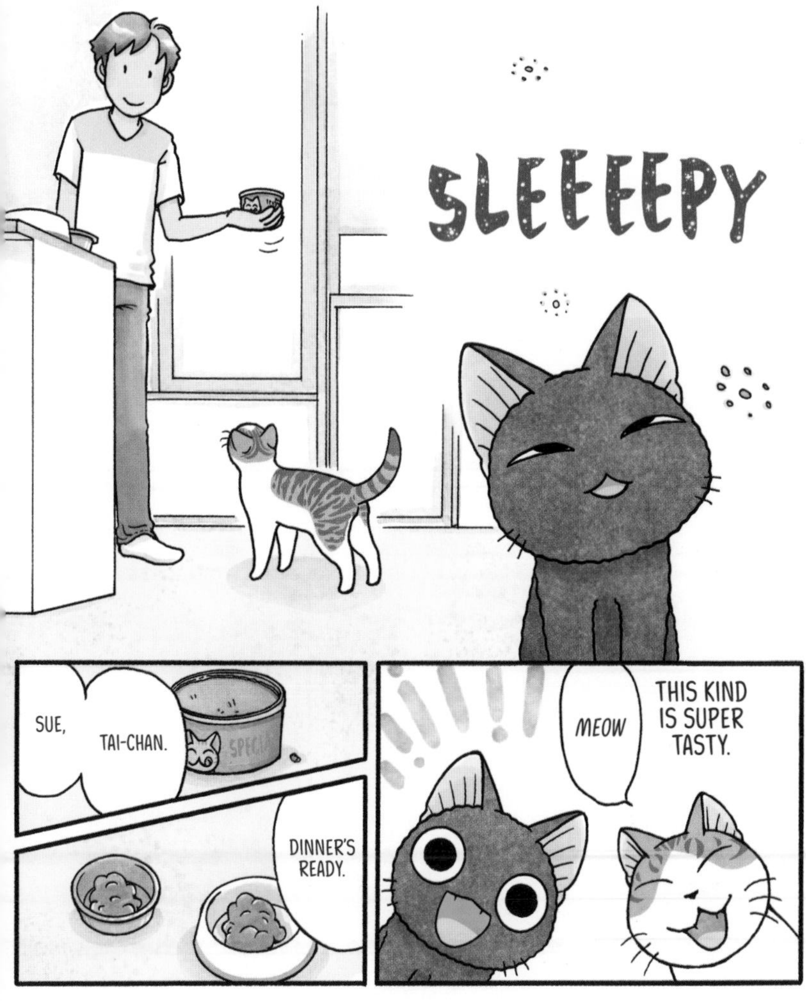
SLEEEEPY
SUE,
TAI-CHAN.
DINNER'S READY.
MEOW
THIS KIND IS SUPER TASTY.

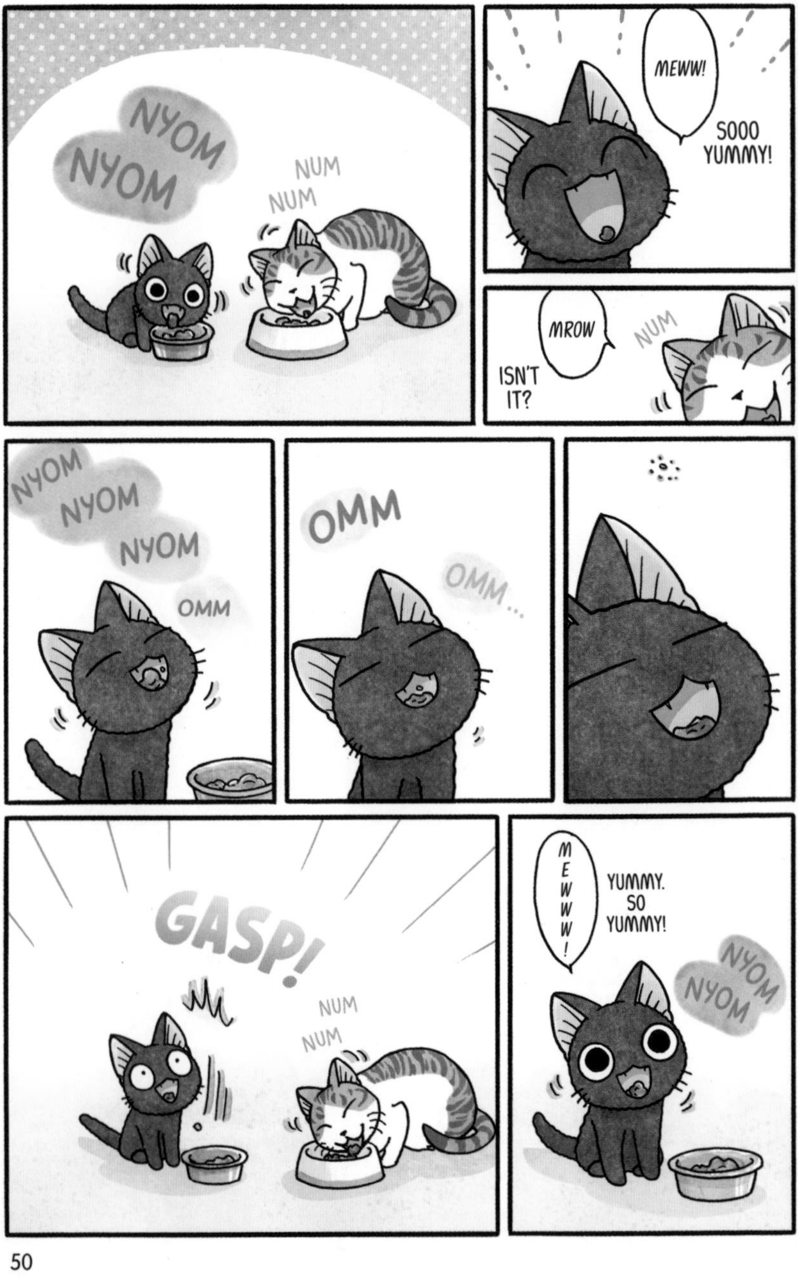
NYOM
NYOM
NUM
NUM
MEWW!
SOOO YUMMY!
MROW
ISN'T IT?
NUM
NYOM
NYOM
NYOM
OMM
OMM
OMM...
GASP!
NUM
NUM
MEWWW!
YUMMY. SO YUMMY!
NYOM
NYOM

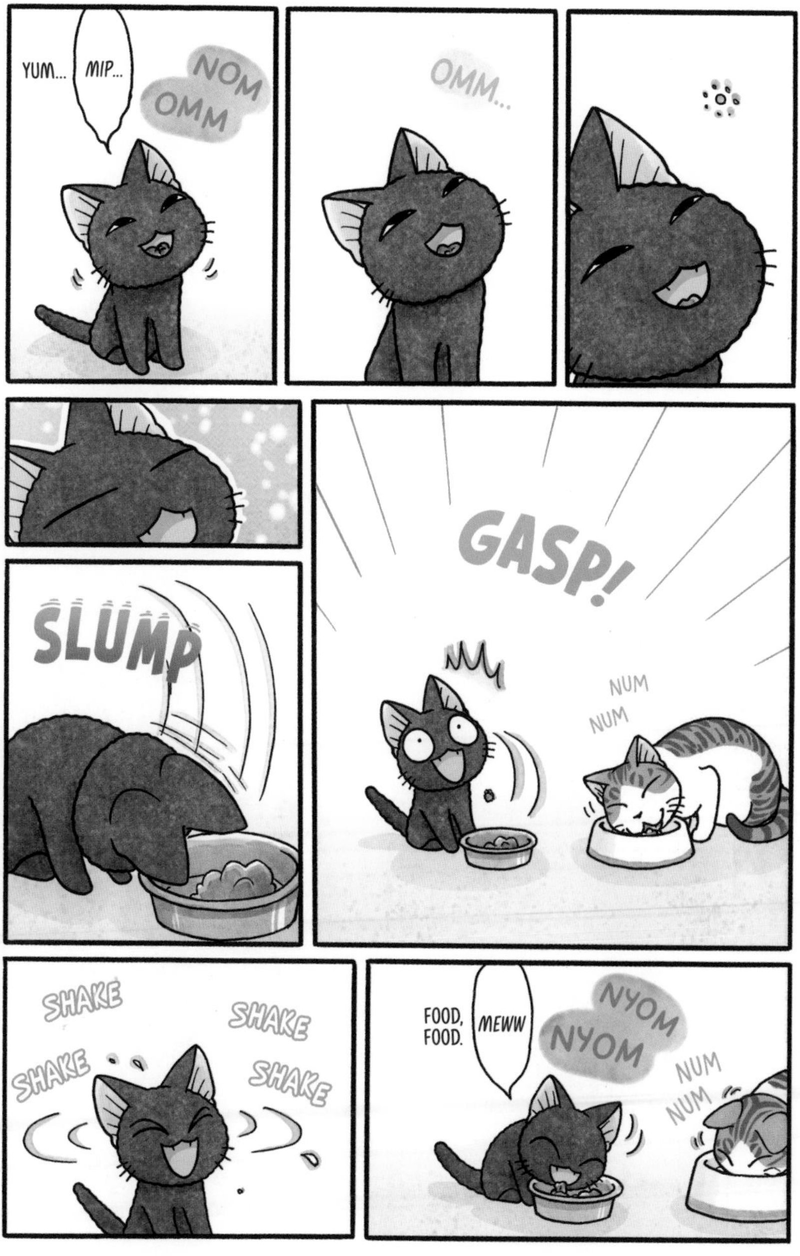
YUM...
MIP...
NOM OMM
OMM...
SLUMP
GASP!
NUM NUM
SHAKE
SHAKE
SHAKE
SHAKE
FOOD, FOOD.
MEWW
NYOM NYOM
NUM NUM

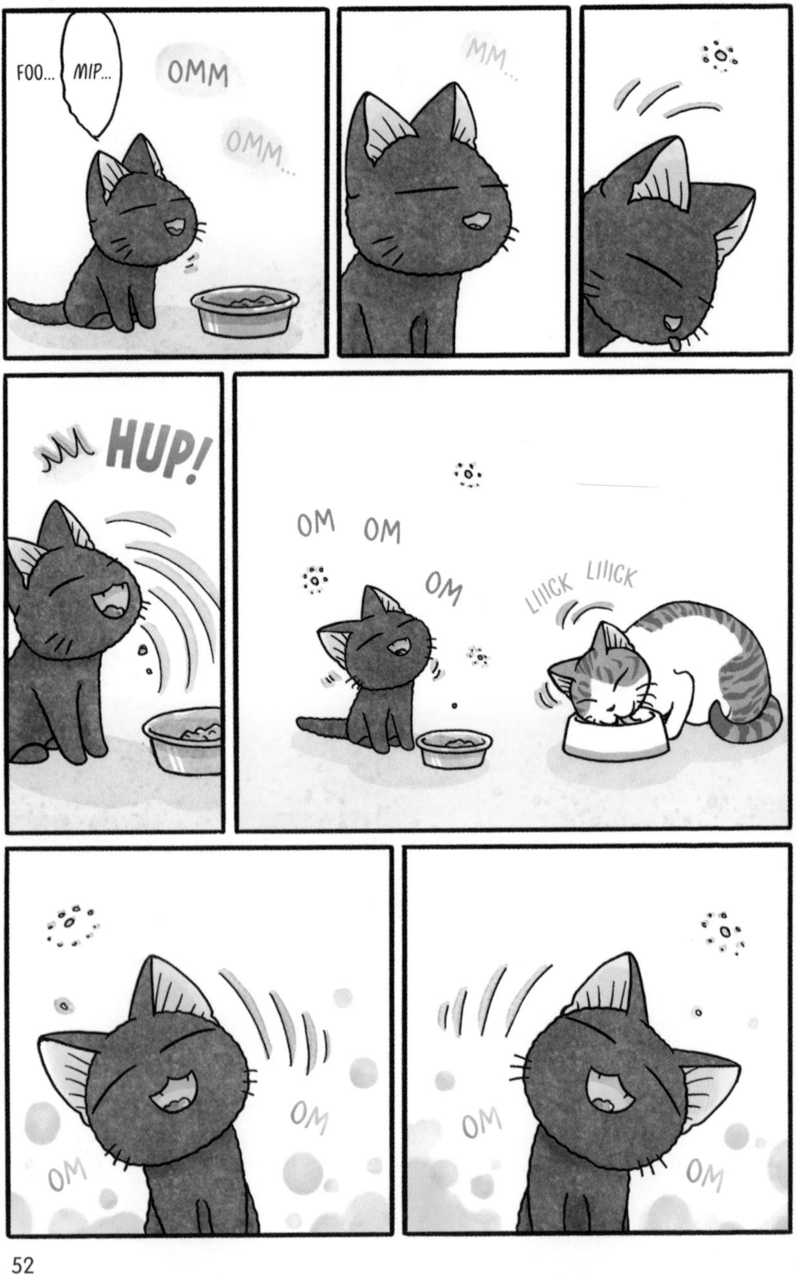
FOO...
MIP...
OMM
OMM...
MM...
HUP!
OM
OM
OM
LIIICK
LIIICK
OM
OM
OM
OM

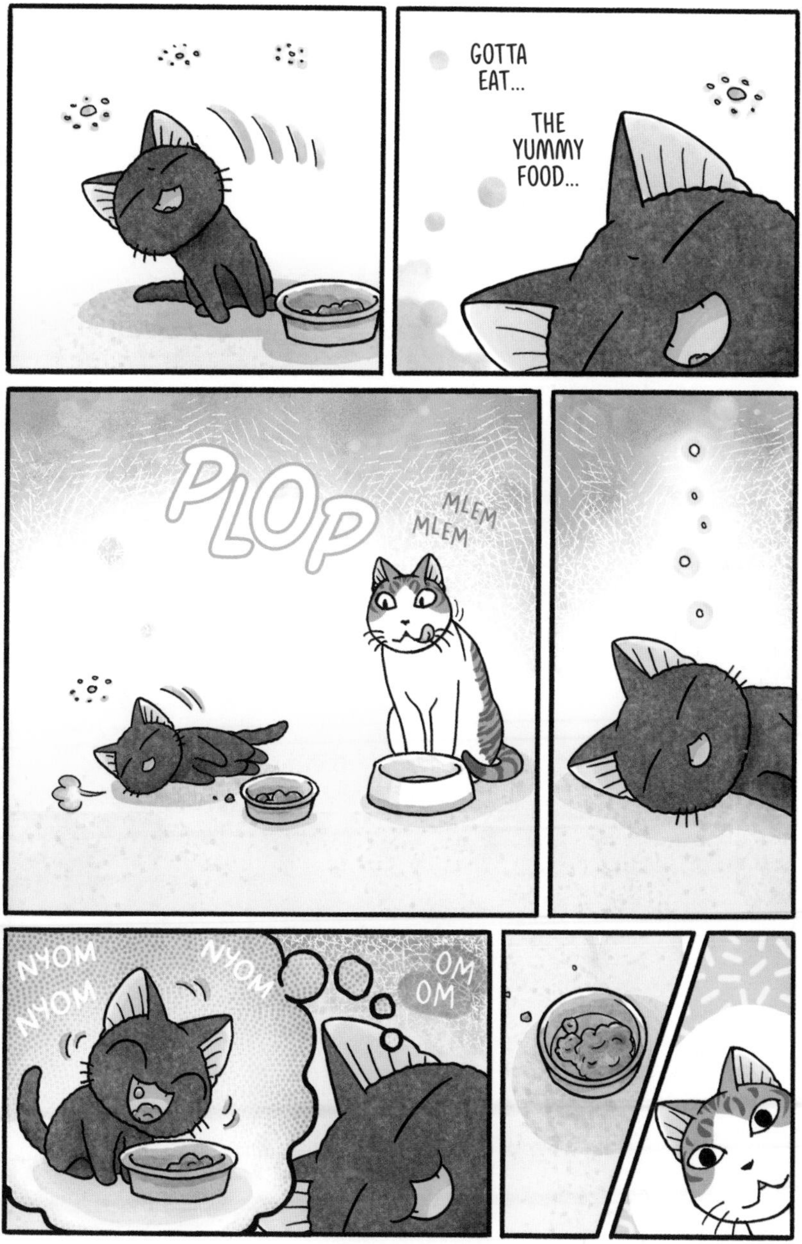
GOTTA EAT...
THE YUMMY FOOD...
PLOP
MLEM MLEM
NYOM NYOM
NYOM
OM OM

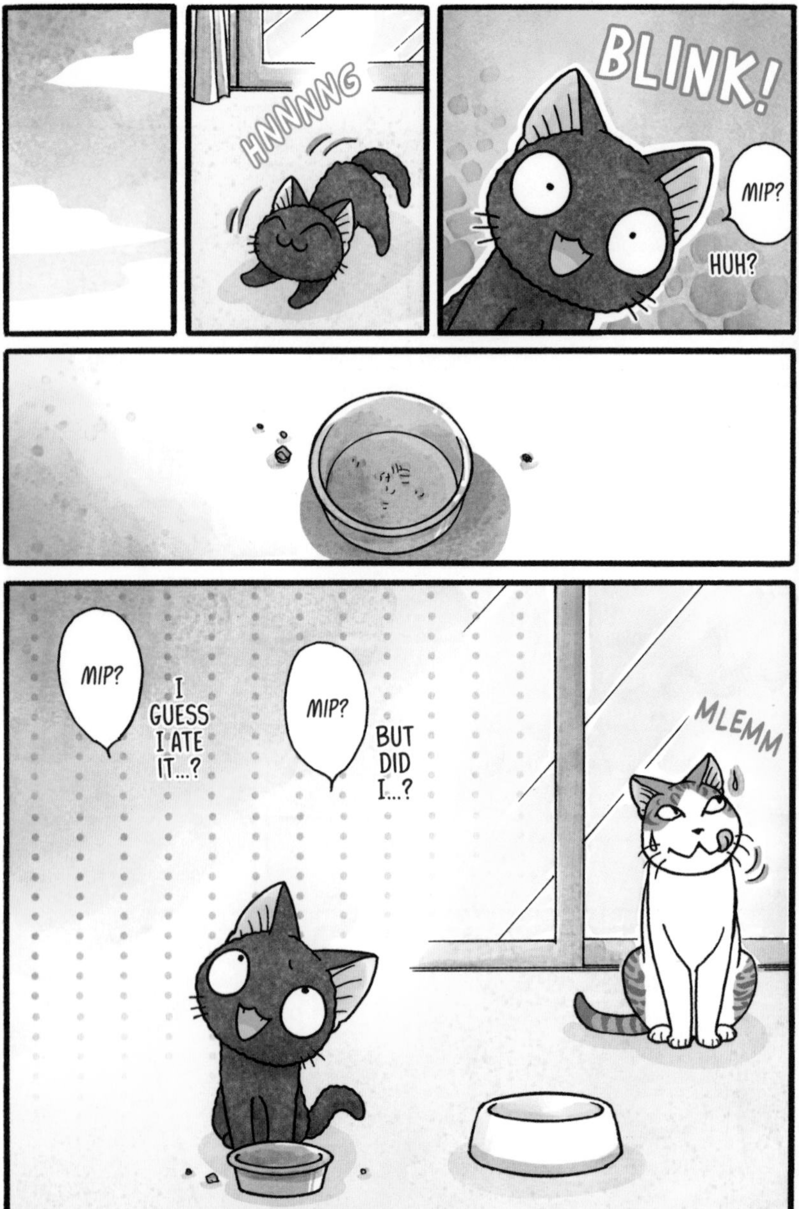
HNNNNG
BLINK!
MIP?
HUH?
MIP?
I GUESS I ATE IT...?
MIP?
BUT DID I...?
MLEMM

CHAPTER 42 Surprise Tactics!

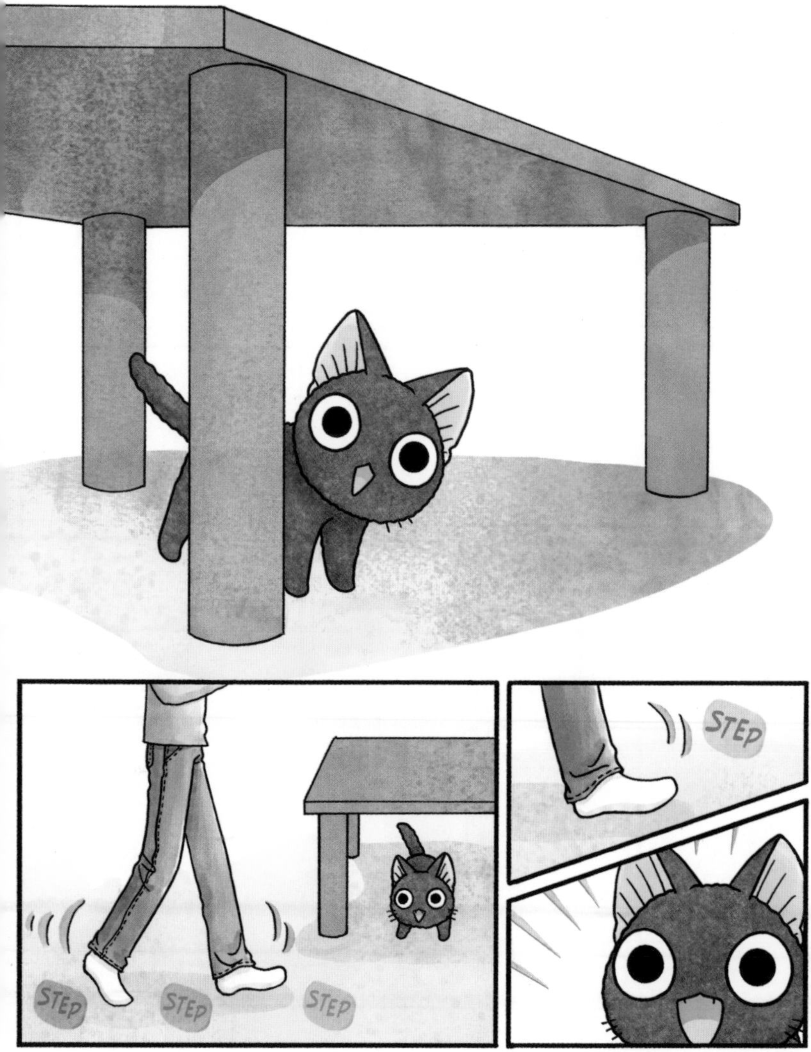
STEP
STEP
STEP
STEP

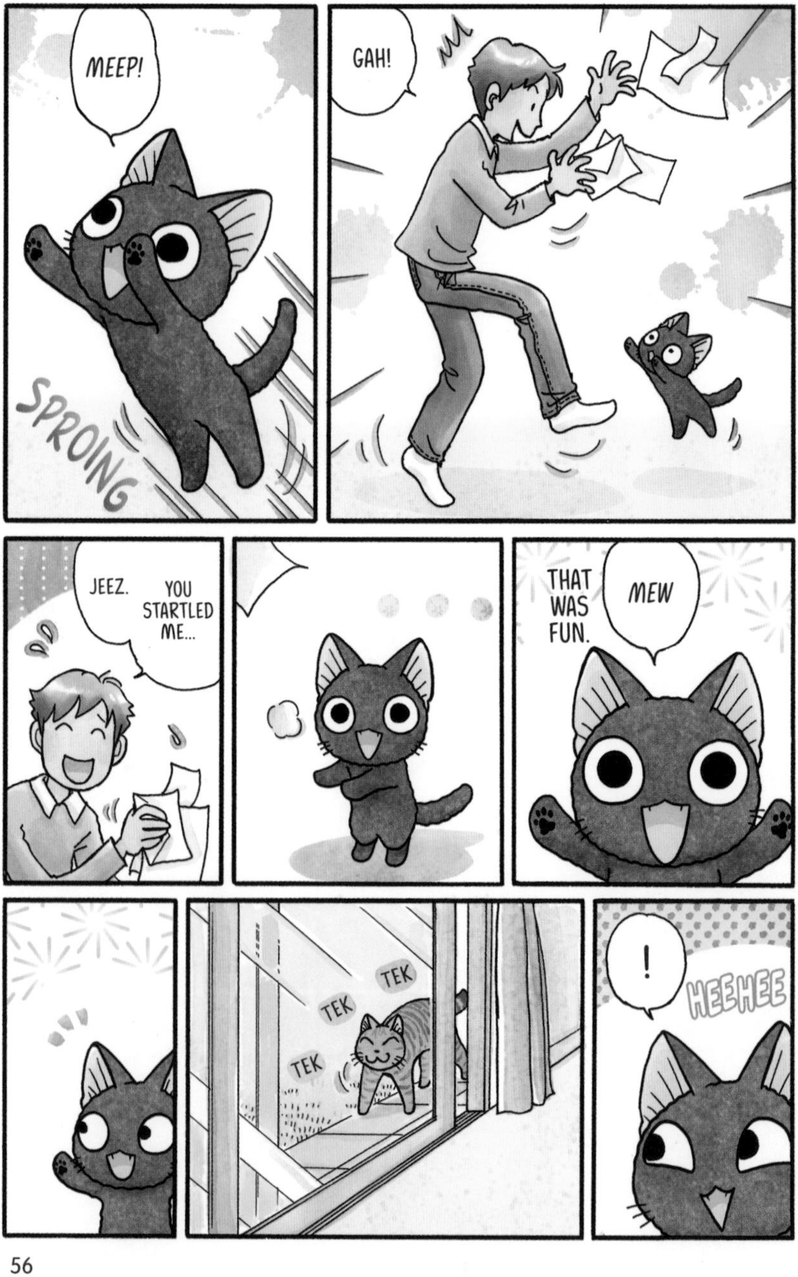
MEEP!
SPROING
GAH!
JEEZ.
YOU STARTLED ME...
THAT WAS FUN.
MEW
TEK
TEK
TEK
!
HEEHEE

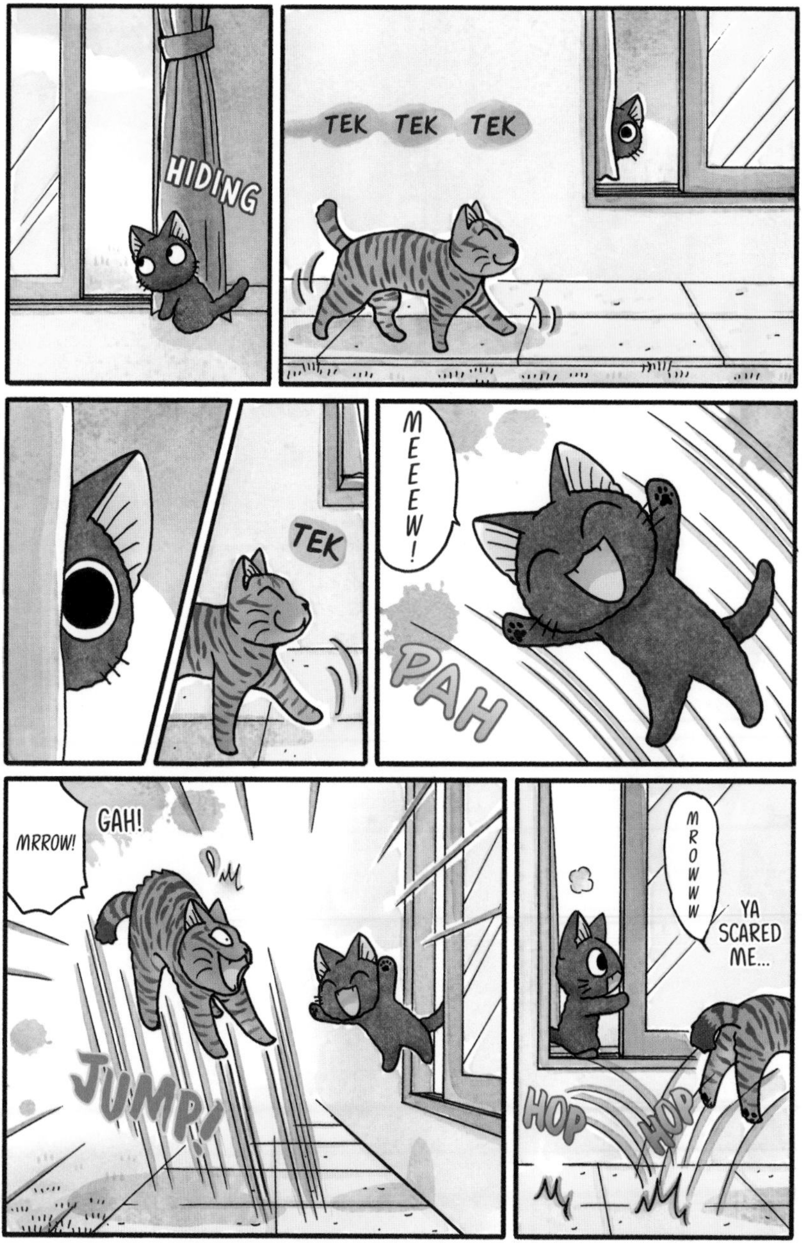
HIDING
TEK TEK TEK
TEK
MEEEEW!
PAH
MRROW!
GAH!
JUMP!
MROWWW
YA SCARED ME...
HOP
HOP

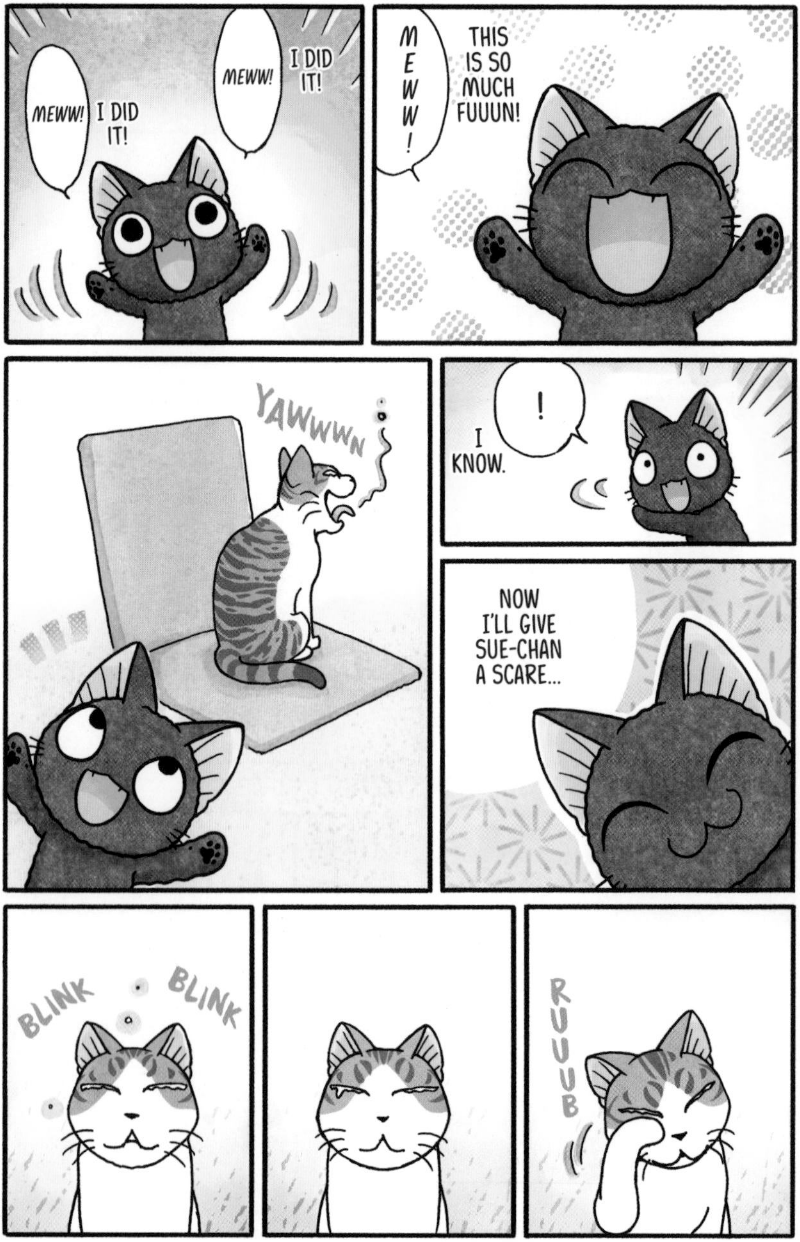
MEWW!
I DID IT!
MEWW!
I DID IT!
MEWW!
THIS IS SO MUCH FUUUN!
YAWWWN
!
I KNOW.
NOW I'LL GIVE SUE-CHAN A SCARE...
BLINK
BLINK
RUUUB

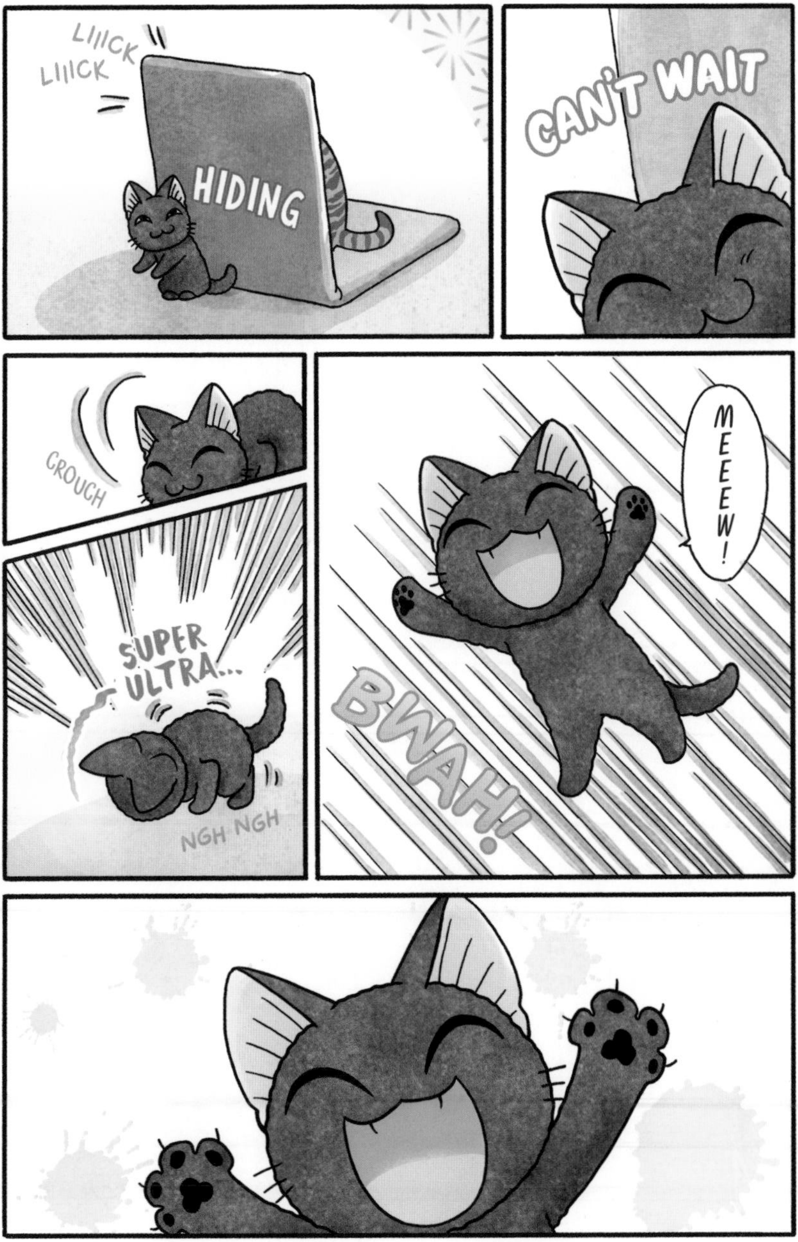
LIIICK
LIIICK
HIDING
CAN'T WAIT
CROUCH
SUPER ULTRA...
NGH NGH
MEEEW!
BWAH!

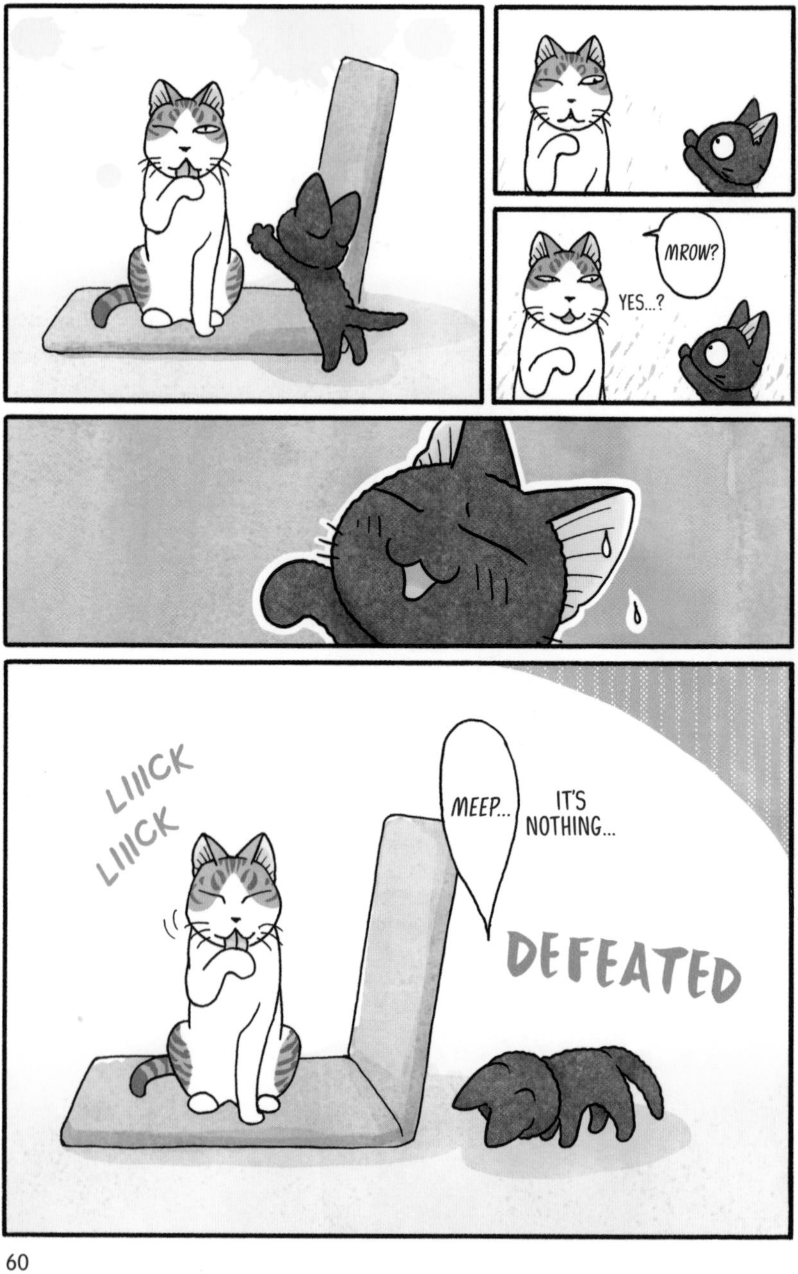
MROW?
YES...?
LIIICK
LIIICK
MEEP...
IT'S NOTHING...
DEFEATED

Sue & Tai-chan

CHAPTER 43 A Good Game?!

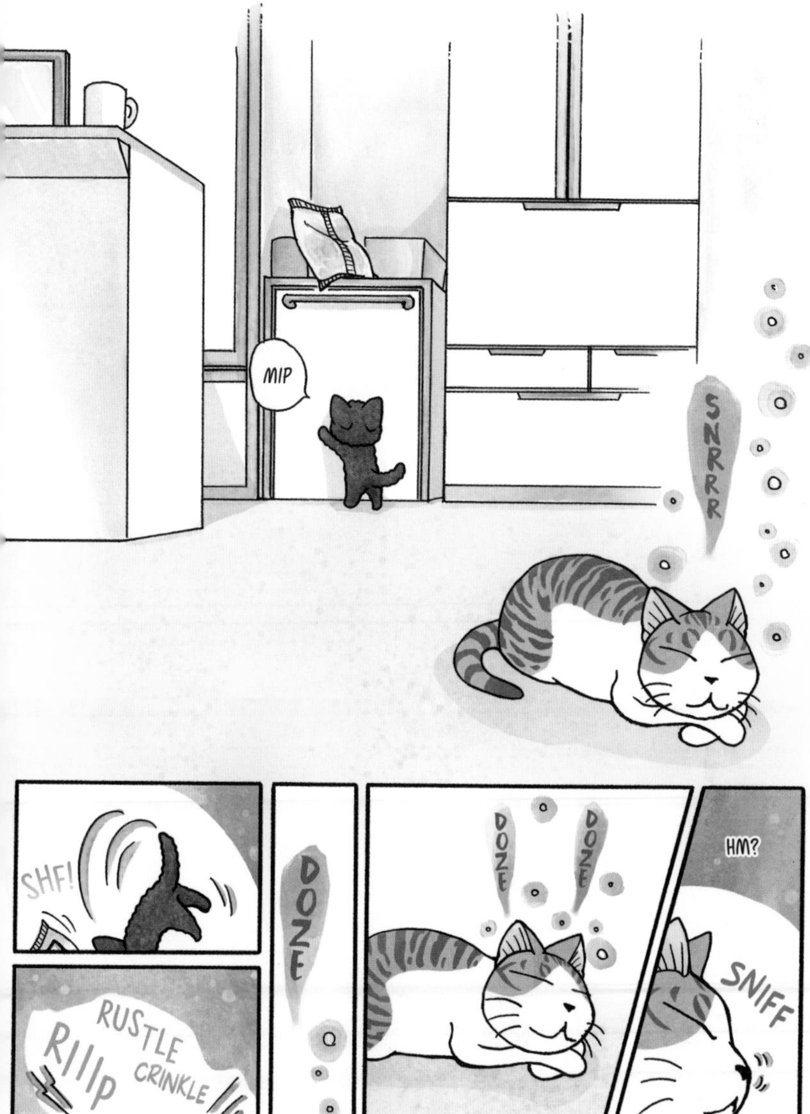
MIP
SNRRR
SHF!
RUSTLE
RIIIP
CRINKLE
DOZE
DOZE
DOZE
HM?
SNIFF

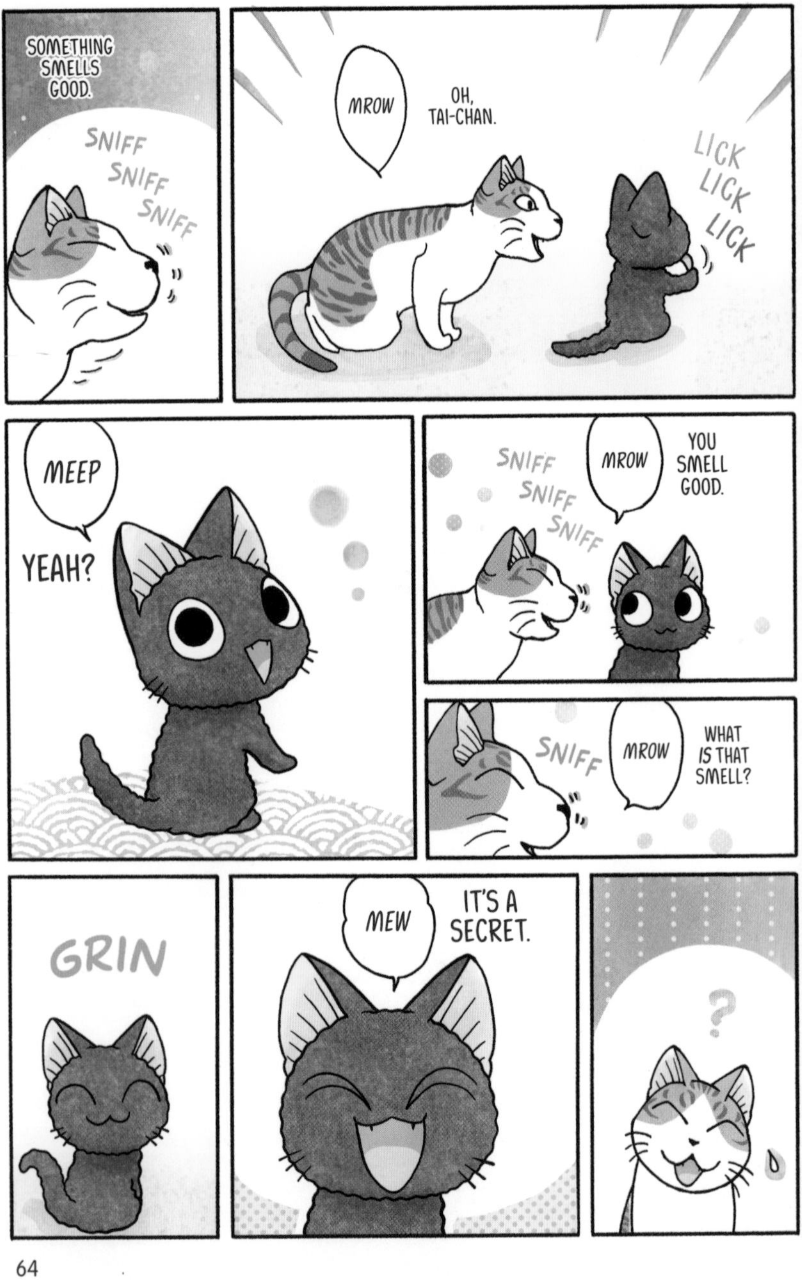
SOMETHING SMELLS GOOD.
SNIFF SNIFF SNIFF
MROW
OH, TAI-CHAN.
LICK LICK LICK
MEEP
YEAH?
SNIFF SNIFF SNIFF
MROW
YOU SMELL GOOD.
SNIFF
MROW
WHAT IS THAT SMELL?
GRIN
MEW
IT'S A SECRET.
?

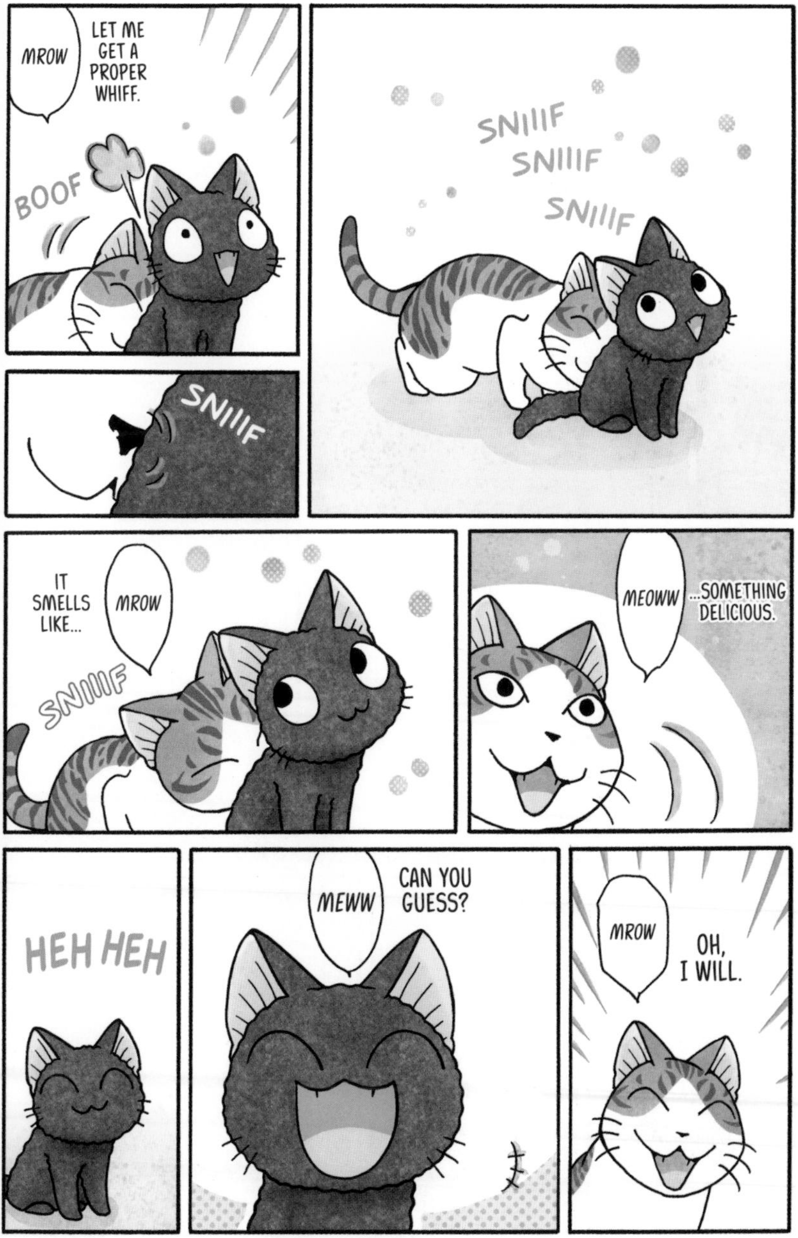
MROW
LET ME GET A PROPER WHIFF.
BOOF
SNIIIF
SNIIIF
SNIIIF
SNIIIF
IT SMELLS LIKE...
MROW
SNIIIF
MEOWW
...SOMETHING DELICIOUS.
HEH HEH
MEWW
CAN YOU GUESS?
MROW
OH, I WILL.

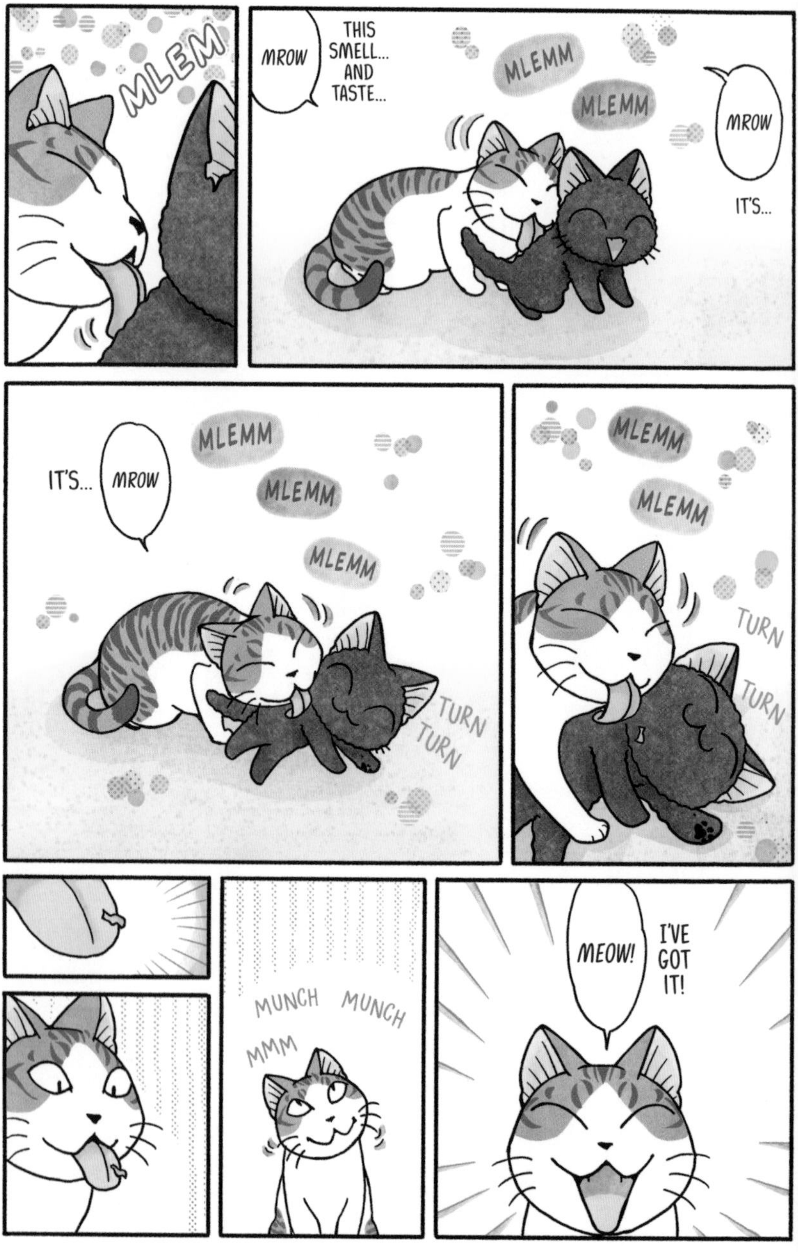
MLEM
MROW
THIS SMELL... AND TASTE...
MLEMM
MLEMM
MROW
IT'S...
IT'S...
MROW
MLEMM
MLEMM
MLEMM
TURN TURN
MLEMM
MLEMM
TURN
TURN
MUNCH MUNCH
MMM
MEOW!
I'VE GOT IT!

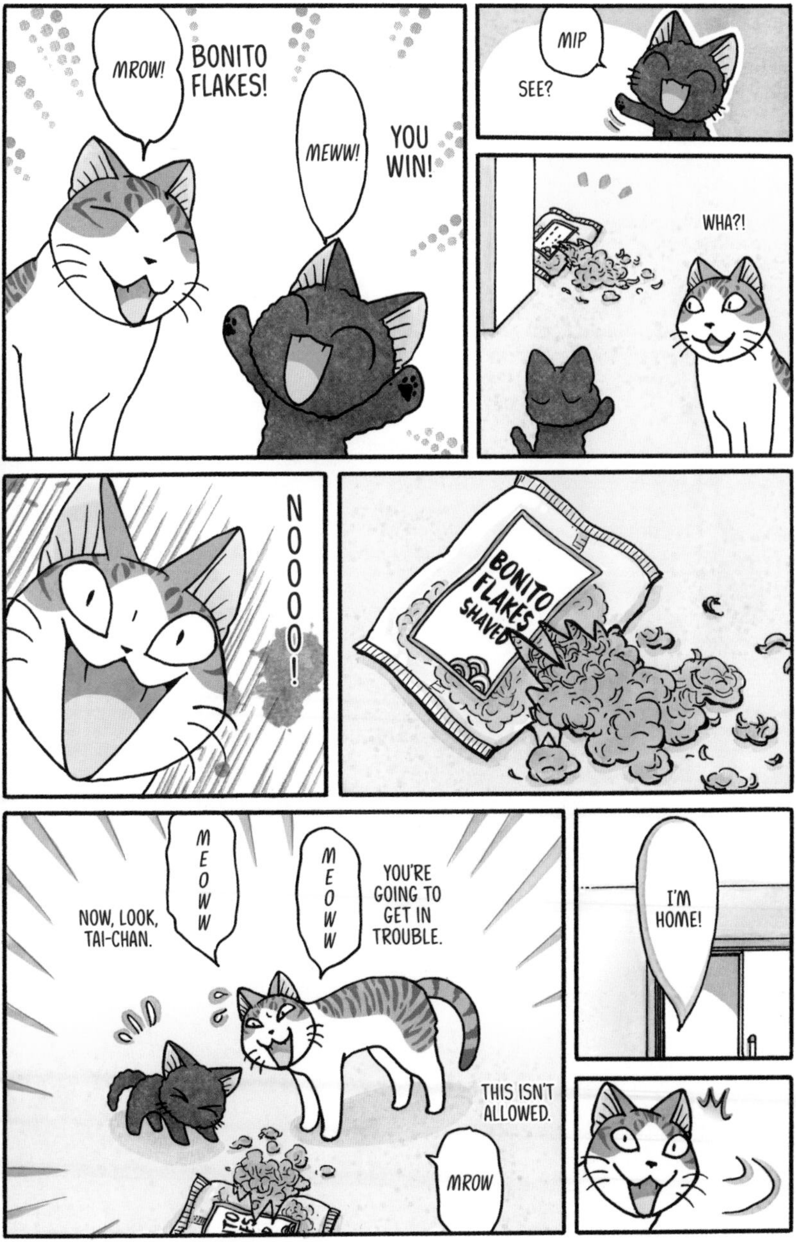
MROW!
BONITO FLAKES!
MEWW!
YOU WIN!
MIP
SEE?
WHA?!
NOOOOO!
BONITO FLAKES SHAVED
MEOWW
NOW, LOOK, TAI-CHAN.
MEOWW
YOU'RE GOING TO GET IN TROUBLE.
THIS ISN'T ALLOWED.
MROW
I'M HOME!

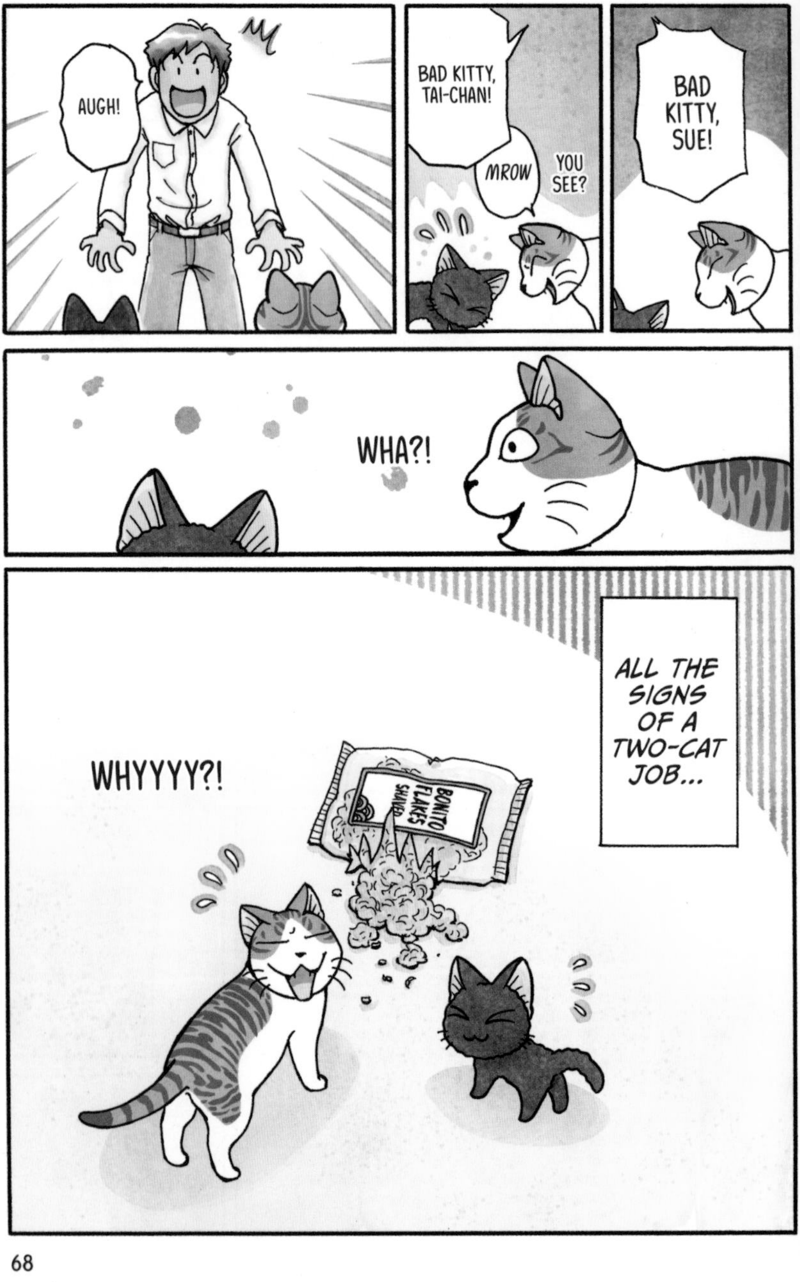
AUGH!
BAD KITTY, TAI-CHAN!
MROW
YOU SEE?
BAD KITTY, SUE!
WHA?!
WHYYYY?!
BONITO FLAKES
SHAVED
ALL THE SIGNS OF A TWO-CAT JOB...

CHAPTER 44 Tai-chan Explosion

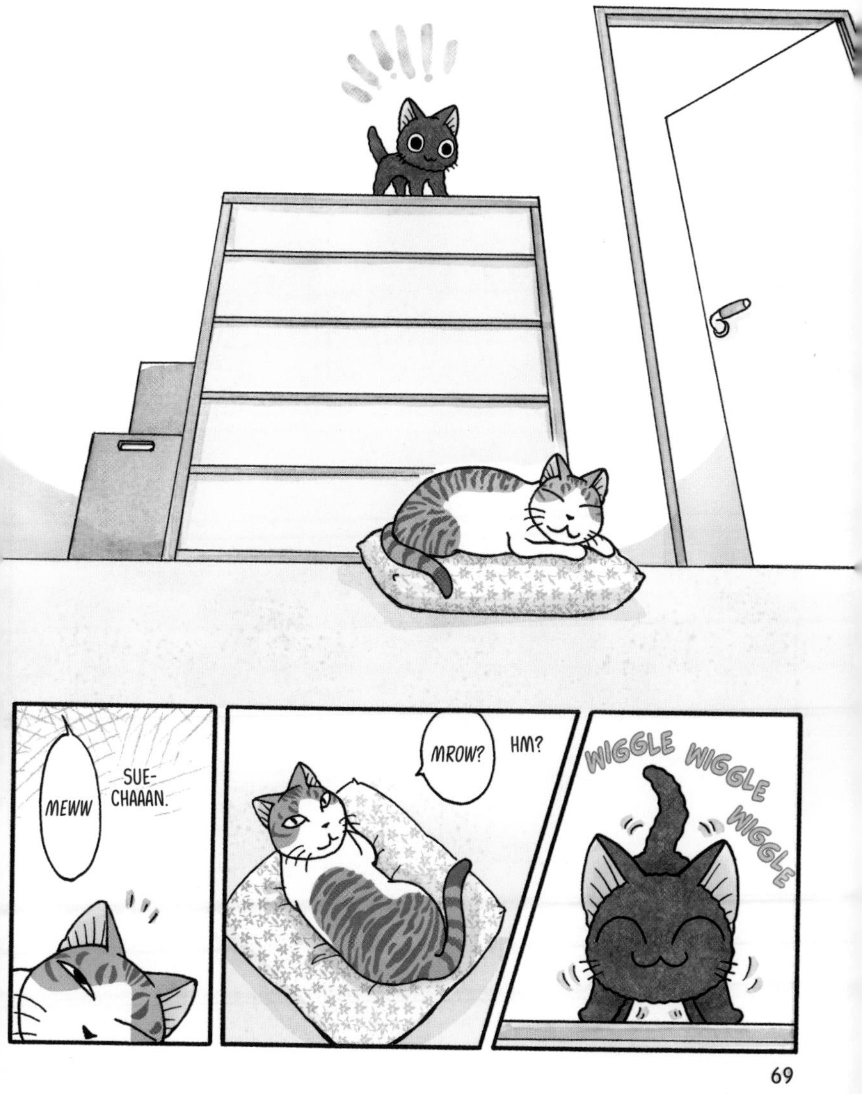
MEWW
SUE-CHAAAN.
MROW?
HM?
WIGGLE WIGGLE WIGGLE

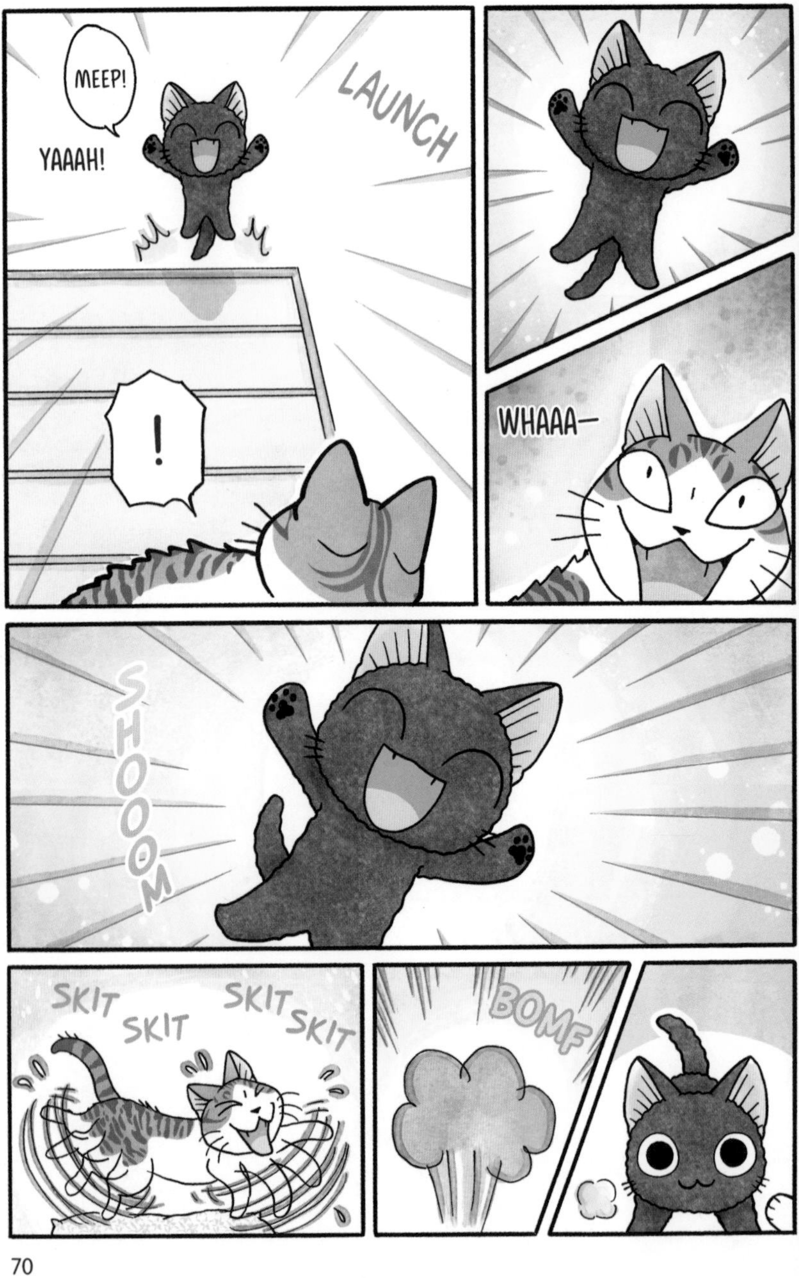
MEEP!
YAAAH!
LAUNCH
!
WHAAA–
SHOOOOM
SKIT
SKIT
SKIT SKIT
BOMF

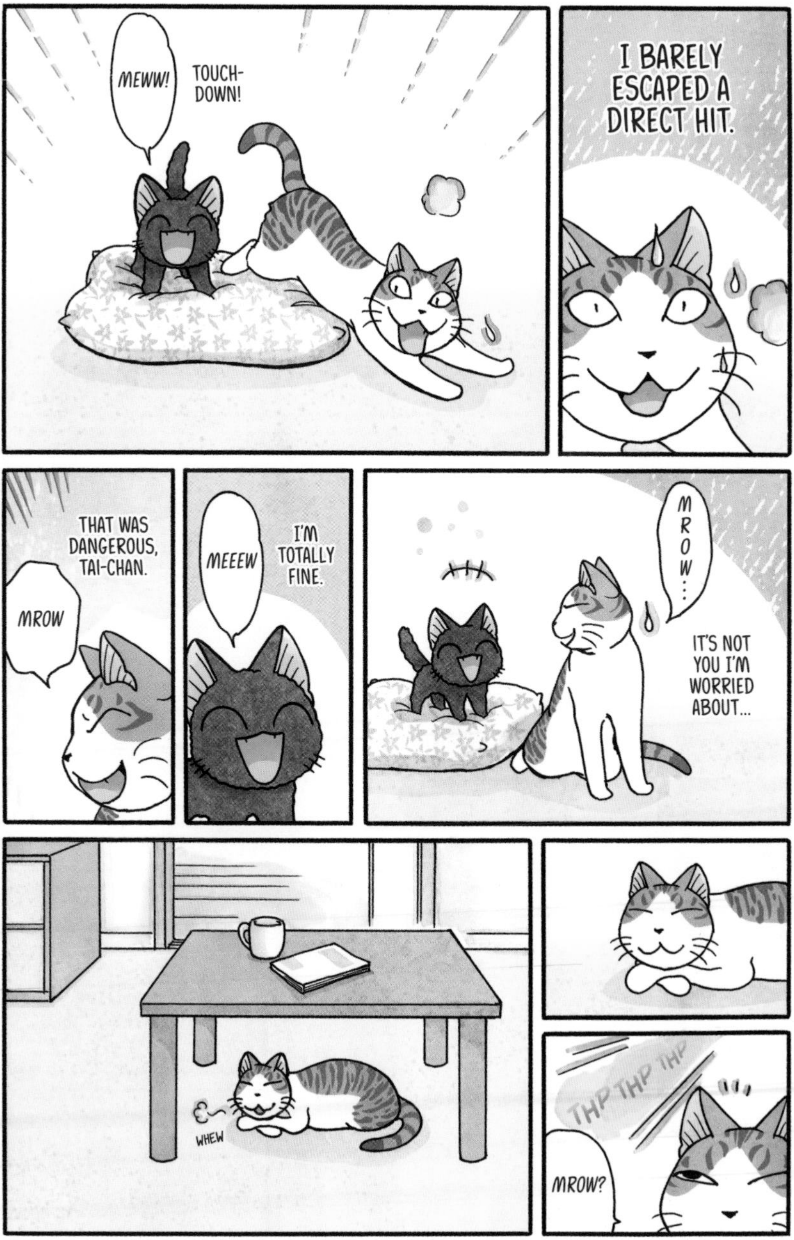
MEWW!
TOUCH-DOWN!
I BARELY ESCAPED A DIRECT HIT.
THAT WAS DANGEROUS, TAI-CHAN.
MROW
MEEEW
I'M TOTALLY FINE.
MROW...
IT'S NOT YOU I'M WORRIED ABOUT...
WHEW
THP THP THP
MROW?

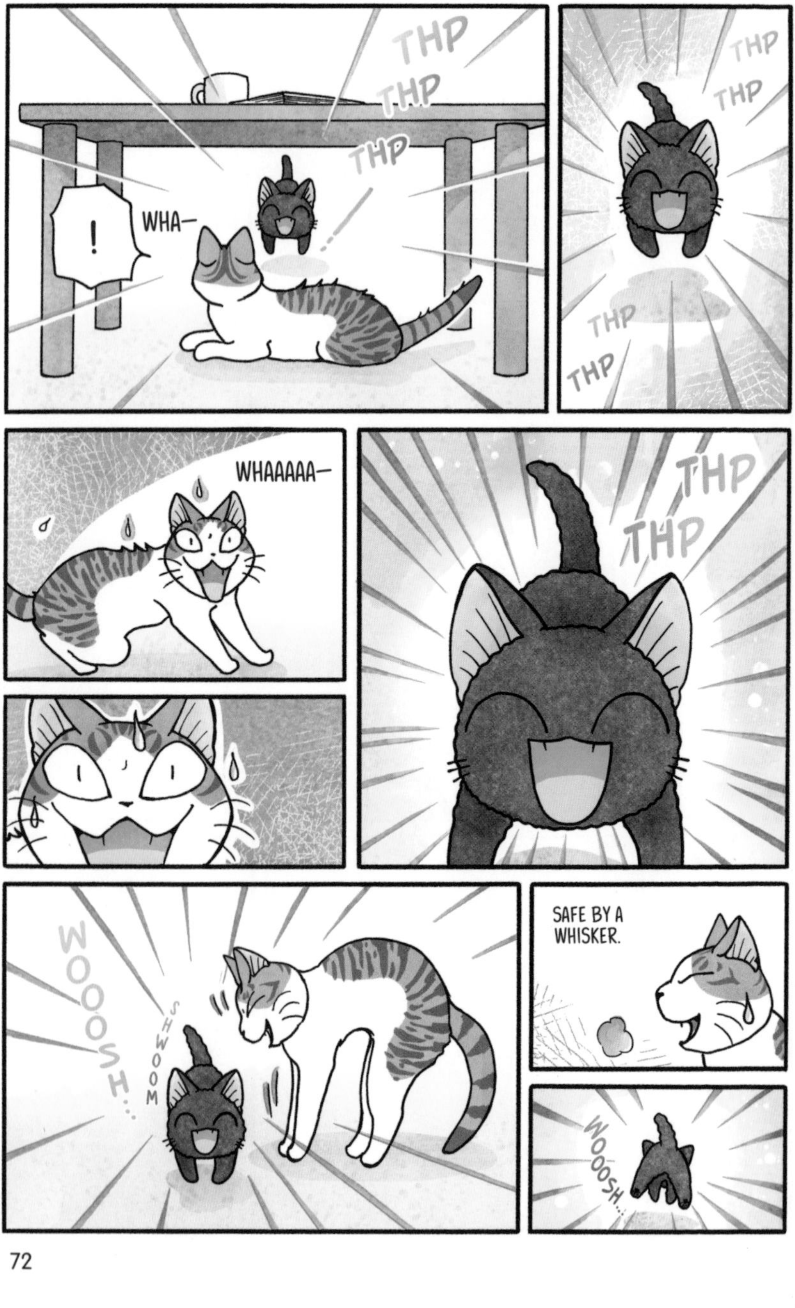
THP
THP
THP
!
WHA—
THP
THP
THP
THP
WHAAAAA—
THP
THP
WOOOSH...
SHWOOM
SAFE BY A WHISKER.
WOOOSH...

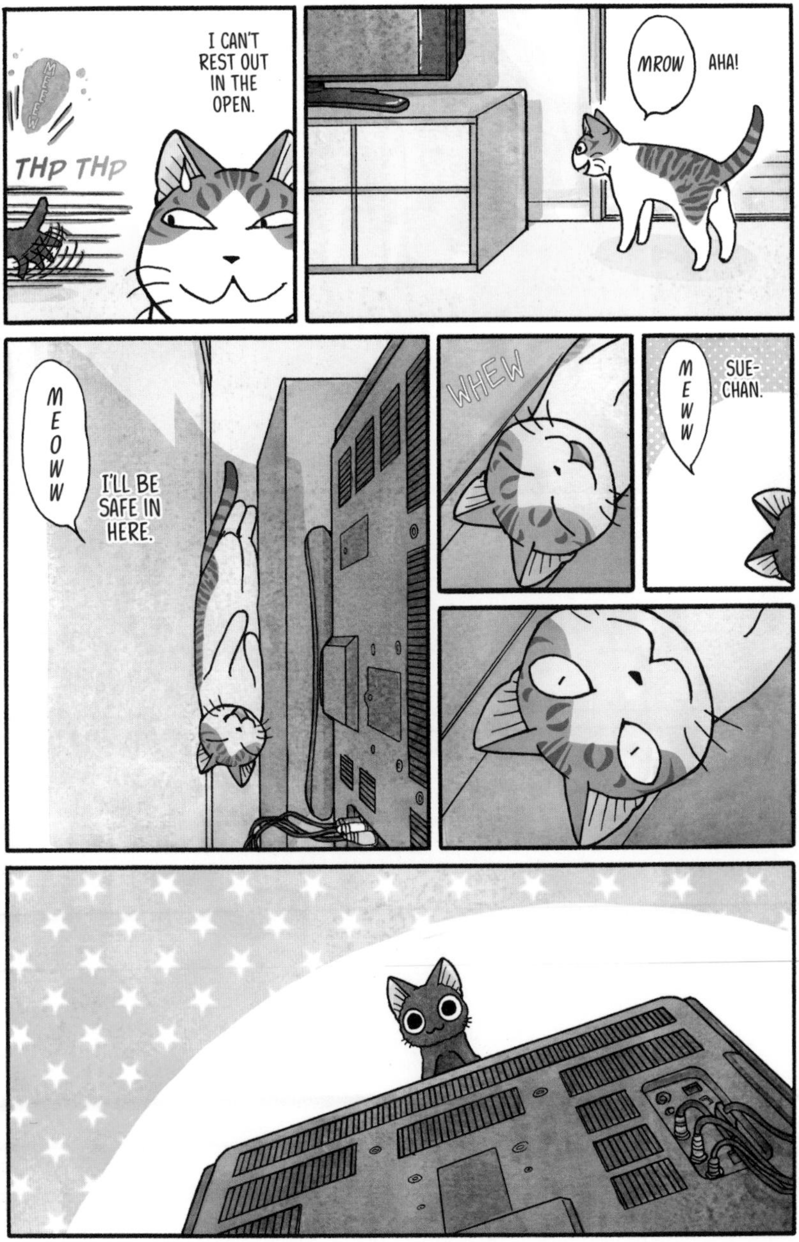
MEEEEW
THP THP
I CAN'T REST OUT IN THE OPEN.
MROW
AHA!
MEOWW
I'LL BE SAFE IN HERE.
WHEW
MEWW
SUE-CHAN.

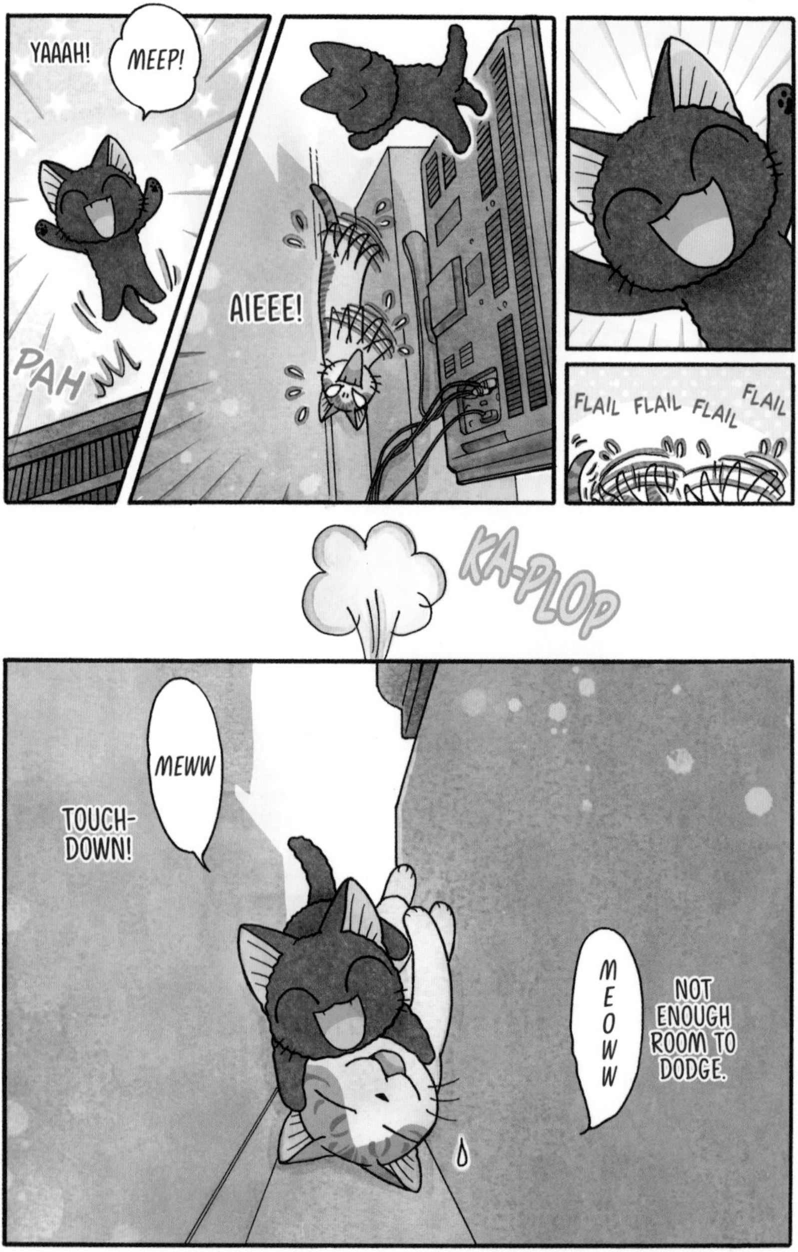
YAAAH!
MEEP!
PAH
AIEEE!
FLAIL FLAIL FLAIL FLAIL
KA-PLOP
MEWW
TOUCH-DOWN!
MEOWW
NOT ENOUGH ROOM TO DODGE.

COZY

COZY

COZY

COZY

COZY

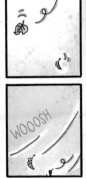

WOOOSH

MEOW

IT'S GETTING COLD.

SHIVER

SHIVER

SHIVER

SHIVER

MEWW

LET'S FIND SOMEPLACE WARM.

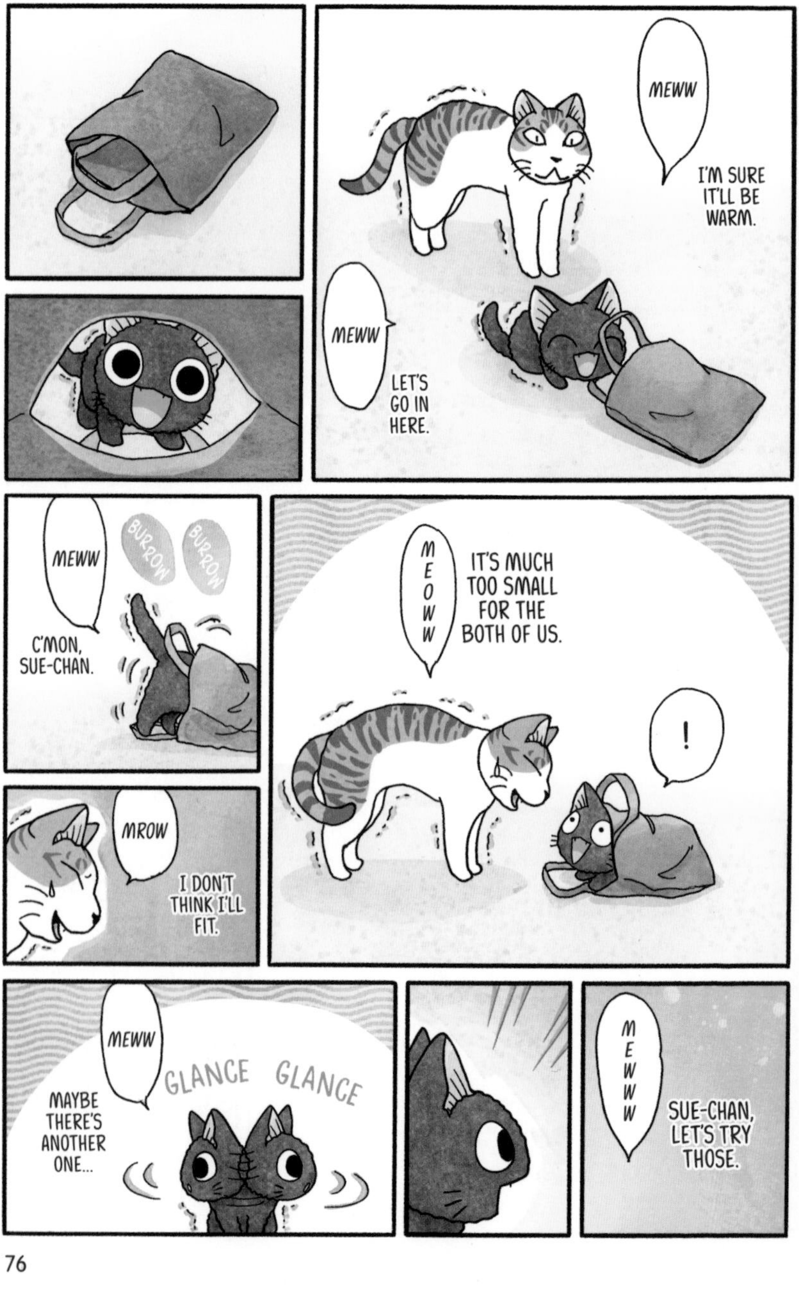
MEWW
I'M SURE IT'LL BE WARM.
MEWW
LET'S GO IN HERE.
MEWW
BURROW
BURROW
C'MON, SUE-CHAN.
MROW
I DON'T THINK I'LL FIT.
MEOWW
IT'S MUCH TOO SMALL FOR THE BOTH OF US.
!
MEWW
GLANCE GLANCE
MAYBE THERE'S ANOTHER ONE...
MEWWW
SUE-CHAN, LET'S TRY THOSE.

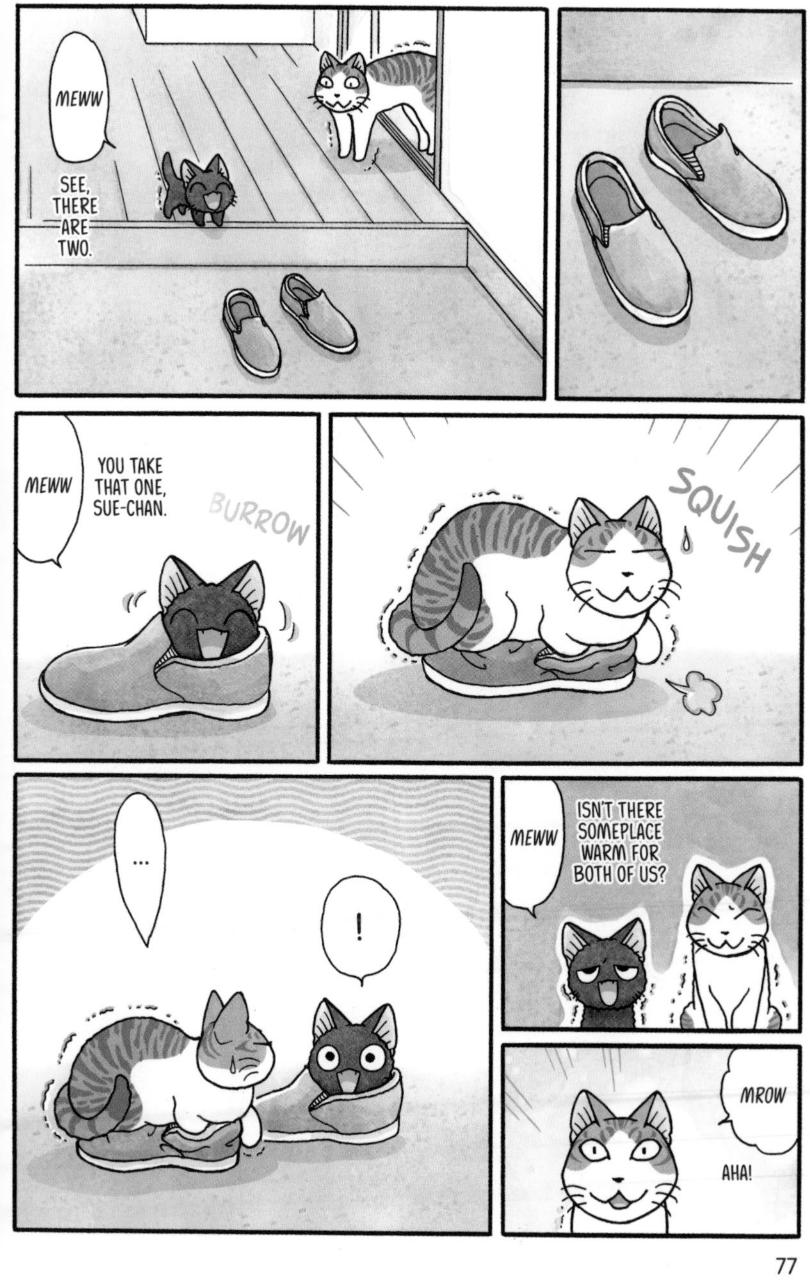
MEWW
SEE, THERE ARE TWO.
MEWW
YOU TAKE THAT ONE, SUE-CHAN.
BURROW
SQUISH
...
!
MEWW
ISN'T THERE SOMEPLACE WARM FOR BOTH OF US?
MROW
AHA!

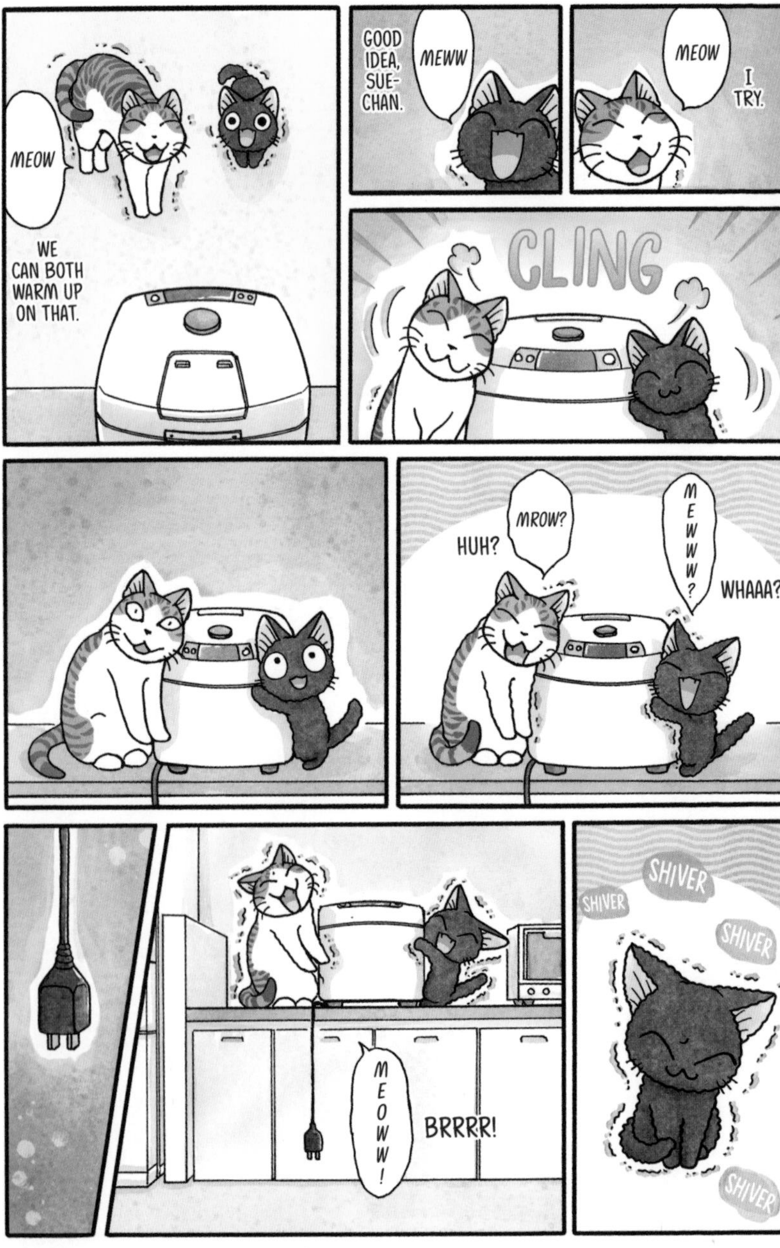
MEOW
WE CAN BOTH WARM UP ON THAT.
GOOD IDEA, SUE-CHAN.
MEWW
MEOW
I TRY.
CLING
MROW?
HUH?
MEWWW?
WHAAA?
MEOWW!
BRRRR!
SHIVER
SHIVER
SHIVER
SHIVER

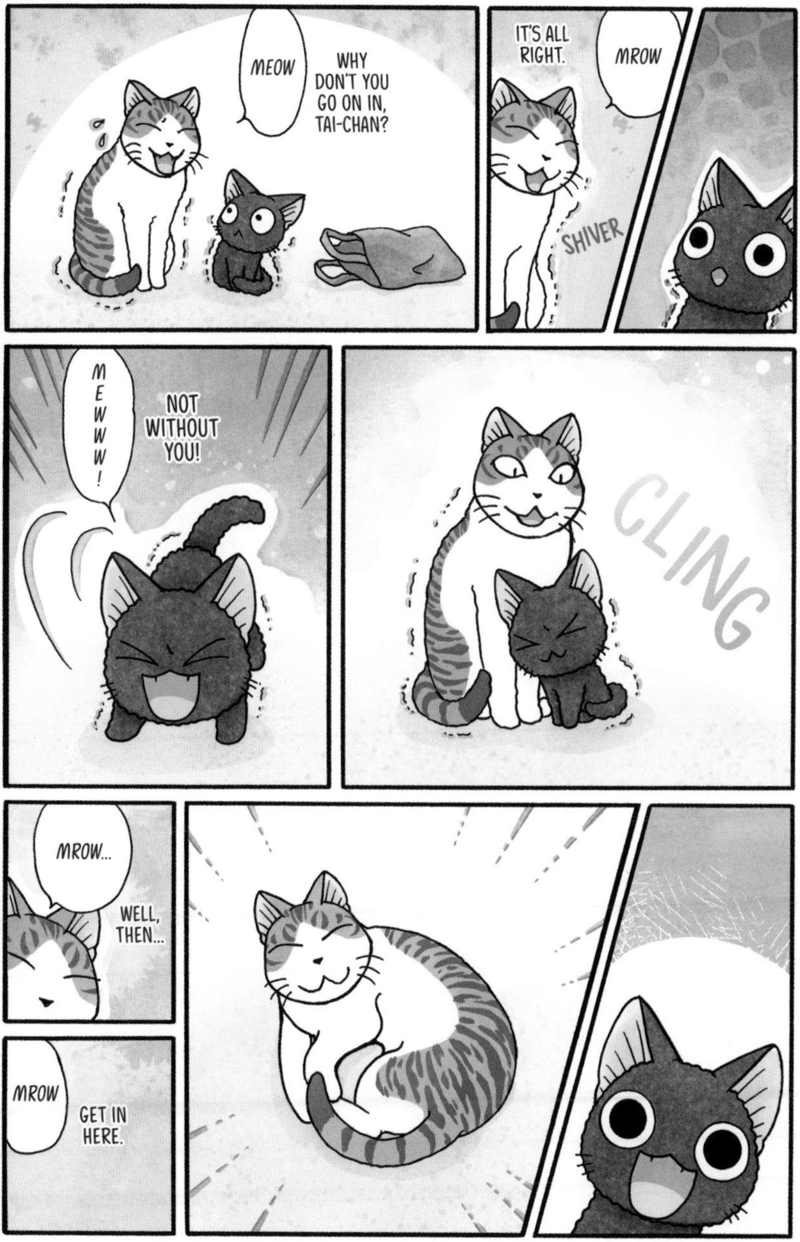
MEOW
WHY DON'T YOU GO ON IN, TAI-CHAN?
IT'S ALL RIGHT.
MROW
SHIVER
MEWWWW!
NOT WITHOUT YOU!
CLING
MROW...
WELL, THEN...
MROW
GET IN HERE.

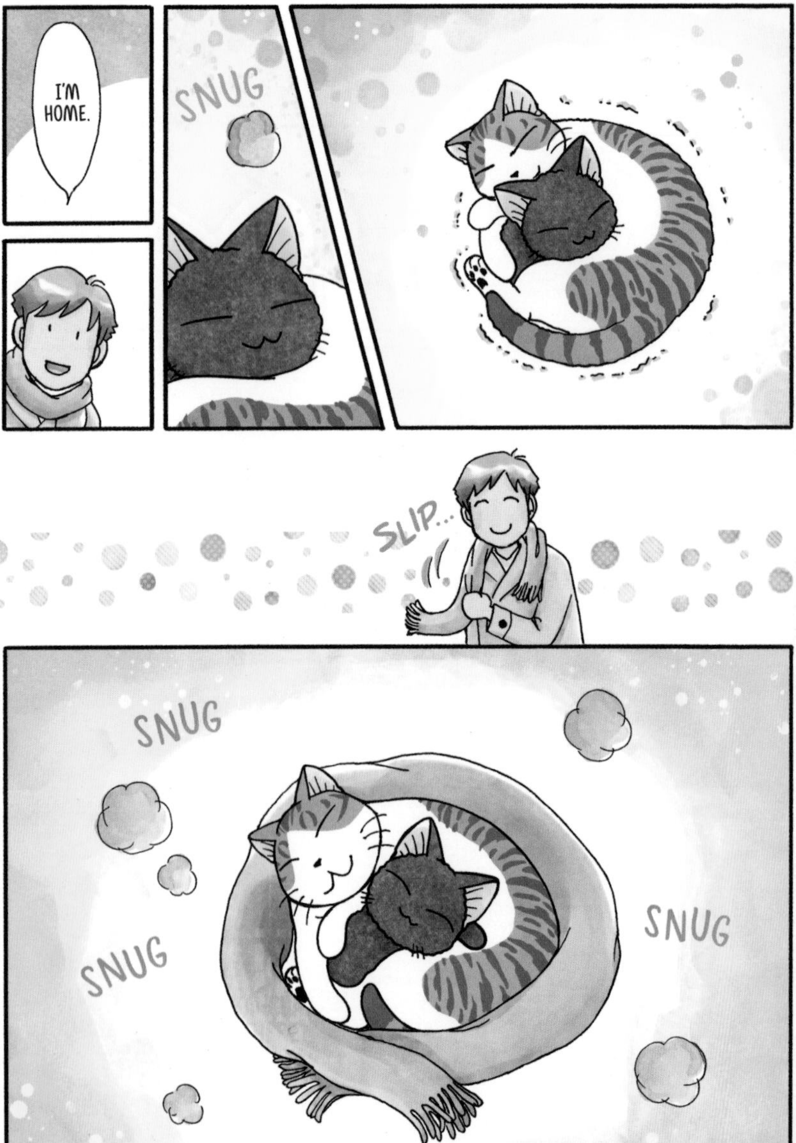
I'M HOME.
SNUG
SLIP...
SNUG
SNUG
SNUG

Sue & Tai-chan

CHAPTER 46 Kitty Christmas

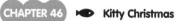

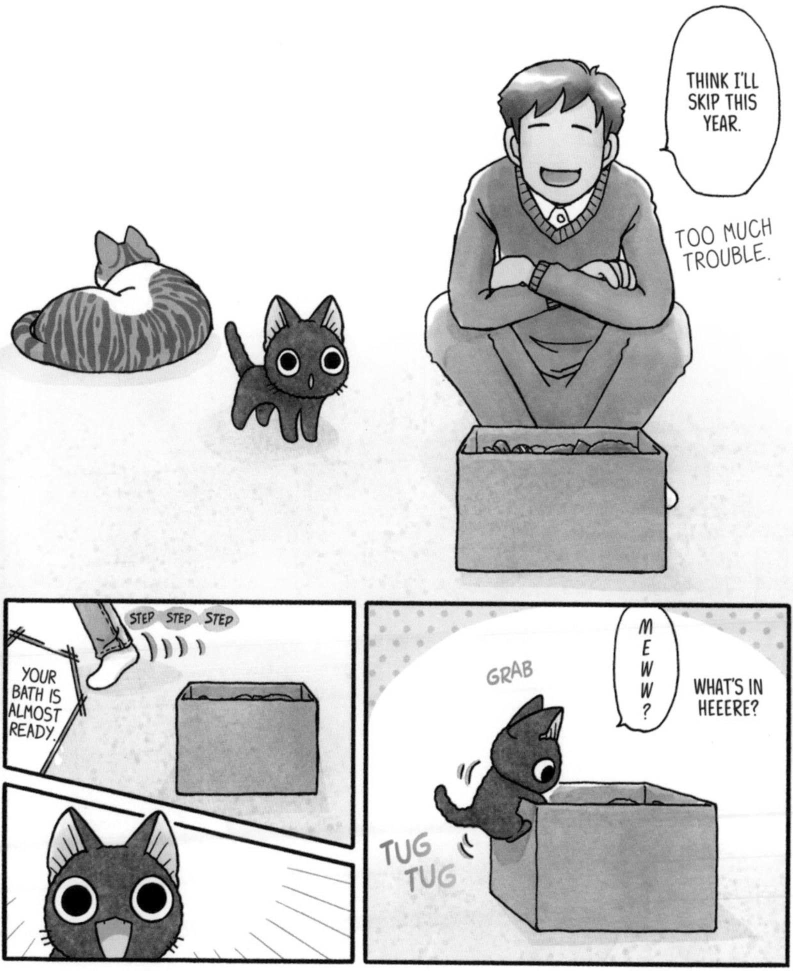
THINK I'LL SKIP THIS YEAR.
TOO MUCH TROUBLE.
STEP STEP STEP
YOUR BATH IS ALMOST READY.
GRAB
MEWW?
WHAT'S IN HEEERE?
TUG TUG

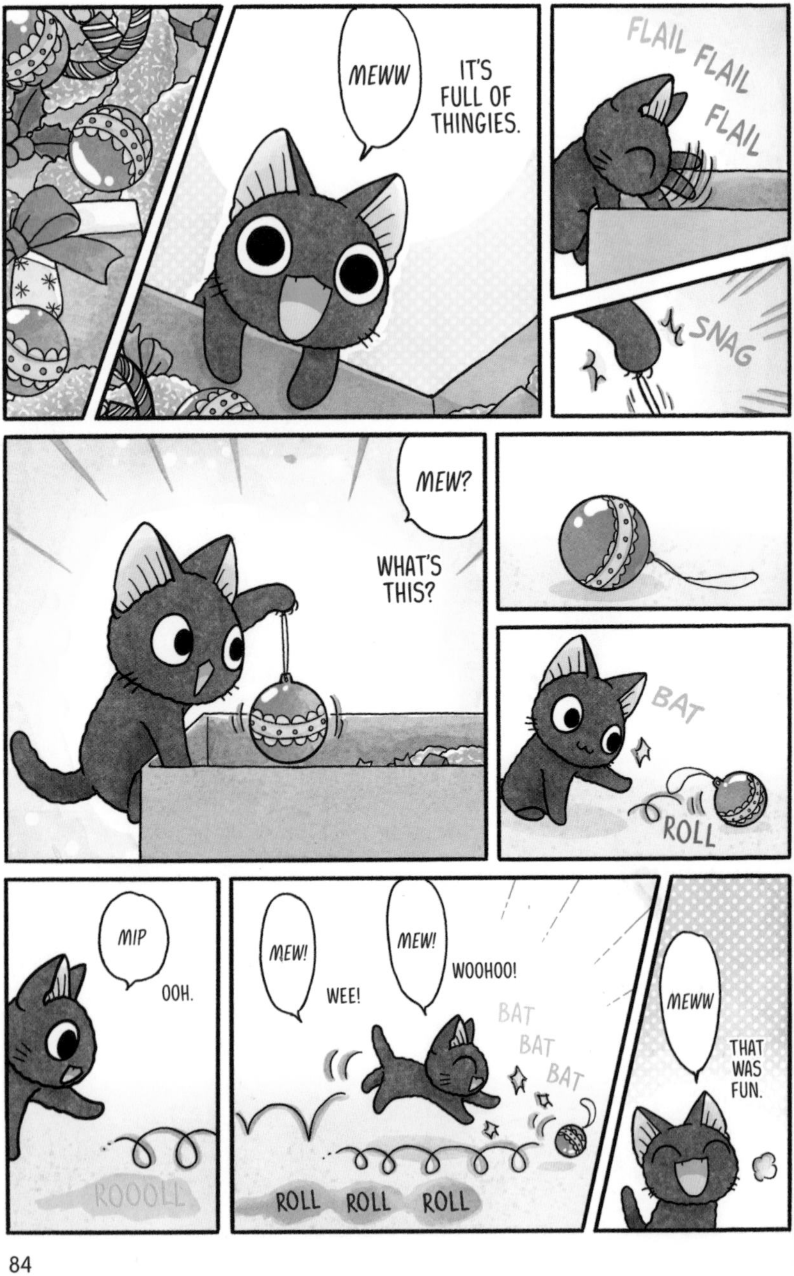
MEWW
IT'S FULL OF THINGIES.
FLAIL FLAIL FLAIL
SNAG
MEW?
WHAT'S THIS?
BAT
ROLL
MIP
OOH.
ROOOLL
MEW!
WEE!
MEW!
WOOHOO!
BAT BAT BAT
ROLL ROLL ROLL
MEWW
THAT WAS FUN.

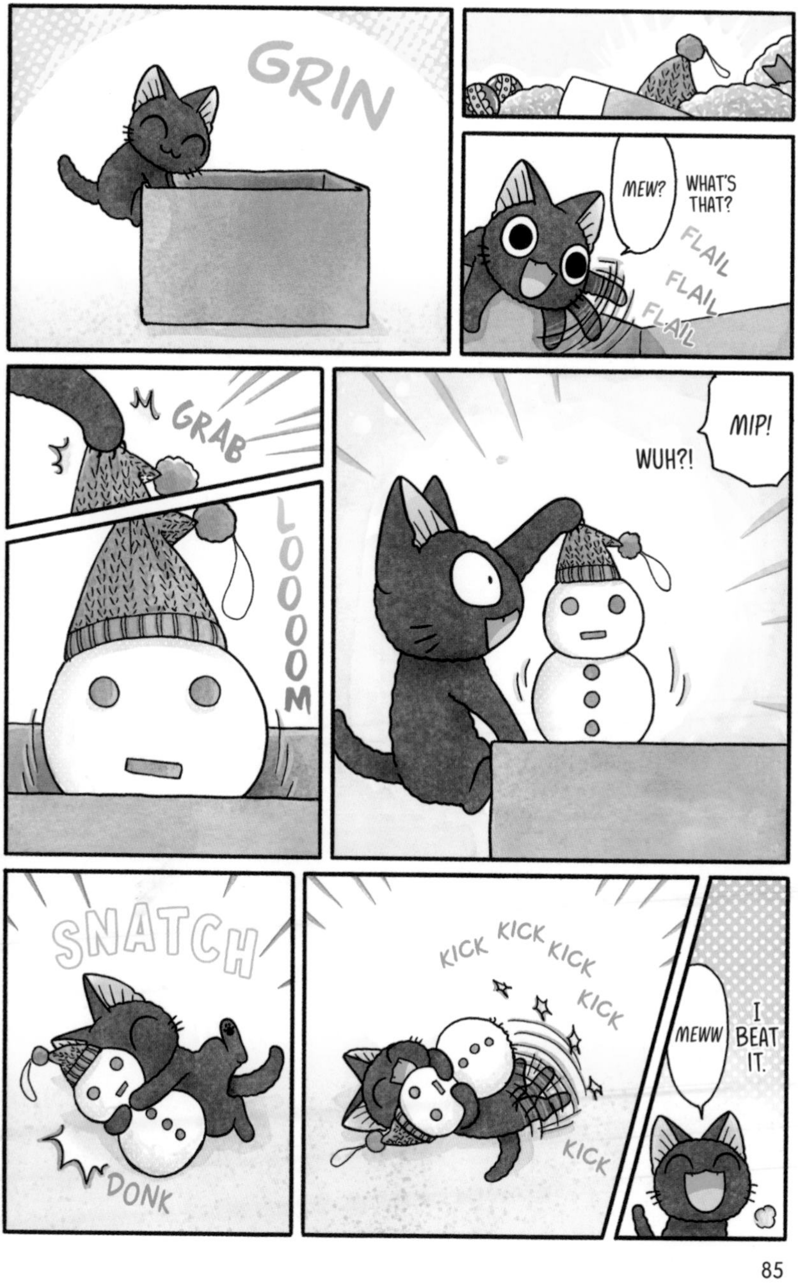
GRIN
MEW?
WHAT'S THAT?
FLAIL
FLAIL
FLAIL
GRAB
LOOOOOM
WUH?!
MIP!
SNATCH
DONK
KICK KICK KICK
KICK
KICK
MEWW
I BEAT IT.

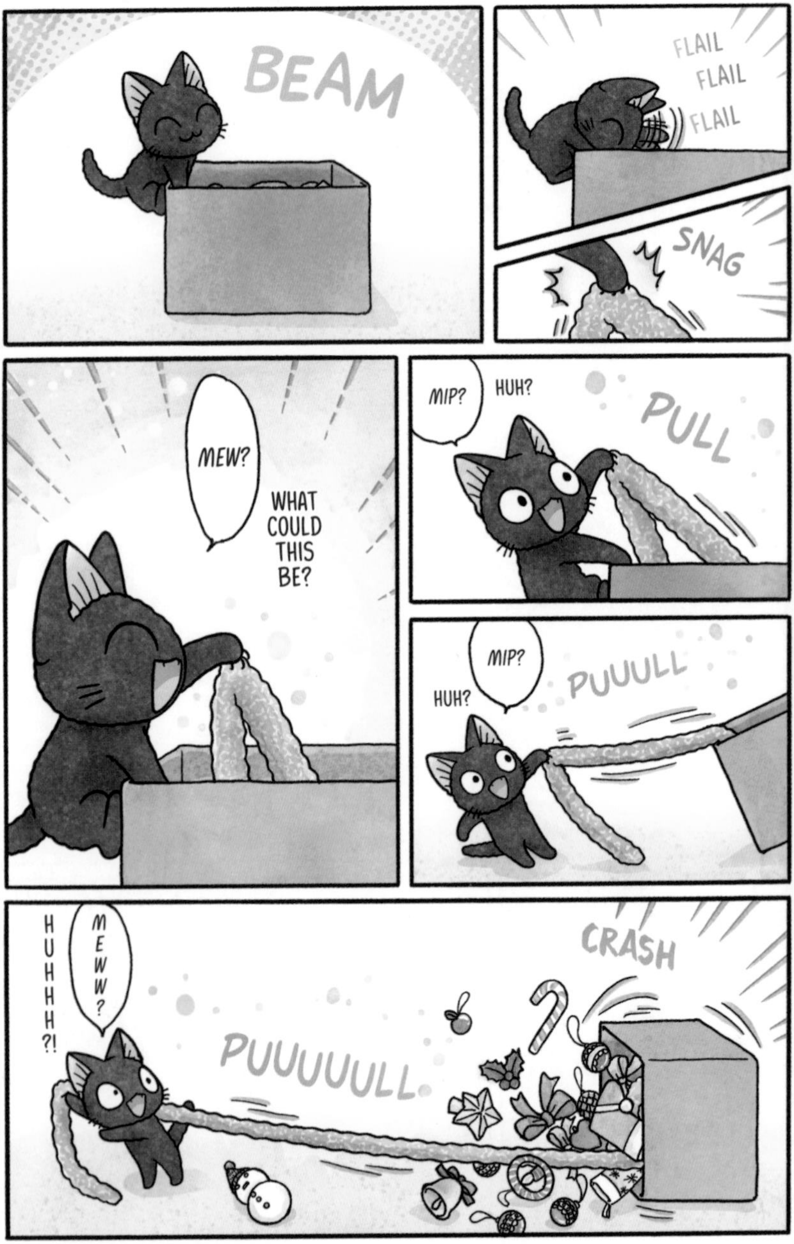
BEAM
FLAIL
FLAIL
FLAIL
SNAG
MEW?
WHAT COULD THIS BE?
MIP?
HUH?
PULL
MIP?
HUH?
PUUULL
MEWW?
HUHHHH?!
PUUUUULL
CRASH

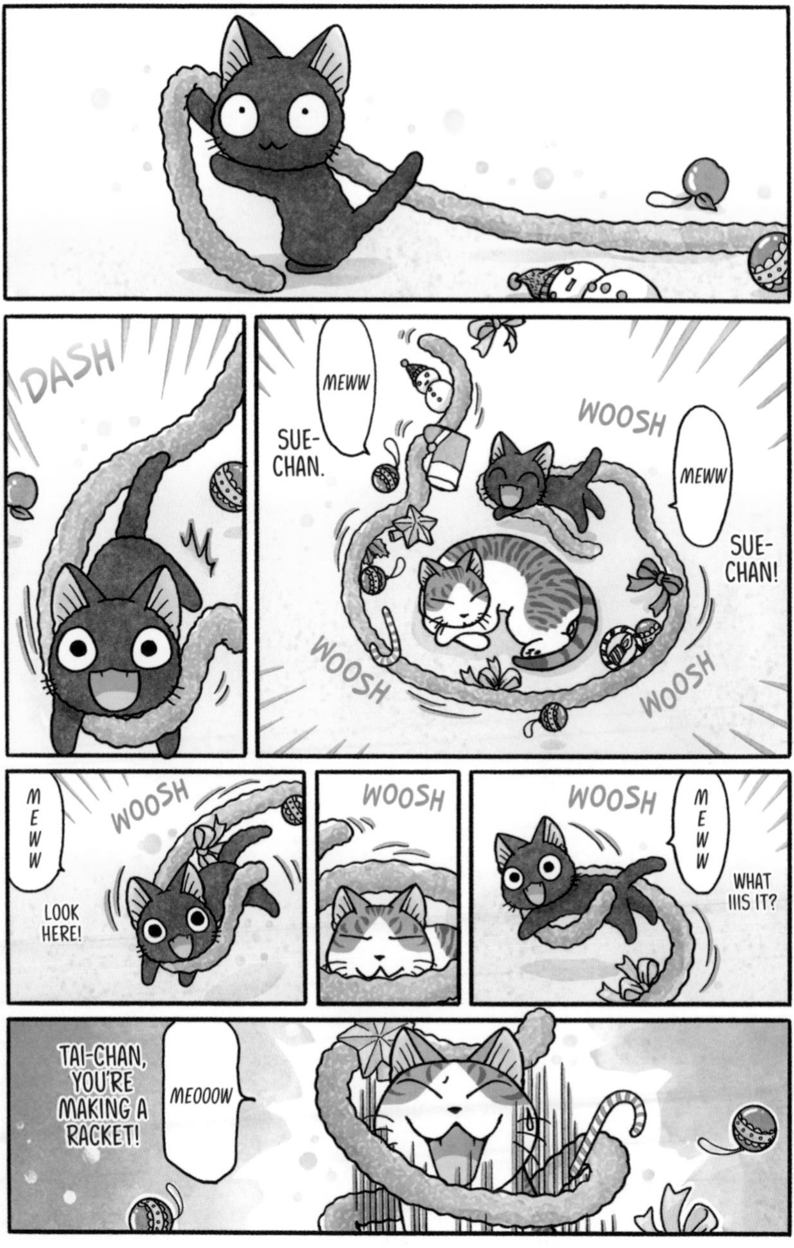
DASH
MEWW
SUE-CHAN.
WOOSH
MEWW
SUE-CHAN!
WOOSH
WOOSH
MEWW
WOOSH
LOOK HERE!
WOOSH
WOOSH
MEWW
WHAT IIIS IT?
TAI-CHAN, YOU'RE MAKING A RACKET!
MEOOOW

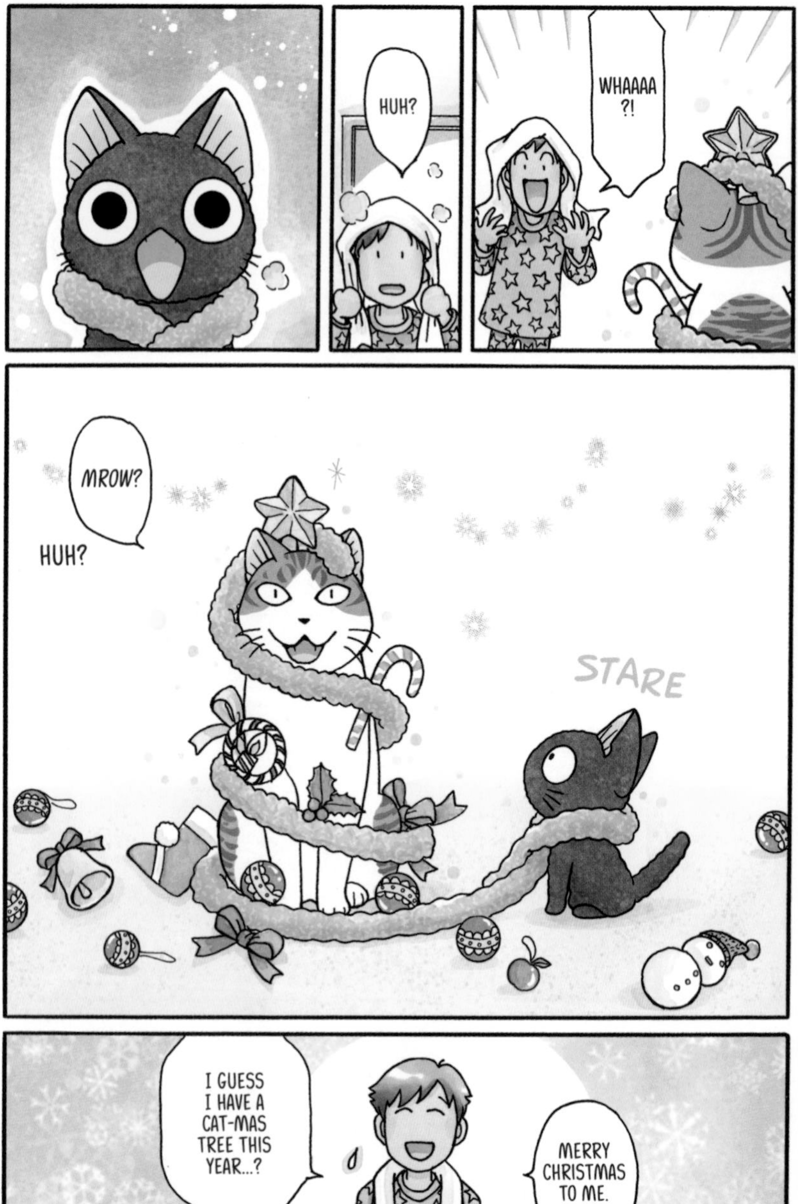
HUH?
WHAAAA ?!
MROW?
HUH?
STARE
I GUESS I HAVE A CAT-MAS TREE THIS YEAR...?
MERRY CHRISTMAS TO ME.

CHAPTER 47 Let's Clean Up ♥

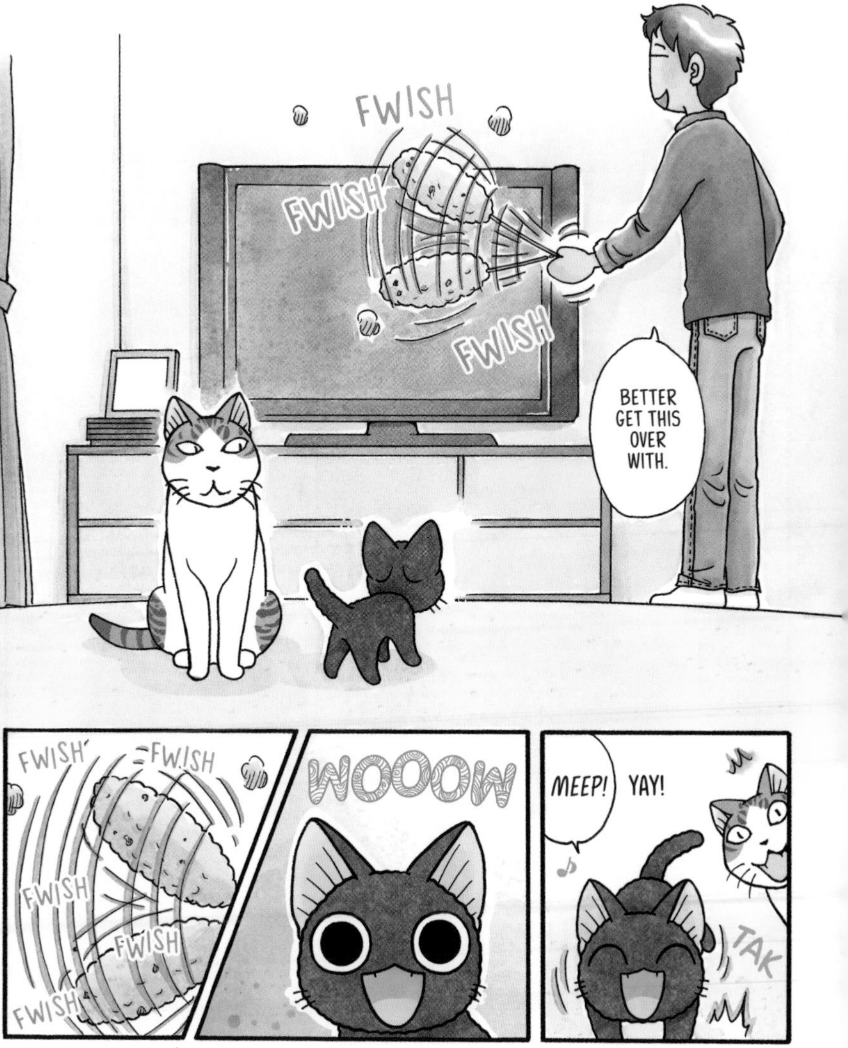
FWISH
FWISH
FWISH
BETTER GET THIS OVER WITH.
FWISH
FWISH
FWISH
FWISH
FWISH
WOOOW
MEEP!
YAY!
TAK

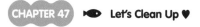

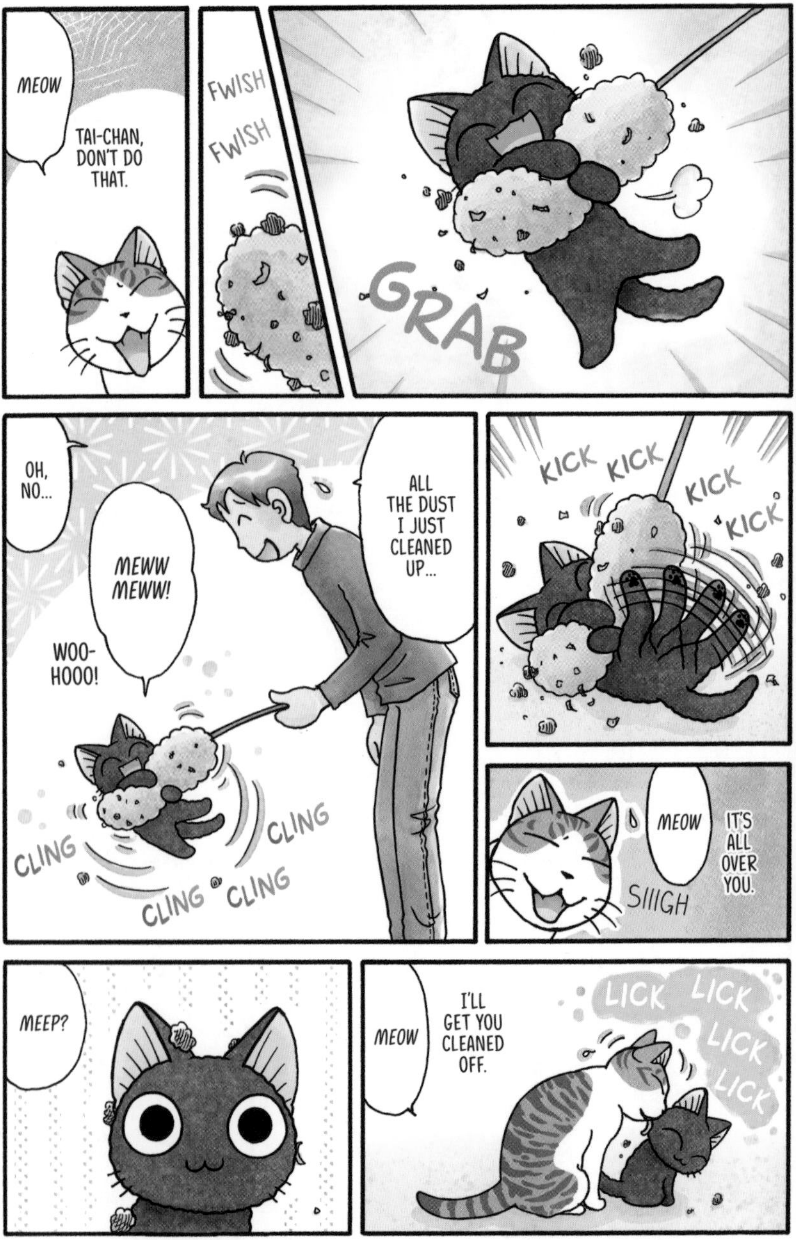
MEOW
TAI-CHAN, DON'T DO THAT.
FWISH
FWISH
GRAB
OH, NO...
MEWW MEWW!
WOO-HOOO!
ALL THE DUST I JUST CLEANED UP...
CLING
CLING
CLING
CLING
KICK
KICK
KICK
KICK
MEOW
IT'S ALL OVER YOU.
SIIIGH
MEEP?
MEOW
I'LL GET YOU CLEANED OFF.
LICK
LICK
LICK
LICK

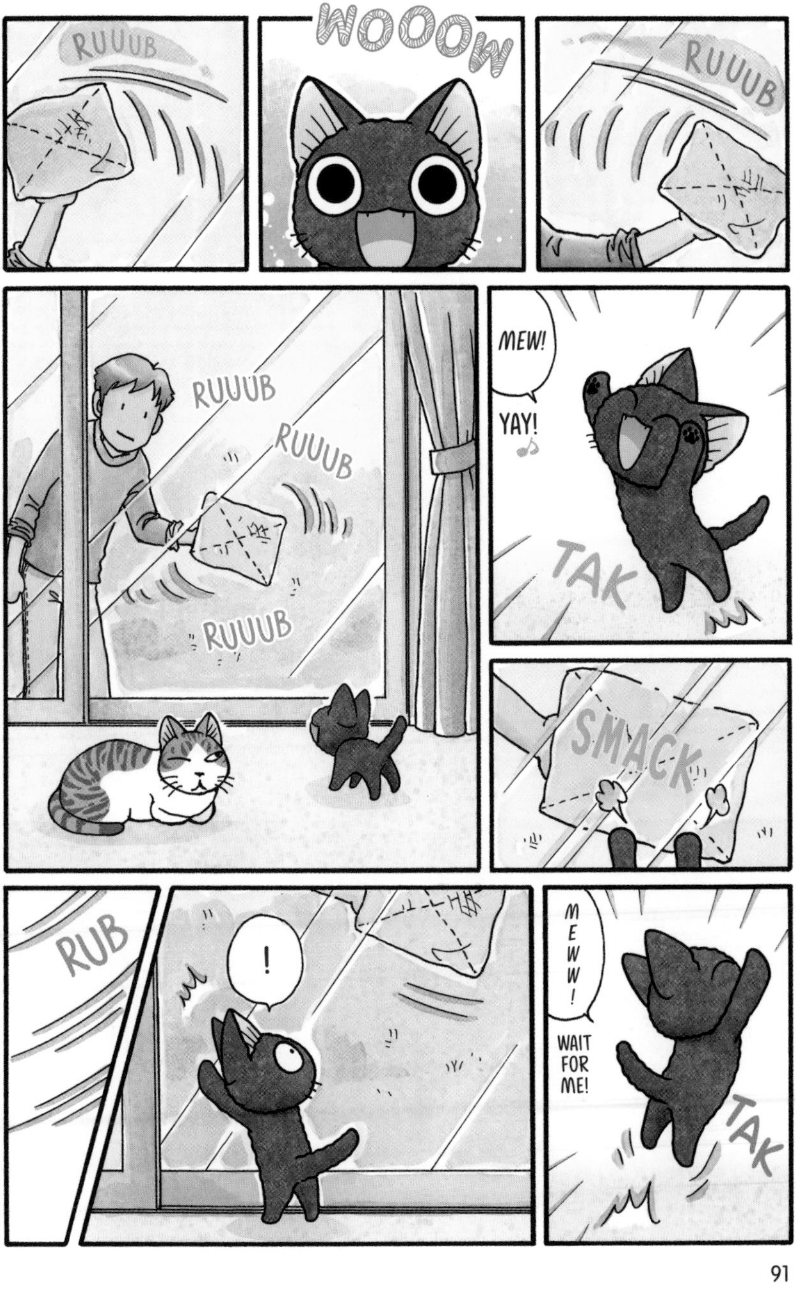

RUUUB
WOOOW
RUUUB
RUUUB
RUUUB
RUUUB
MEW!
YAY!
TAK
SMACK
RUB
!
MEWW!
WAIT FOR ME!
TAK

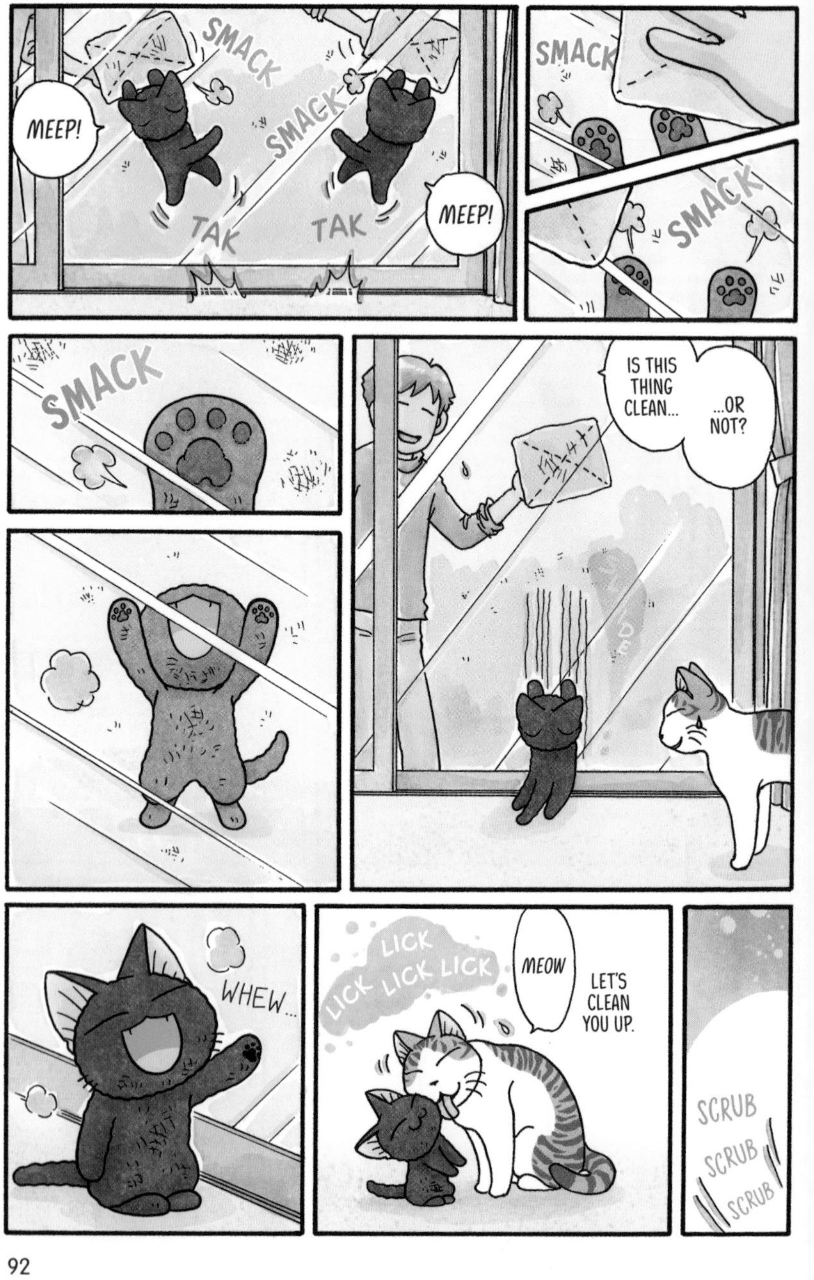

SMACK
MEEP!
SMACK
TAK
TAK
MEEP!
SMACK
SMACK
SMACK
IS THIS THING CLEAN...
...OR NOT?
WHEW...
LICK LICK LICK LICK
MEOW
LET'S CLEAN YOU UP.
SCRUB
SCRUB
SCRUB

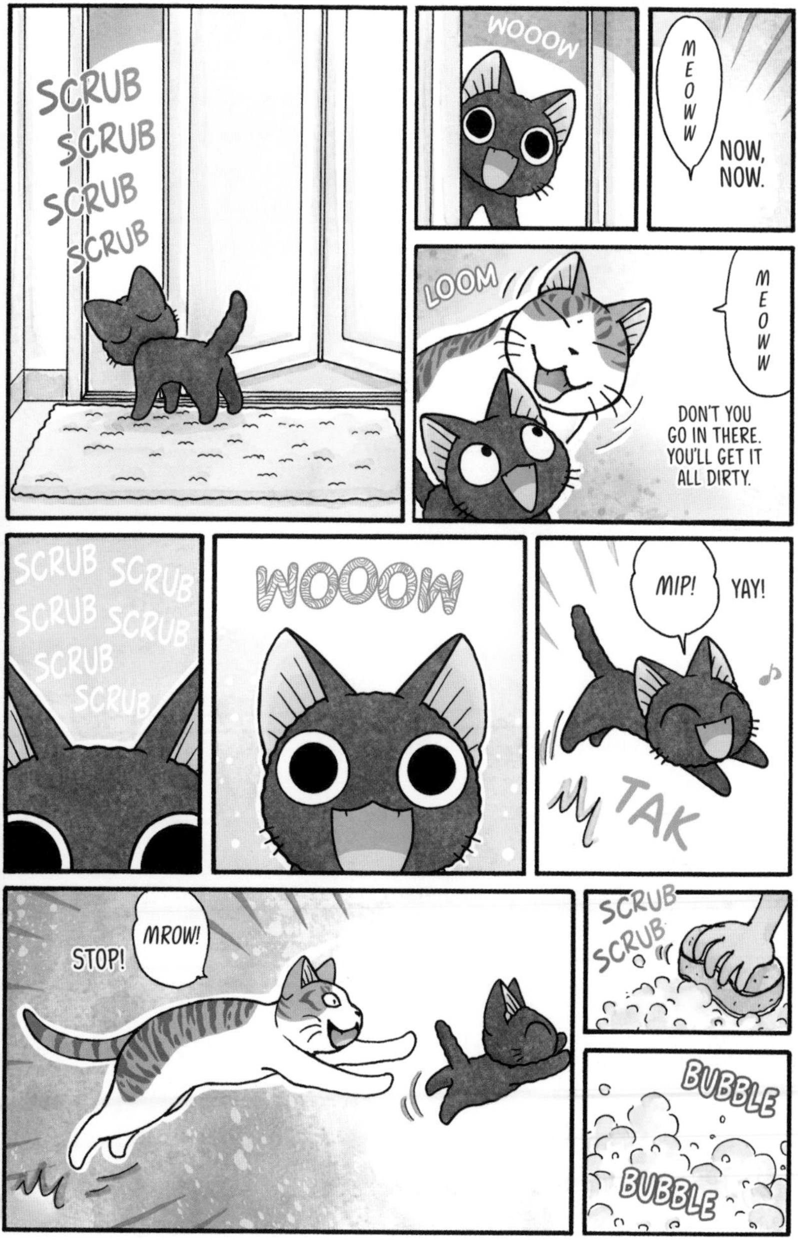
SCRUB
SCRUB
SCRUB
SCRUB
WOOOW
MEOWW
NOW, NOW.
LOOM
MEOWW
DON'T YOU GO IN THERE. YOU'LL GET IT ALL DIRTY.
SCRUB SCRUB
SCRUB SCRUB
SCRUB
SCRUB
WOOOW
MIP!
YAY!
TAK
MROW!
STOP!
SCRUB
SCRUB
BUBBLE
BUBBLE

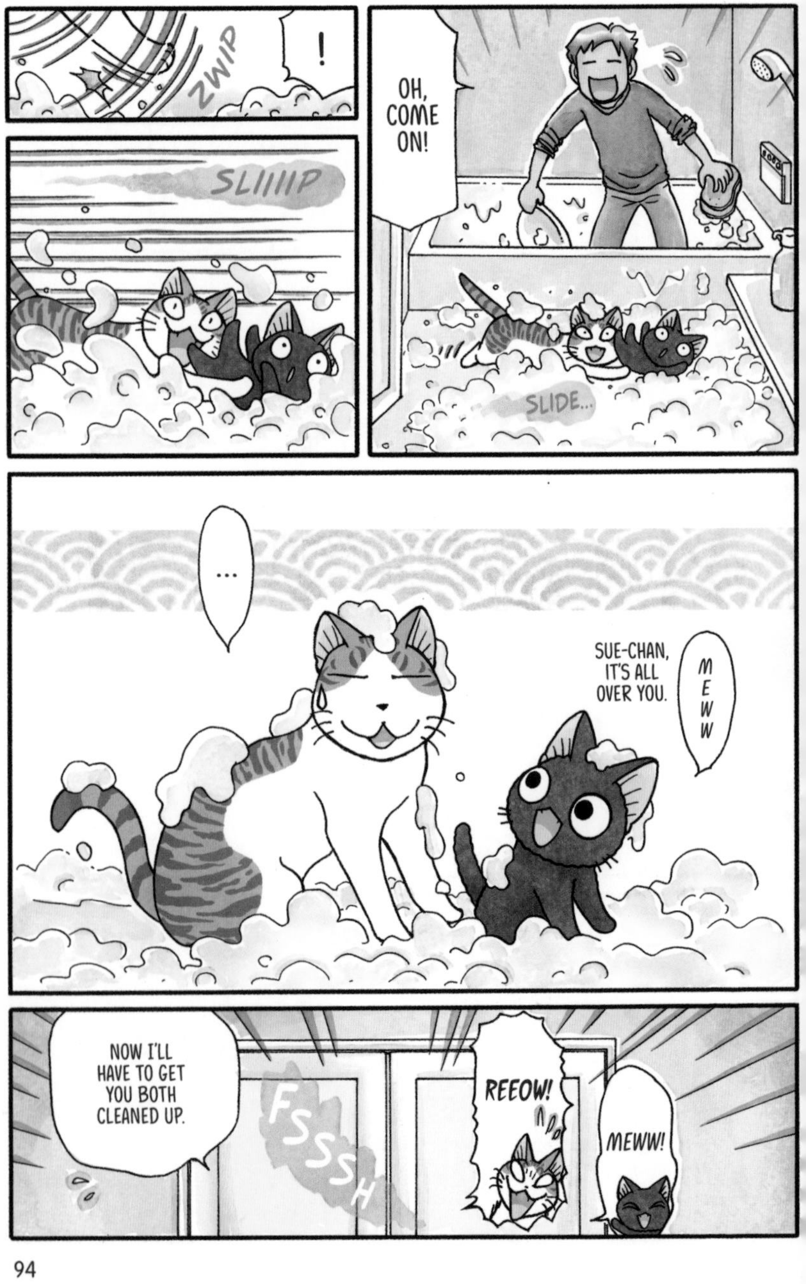
ZWIP
!
SLIIIP
OH, COME ON!
SLIDE...
...
SUE-CHAN, IT'S ALL OVER YOU.
MEWW
NOW I'LL HAVE TO GET YOU BOTH CLEANED UP.
FSSSH
REEOW!
MEWW!

CHAPTER 48 New Year with Cats

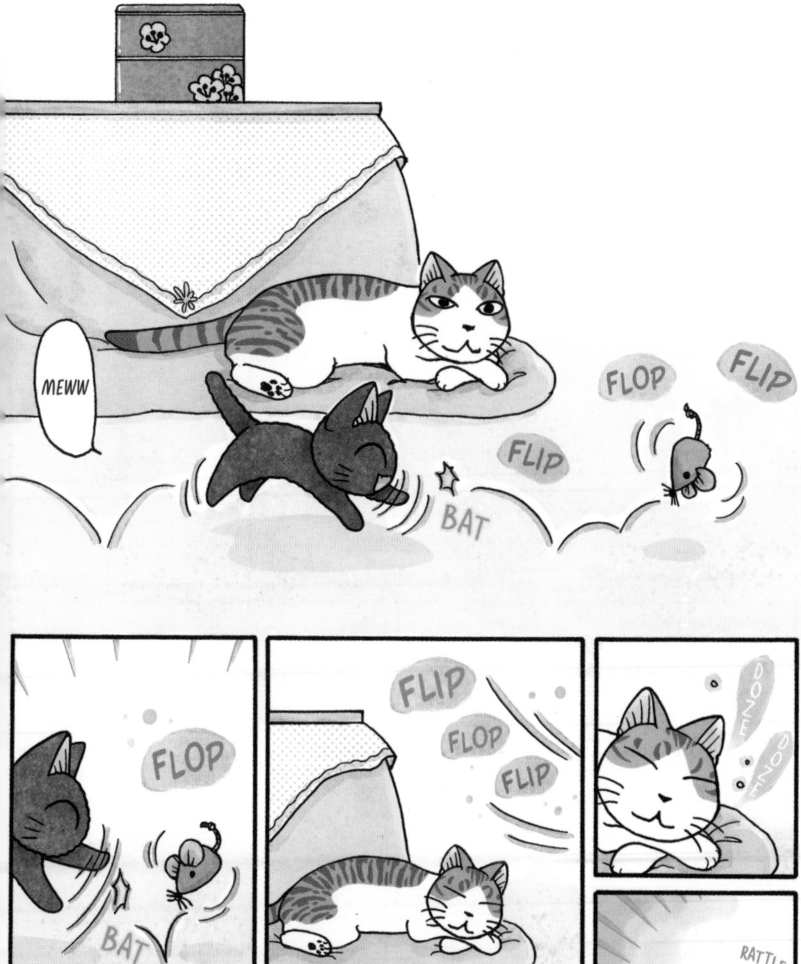
MEWW
FLOP
FLIP
FLIP
BAT
FLOP
BAT
FLIP
FLOP
FLIP
DOZE
DOZE
RATTLE
RATTLE

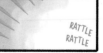

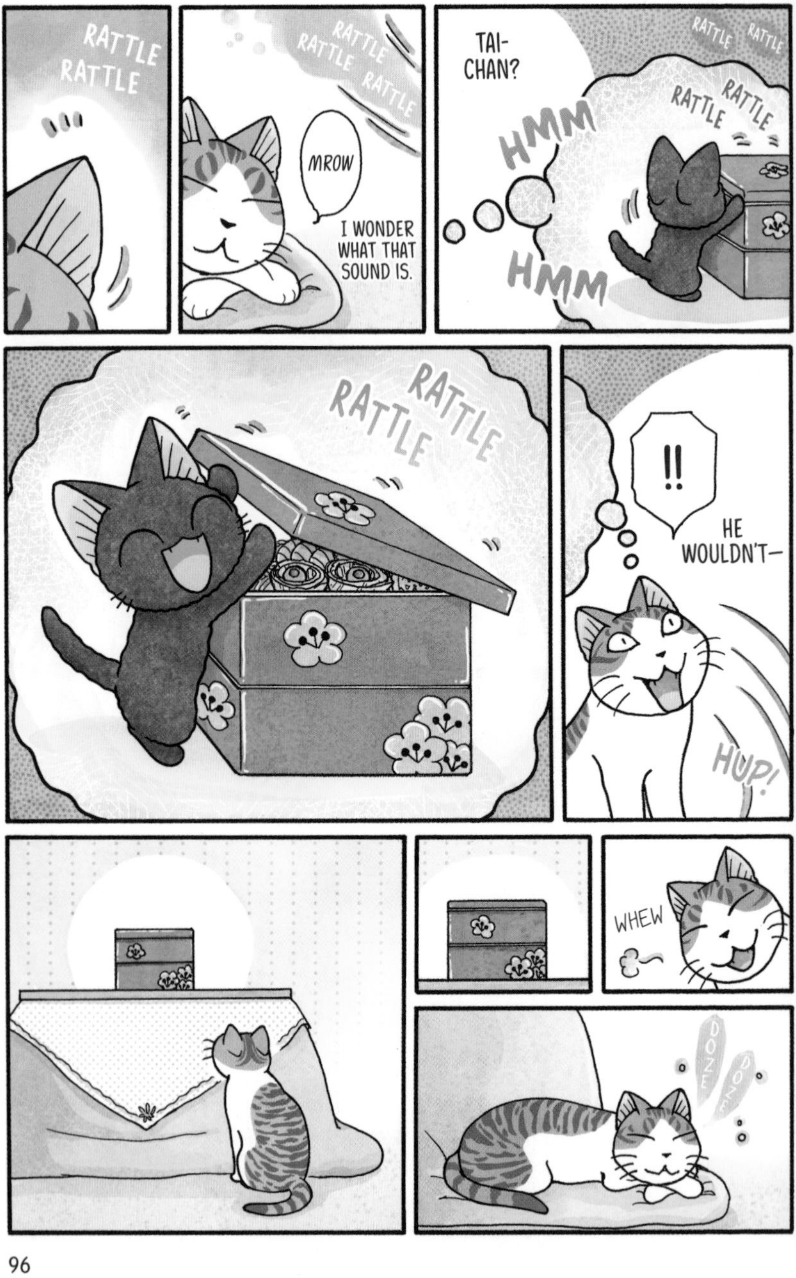

RATTLE RATTLE
...
RATTLE RATTLE RATTLE
MROW
I WONDER WHAT THAT SOUND IS.
TAI-CHAN?
RATTLE RATTLE
RATTLE RATTLE
HMM
HMM
RATTLE RATTLE
!!
HE WOULDN'T—
HUP!
WHEW
DOZE DOZE

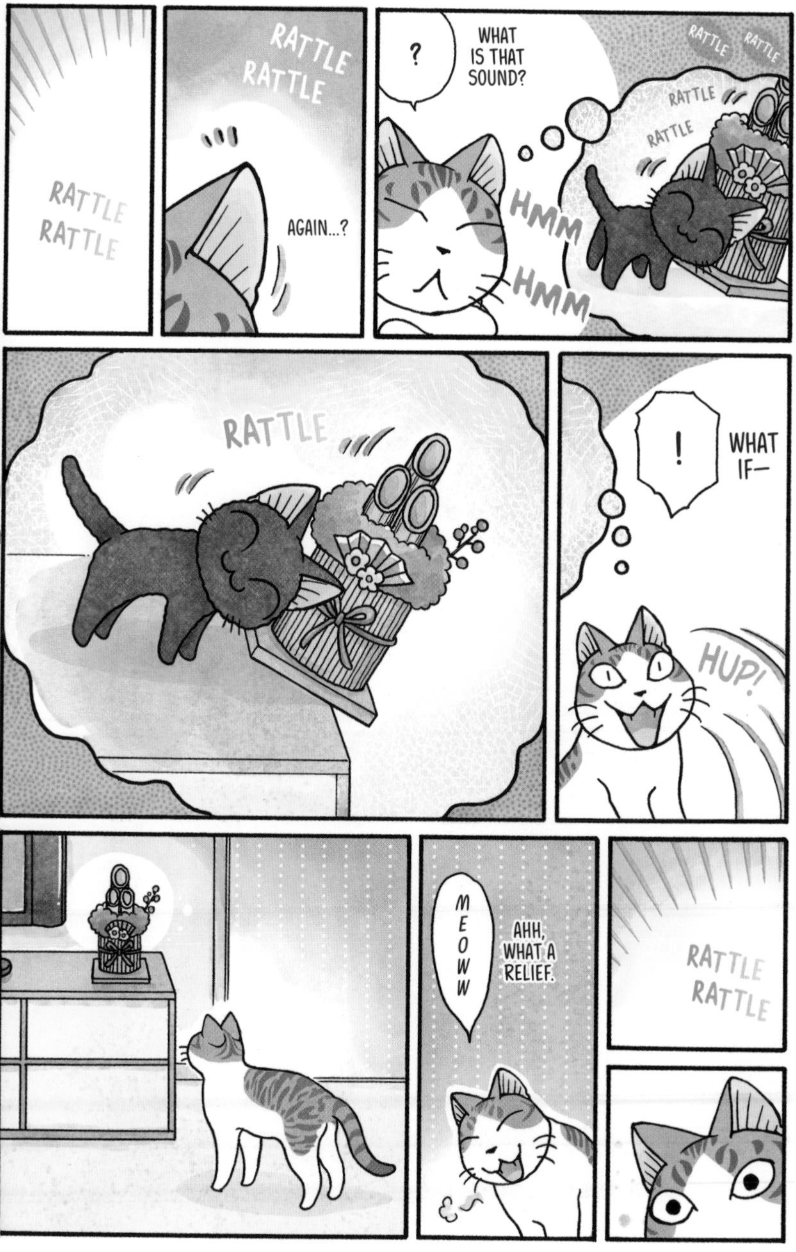
RATTLE RATTLE
RATTLE RATTLE
AGAIN...?
?
WHAT IS THAT SOUND?
HMM HMM
RATTLE RATTLE
RATTLE RATTLE
RATTLE
!
WHAT IF—
HUP!
MEOWW
AHH, WHAT A RELIEF.
RATTLE RATTLE

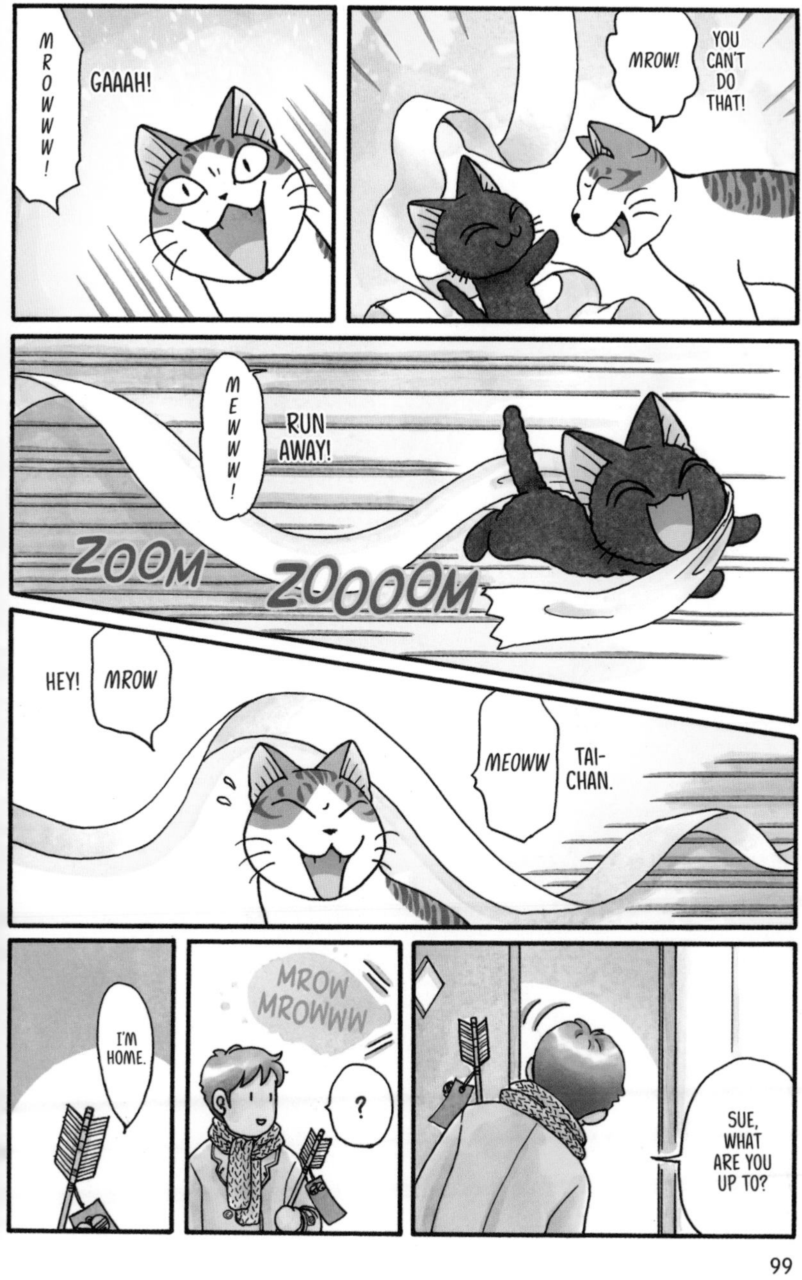
MROWWWW!
GAAAH!
MROW!
YOU CAN'T DO THAT!
MEWWW!
RUN AWAY!
ZOOM
ZOOOOM
HEY!
MROW
MEOWW
TAI-CHAN.
I'M HOME.
MROW MROWWW
?
SUE, WHAT ARE YOU UP TO?

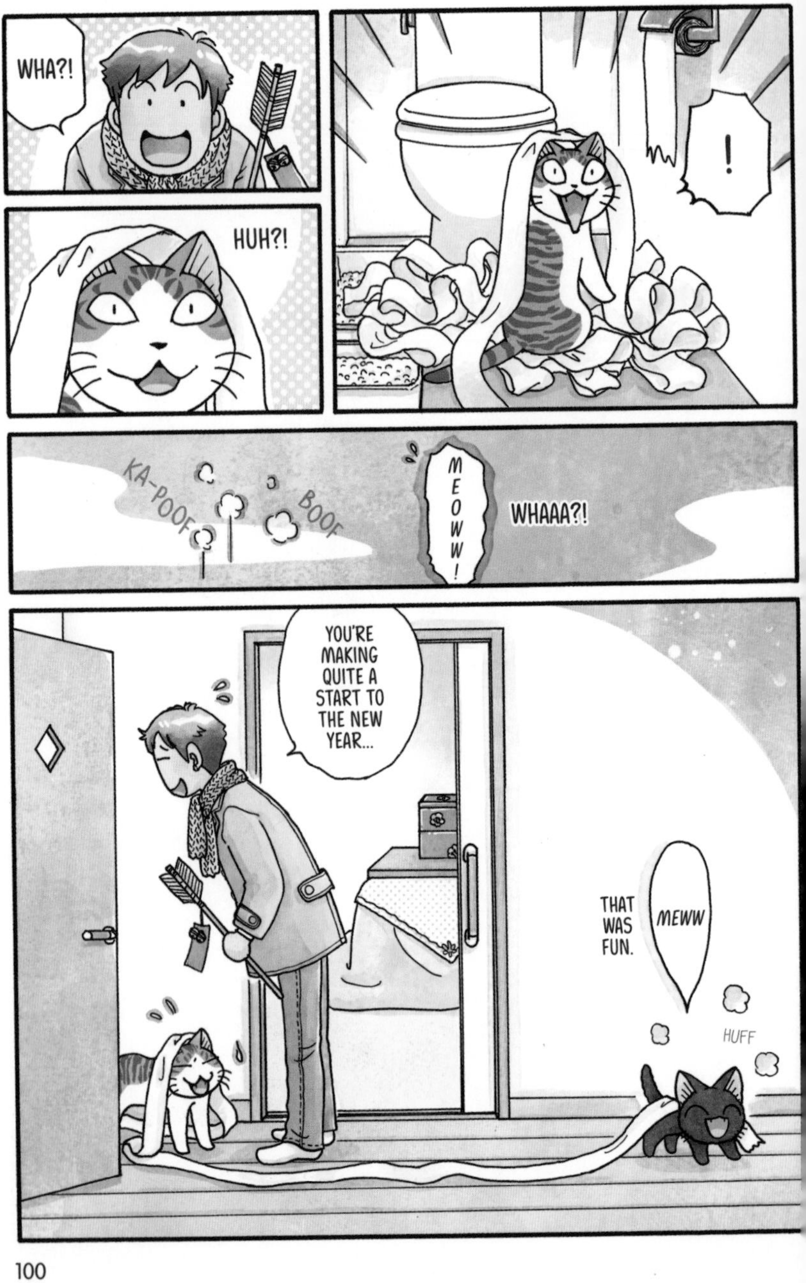
WHA?!
HUH?!
!
KA-POOF
BOOF
MEOWW!
WHAAA?!
YOU'RE MAKING QUITE A START TO THE NEW YEAR...
THAT WAS FUN.
MEWW
HUFF

Sue & Tai-chan

CHAPTER 49 Sue's Happy Dream

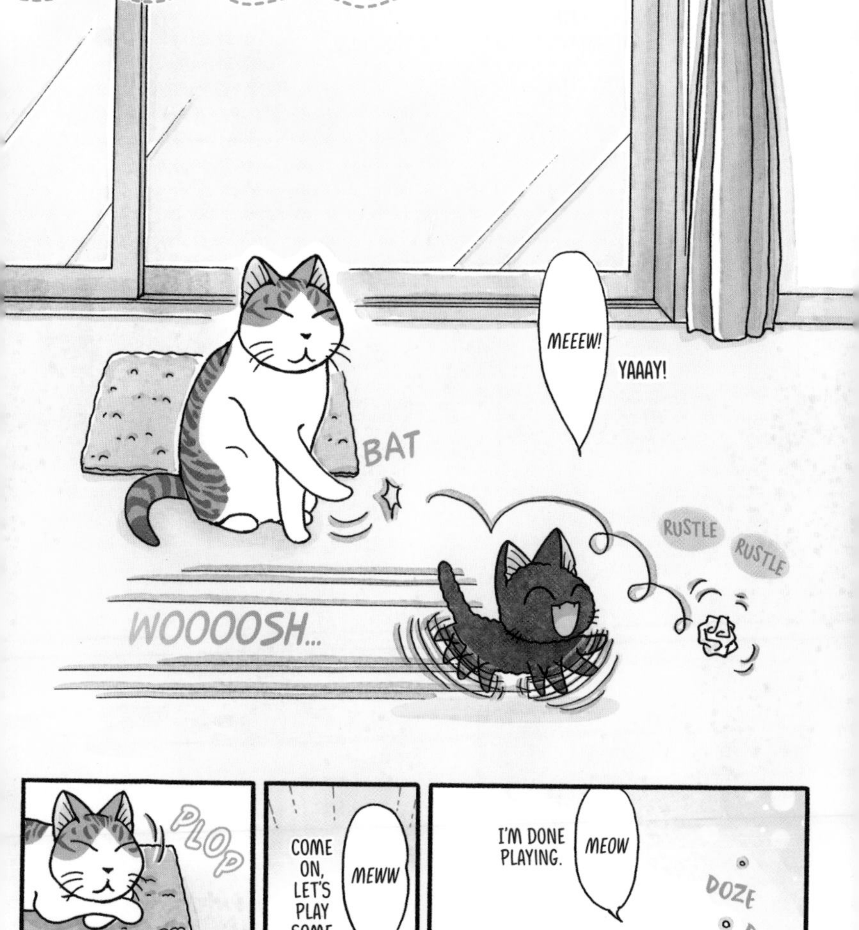
MEEEW!
YAAAY!
BAT
RUSTLE
RUSTLE
WOOOOSH...
PLOP
MEW!
LET'S PLAY!
COME ON, LET'S PLAY SOME MORE!
MEWW
I'M DONE PLAYING.
MEOW
DOZE
DOZE

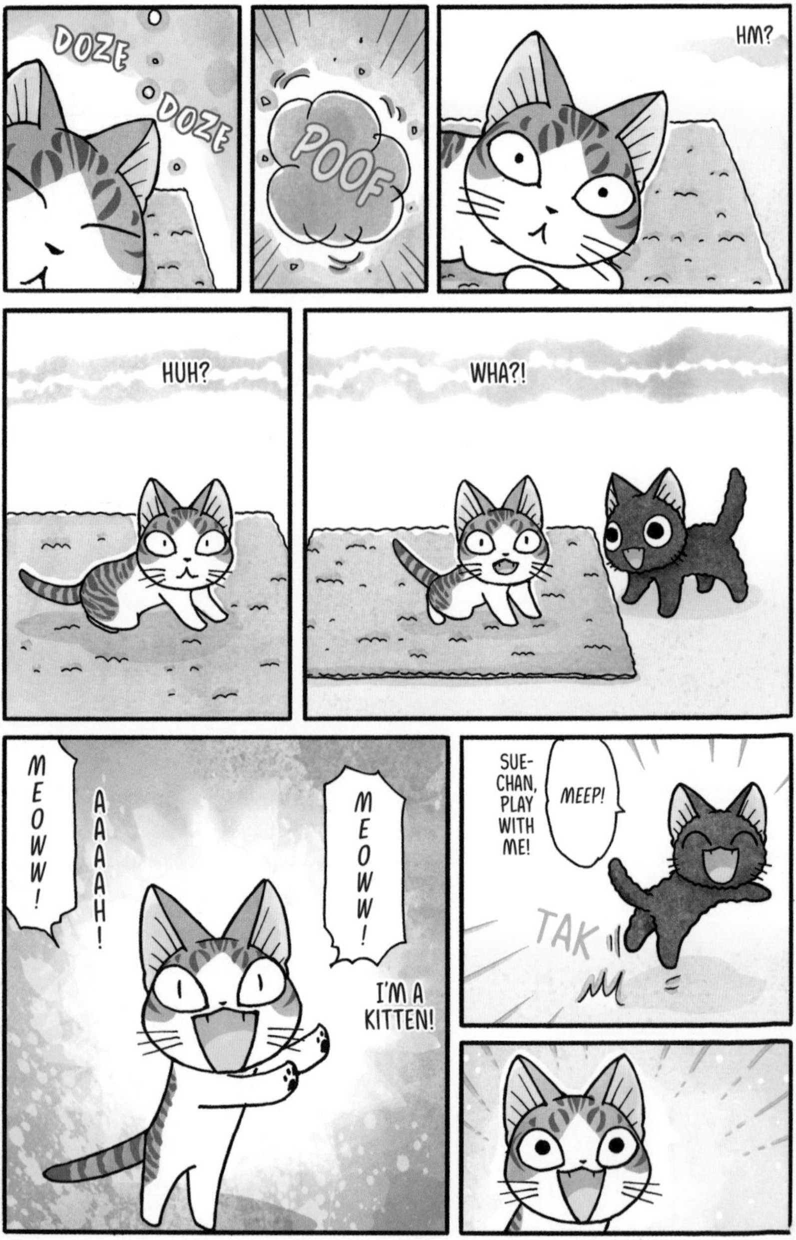
DOZE
DOZE
POOF
HM?
HUH?
WHA?!
MEOWW!
AAAAAH!
MEOWW!
I'M A KITTEN!
SUE-CHAN, PLAY WITH ME!
MEEP!
TAK

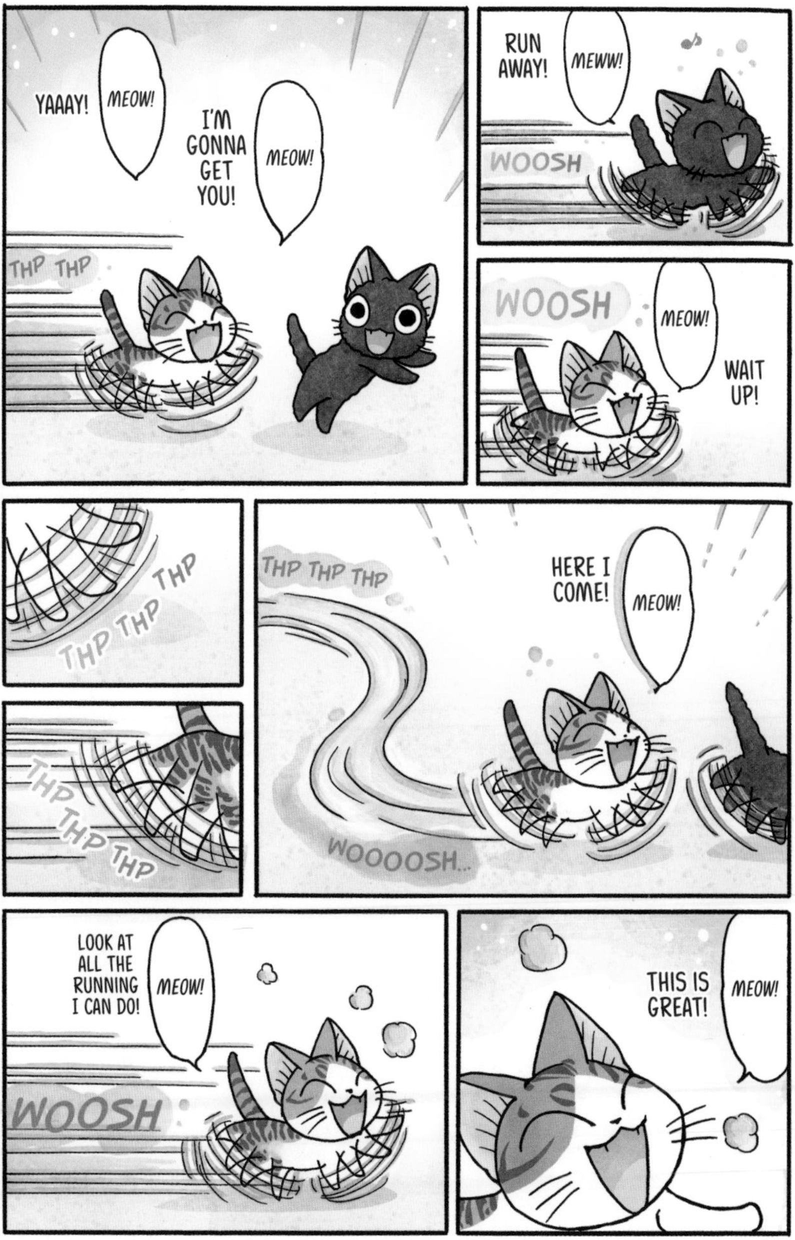
YAAAY!
MEOW!
I'M GONNA GET YOU!
MEOW!
THP THP
RUN AWAY!
MEWW!
WOOSH
WOOSH
MEOW!
WAIT UP!
THP THP THP
THP THP THP
THP THP THP
HERE I COME!
MEOW!
WOOOOSH...
LOOK AT ALL THE RUNNING I CAN DO!
MEOW!
WOOSH
THIS IS GREAT!
MEOW!

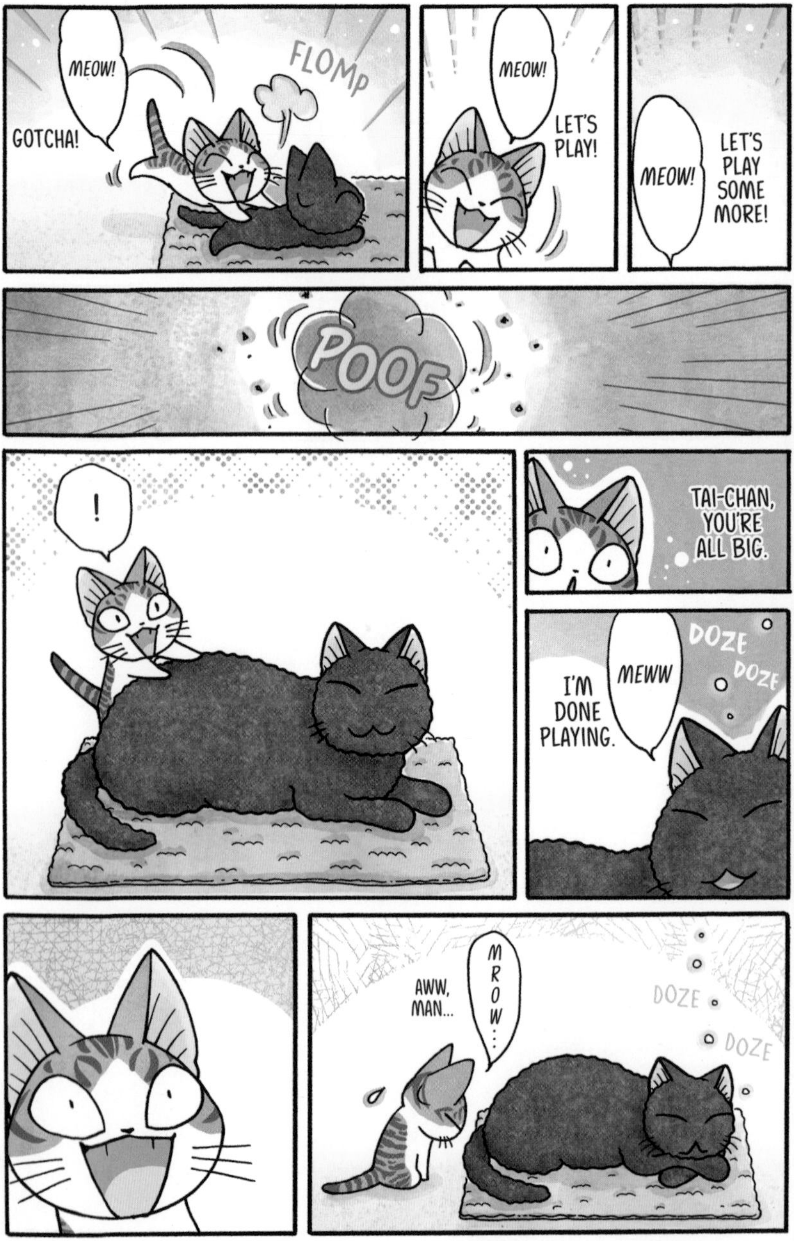
MEOW!
GOTCHA!
FLOMP
MEOW!
LET'S PLAY!
MEOW!
LET'S PLAY SOME MORE!
POOF
!
TAI-CHAN, YOU'RE ALL BIG.
MEWW
I'M DONE PLAYING.
DOZE DOZE
MROW...
AWW, MAN...
DOZE
DOZE

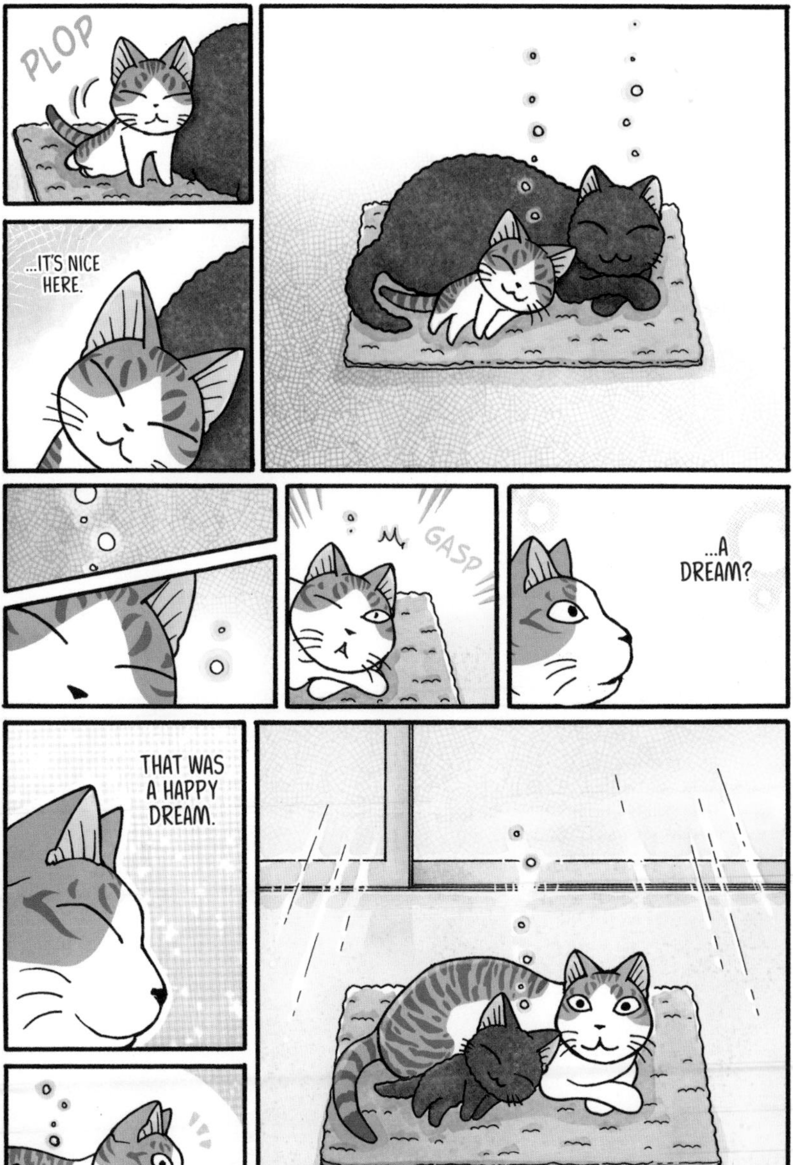
PLOP
...IT'S NICE HERE.
GASP
...A DREAM?
THAT WAS A HAPPY DREAM.

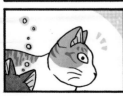

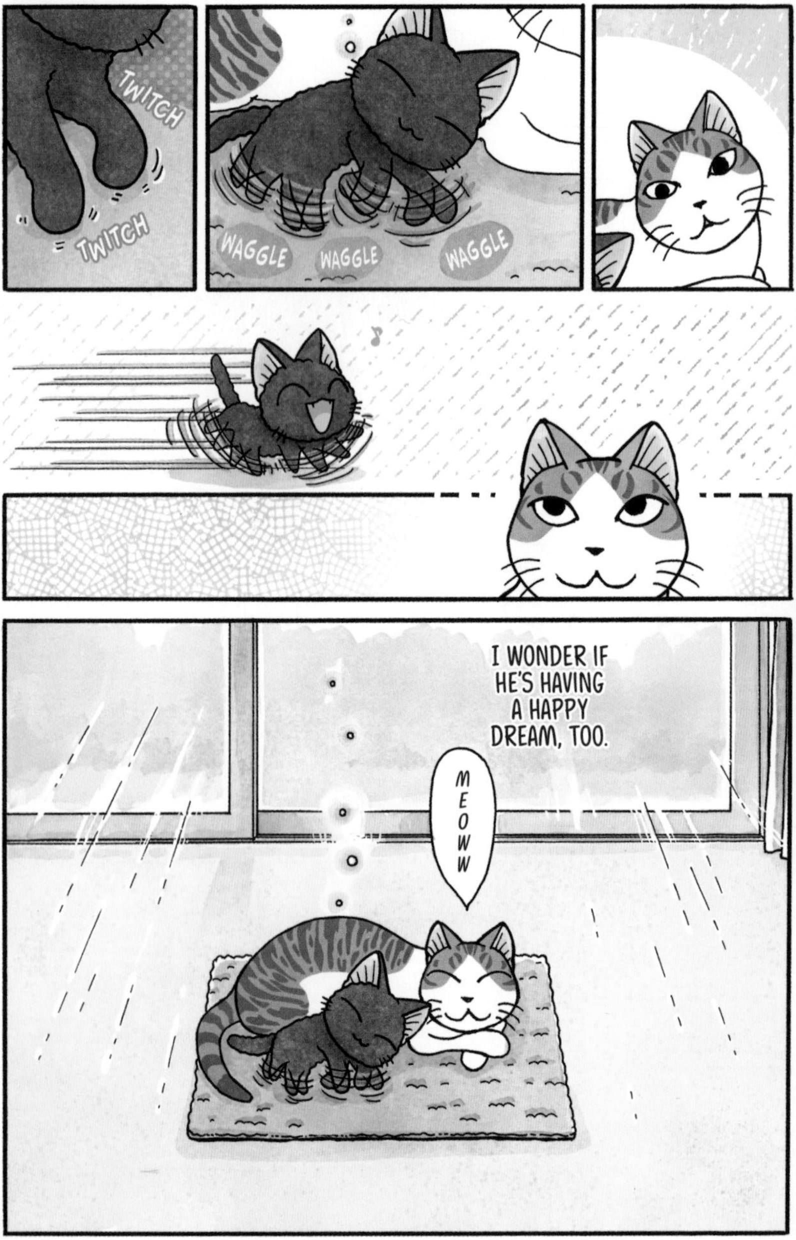
TWITCH
TWITCH
WAGGLE
WAGGLE
WAGGLE
I WONDER IF HE'S HAVING A HAPPY DREAM, TOO.
MEOWW

CHAPTER 50 Cherry Blossoms for Tai-chan

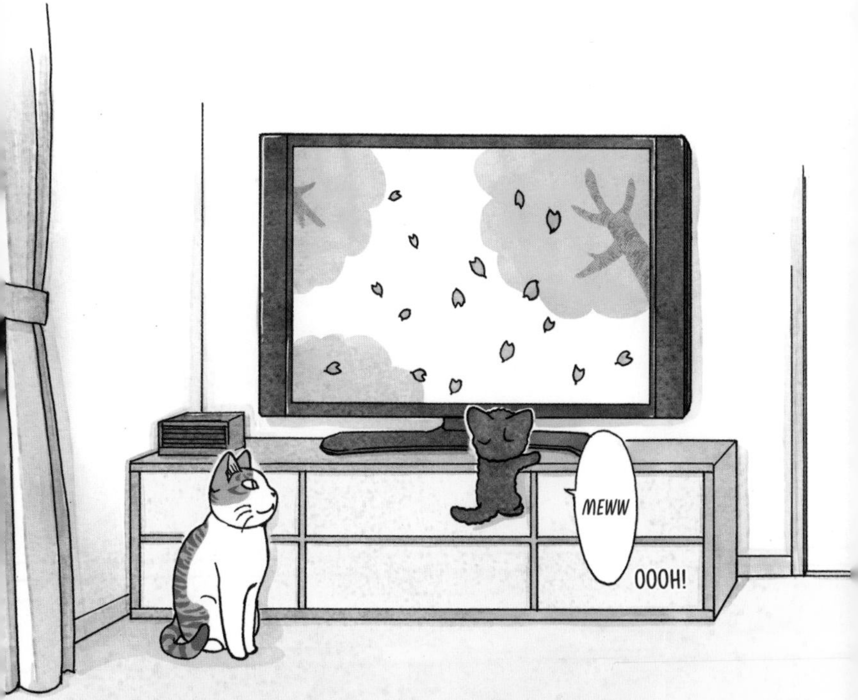
MEWW
OOOH!

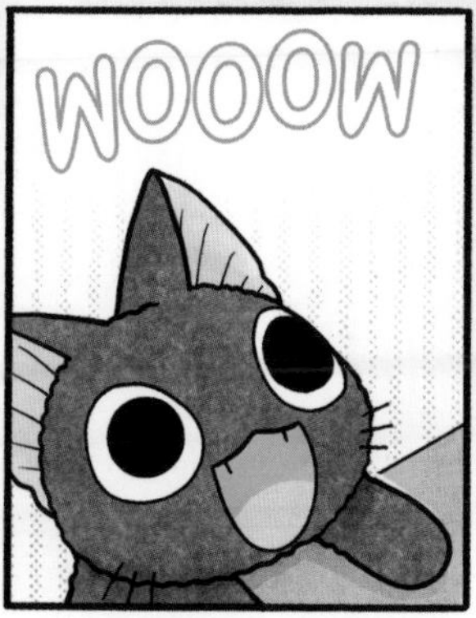
WOOOW

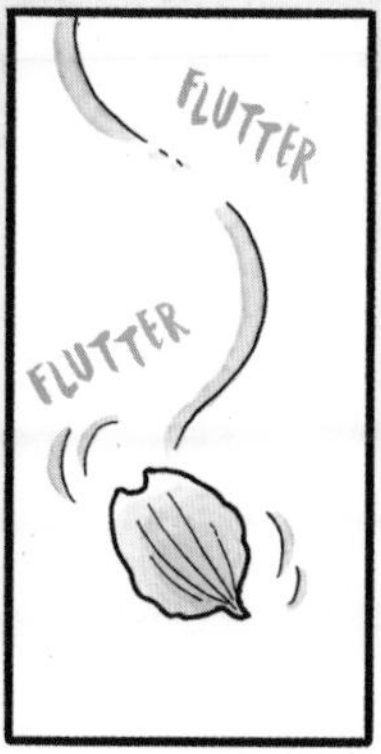
FLUTTER
FLUTTER

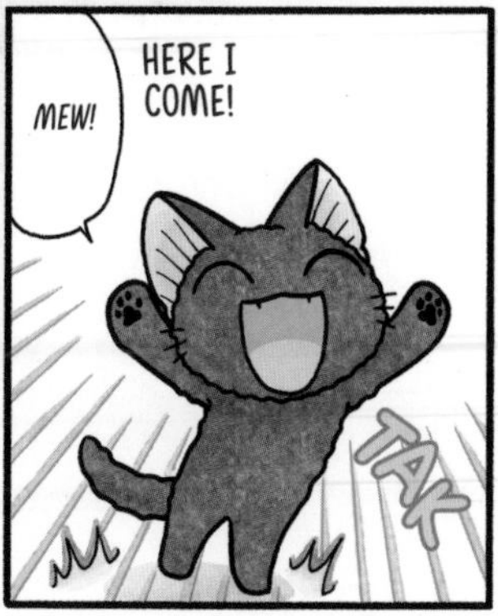
MEW!
HERE I COME!
TAK

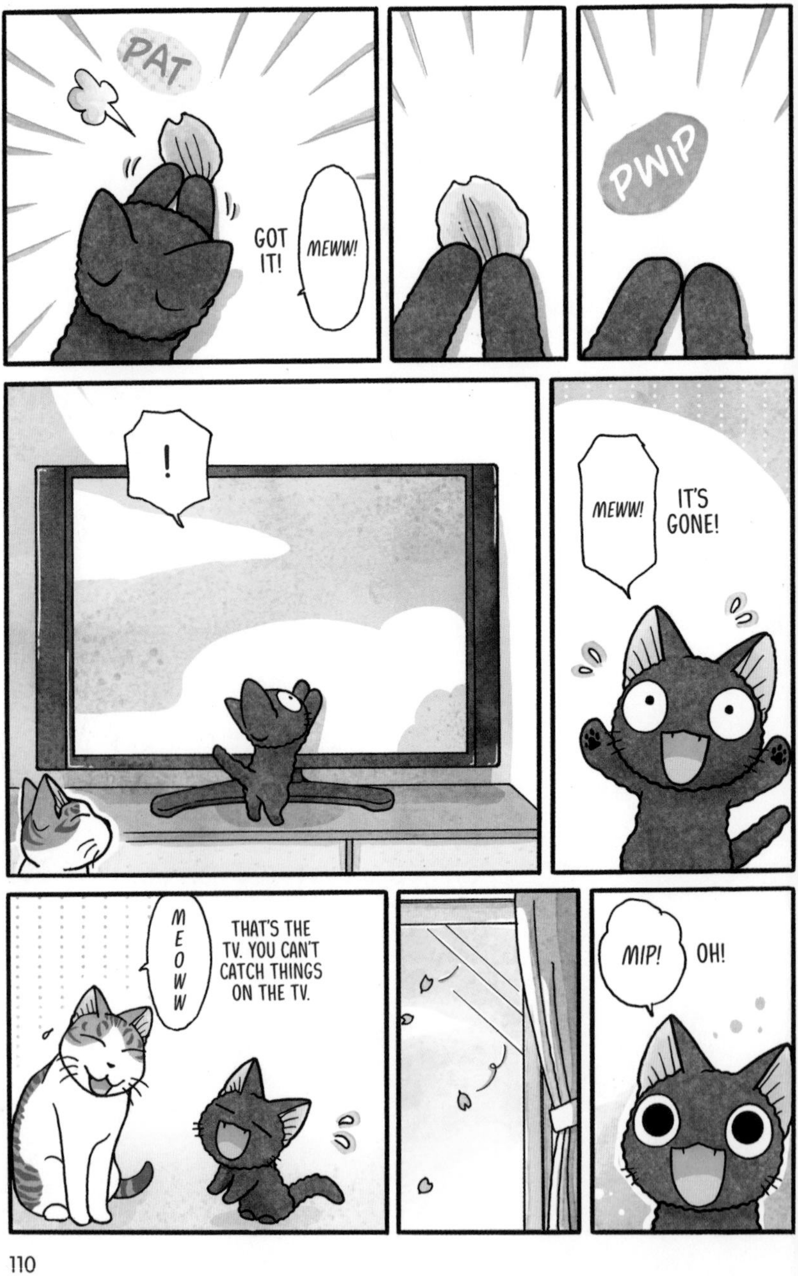
PAT
GOT IT!
MEWW!
PWIP
!
MEWW!
IT'S GONE!
MEOWW
THAT'S THE TV. YOU CAN'T CATCH THINGS ON THE TV.
MIP!
OH!

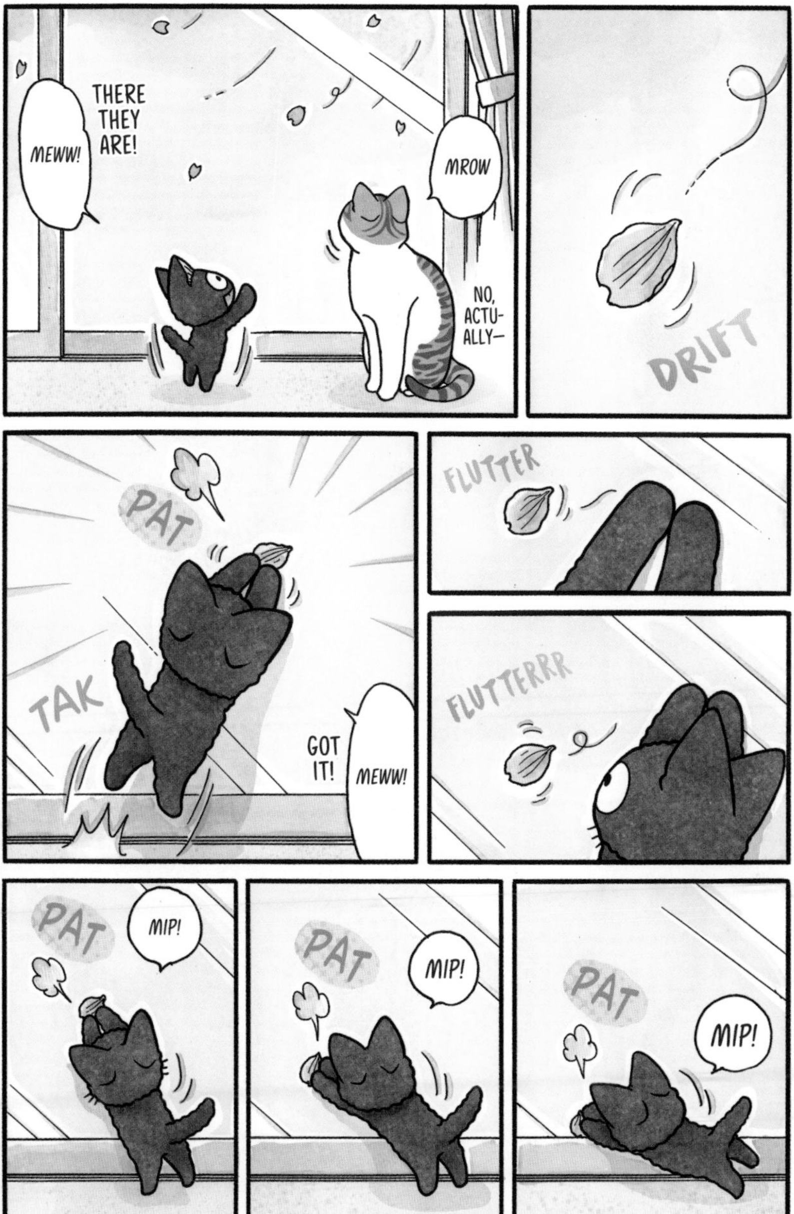
MEWW!
THERE THEY ARE!
MROW
NO, ACTU-ALLY—
DRIFT
PAT
TAK
GOT IT!
MEWW!
FLUTTER
FLUTTERRR
PAT
MIP!
PAT
MIP!
PAT
MIP!

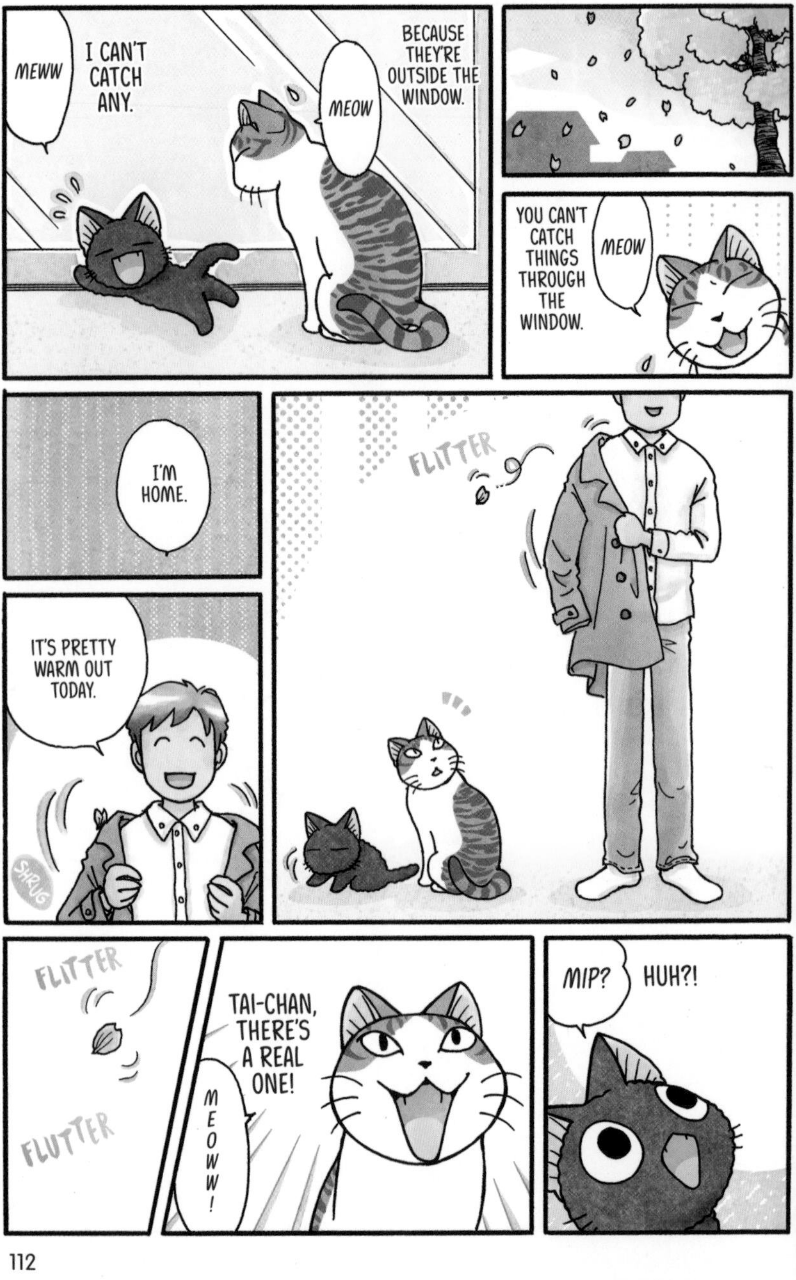
MEWW
I CAN'T CATCH ANY.
MEOW
BECAUSE THEY'RE OUTSIDE THE WINDOW.
YOU CAN'T CATCH THINGS THROUGH THE WINDOW.
MEOW
I'M HOME.
IT'S PRETTY WARM OUT TODAY.
SHRUG
FLITTER
FLITTER
FLUTTER
TAI-CHAN, THERE'S A REAL ONE!
MEOWW!
MIP?
HUH?!

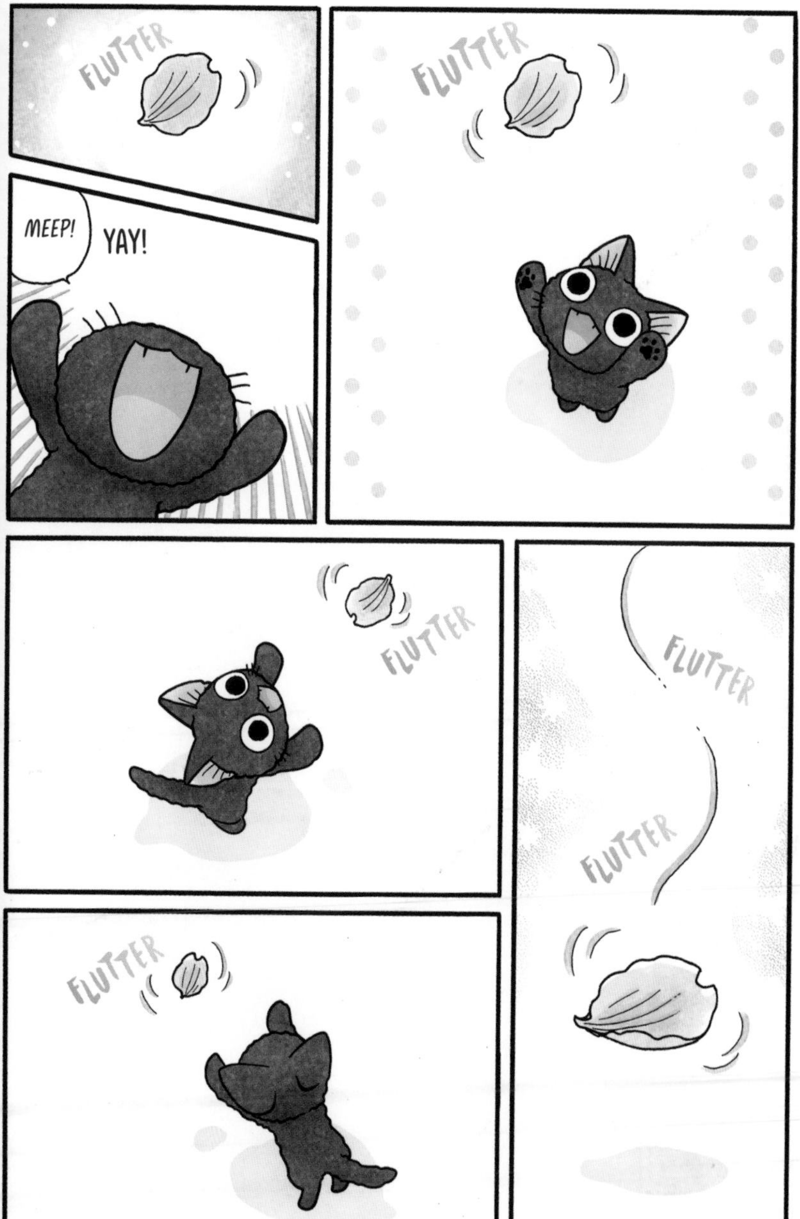
FLUTTER
MEEP!
YAY!
FLUTTER
FLUTTER
FLUTTER
FLUTTER
FLUTTER

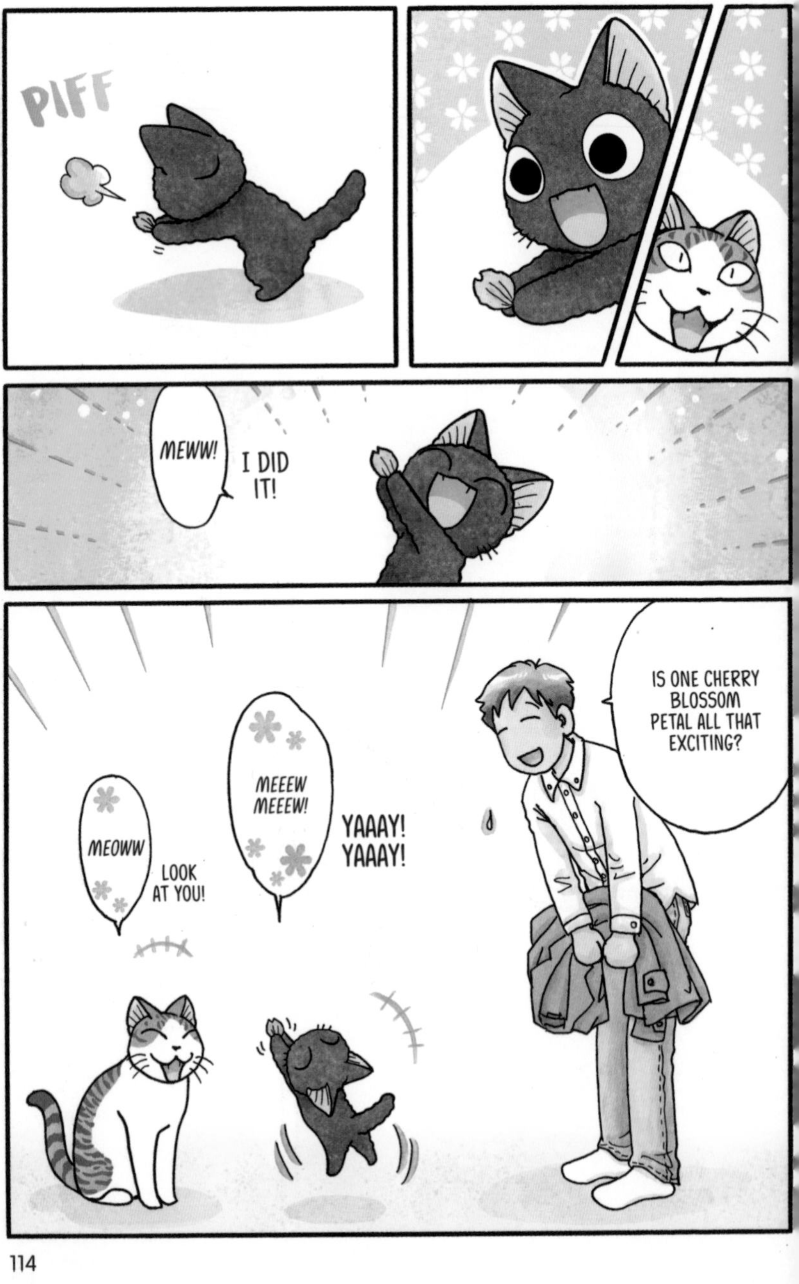
PIFF
MEWW!
I DID IT!
MEOWW
LOOK AT YOU!
MEEEW MEEEW!
YAAAY! YAAAY!
IS ONE CHERRY BLOSSOM PETAL ALL THAT EXCITING?

CHAPTER 51 Something's Not Right?!

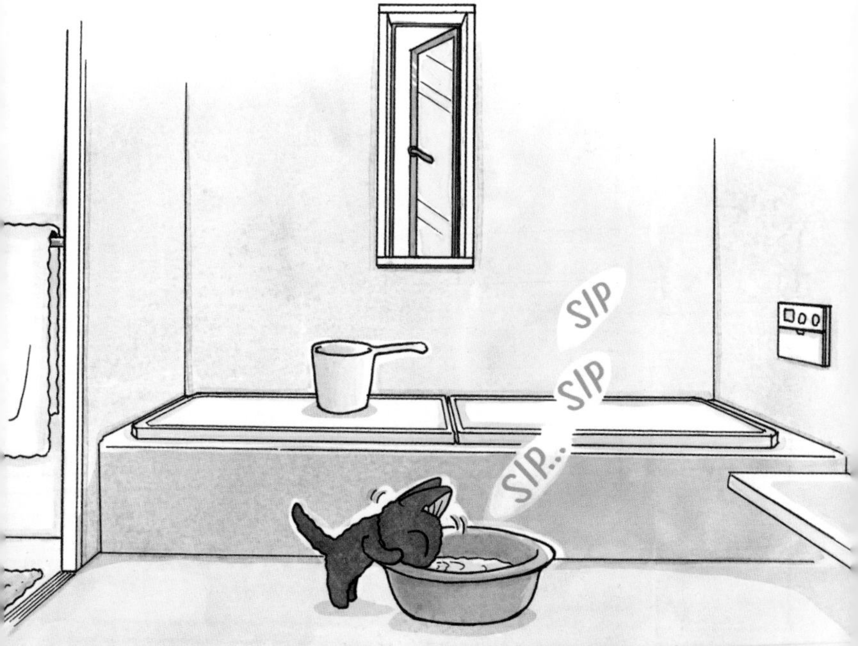
SIP
SIP
SIP...

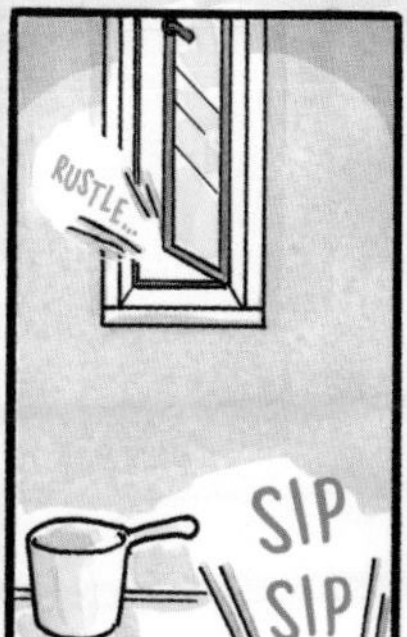
RUSTLE...
SIP
SIP

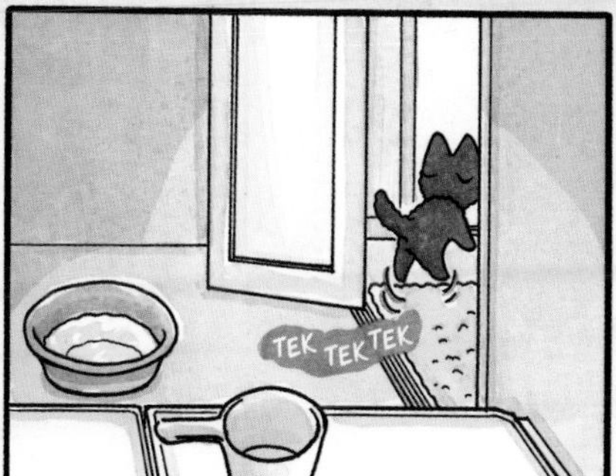
TEK TEK TEK

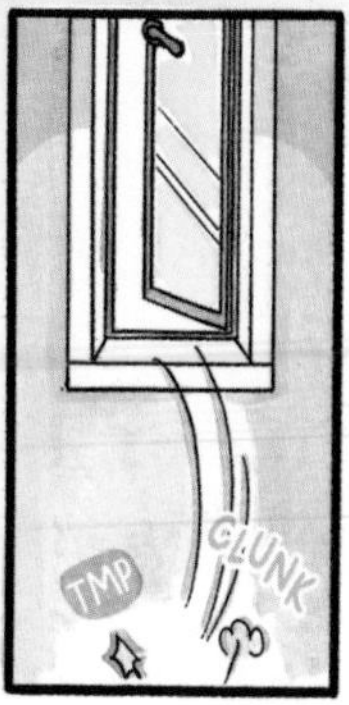
TMP
CLUNK

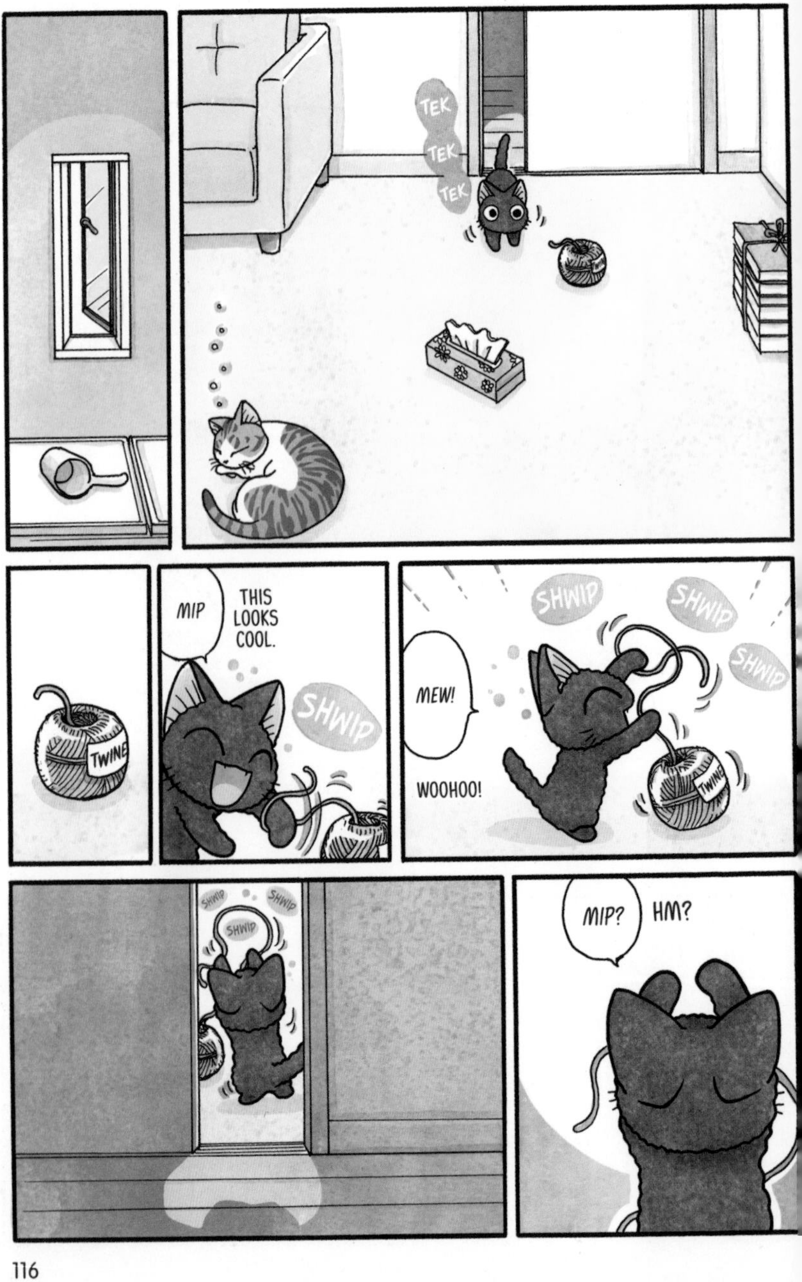
TEK
TEK
TEK
MIP
THIS LOOKS COOL.
SHWIP
SHWIP
SHWIP
SHWIP
MEW!
WOOHOO!
SHWIP
SHWIP
SHWIP
MIP?
HM?

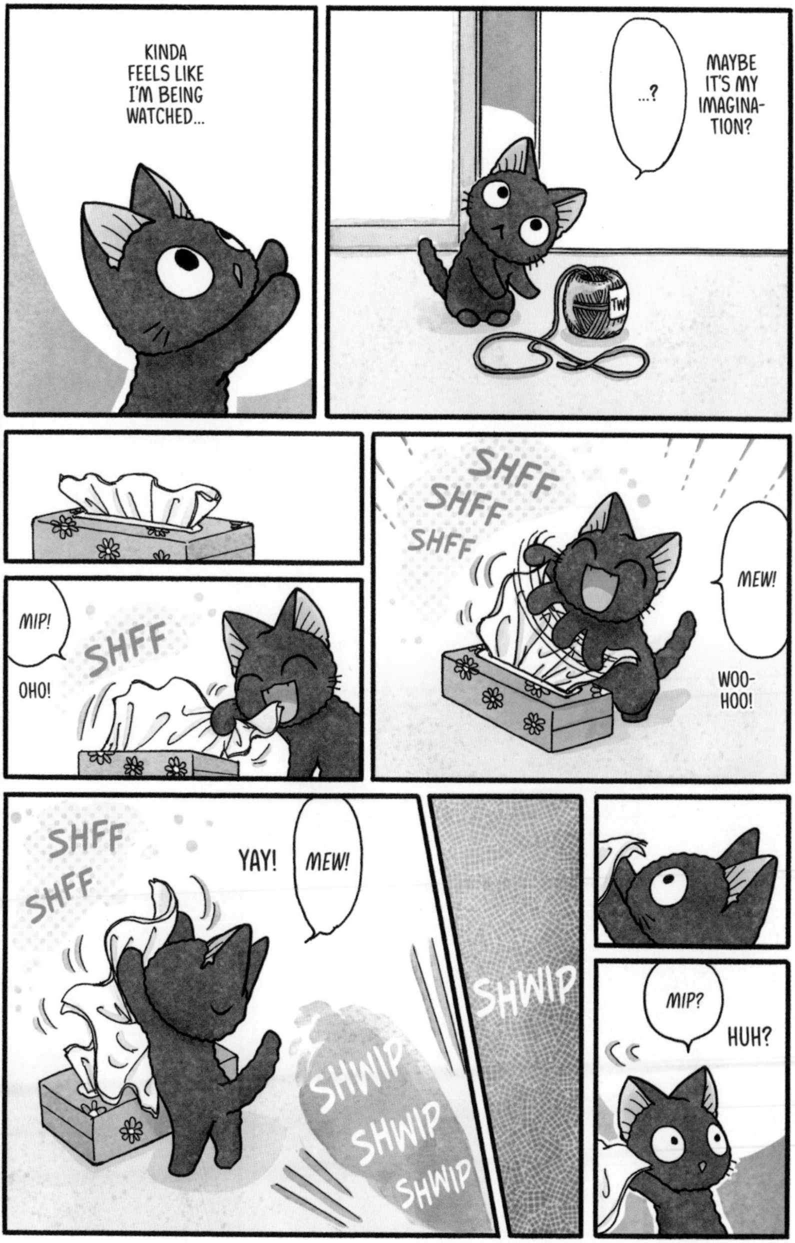
KINDA FEELS LIKE I'M BEING WATCHED...
...?
MAYBE IT'S MY IMAGINA-TION?
MIP!
SHFF
OHO!
SHFF SHFF SHFF
MEW!
WOO-HOO!
SHFF SHFF
YAY!
MEW!
SHWIP SHWIP SHWIP
SHWIP
MIP?
HUH?

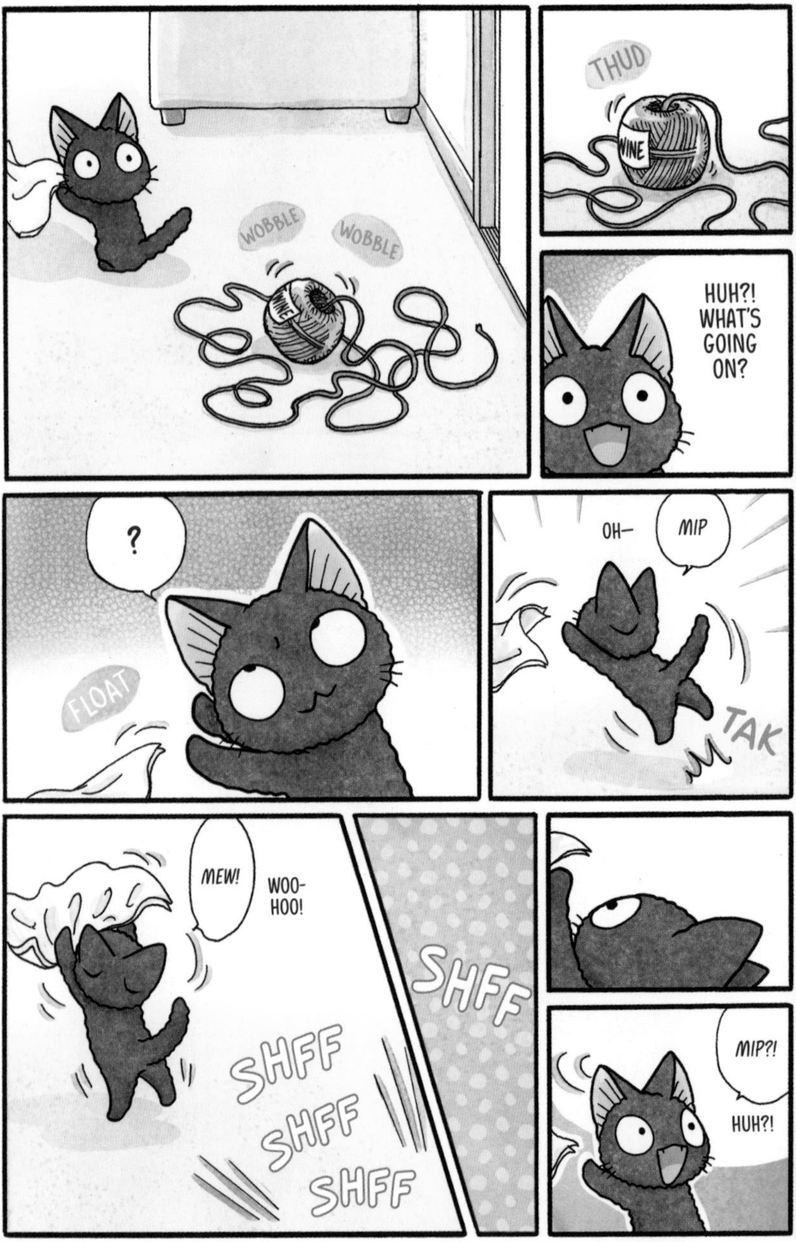
WOBBLE
WOBBLE
THUD
WINE
HUH?! WHAT'S GOING ON?
?
FLOAT
OH—
MIP
TAK
MEW!
WOO-HOO!
SHFF
SHFF
SHFF
SHFF
MIP?!
HUH?!

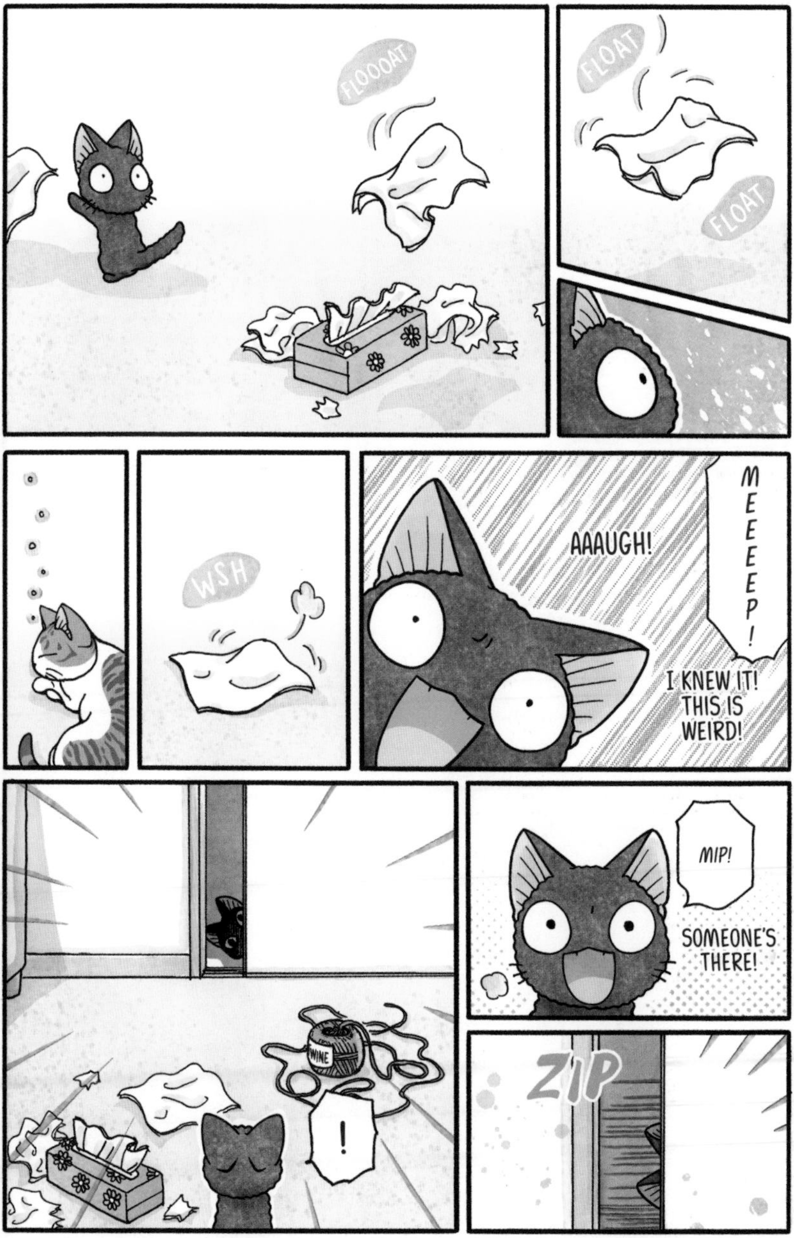
FLOOOAT
FLOAT
FLOAT
WSH
AAAUGH!
MEEEEEP!
I KNEW IT! THIS IS WEIRD!
!
MIP!
SOMEONE'S THERE!
ZIP

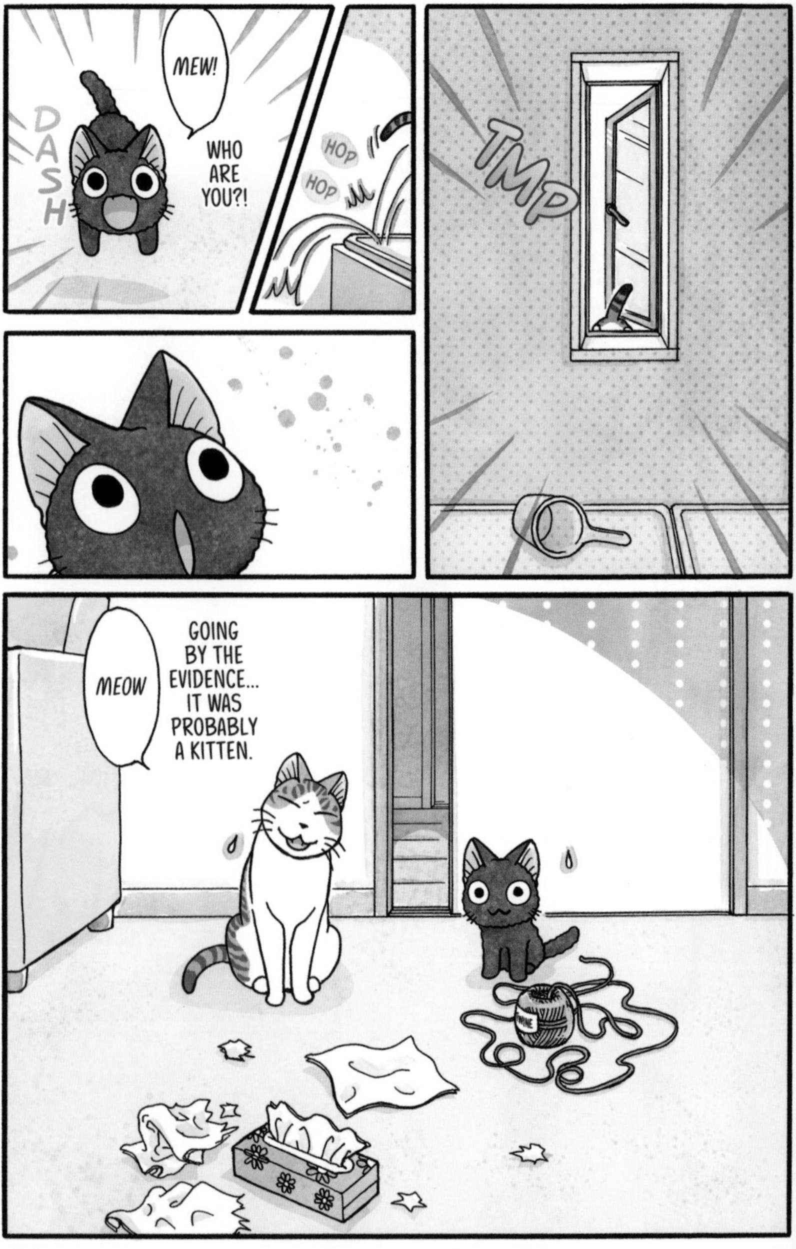
DASH
MEW!
WHO ARE YOU?!
HOP
HOP
TMP
MEOW
GOING BY THE EVIDENCE... IT WAS PROBABLY A KITTEN.
TWINE

TO BE CONTINUED IN *SUE & TAI-CHAN* 4!

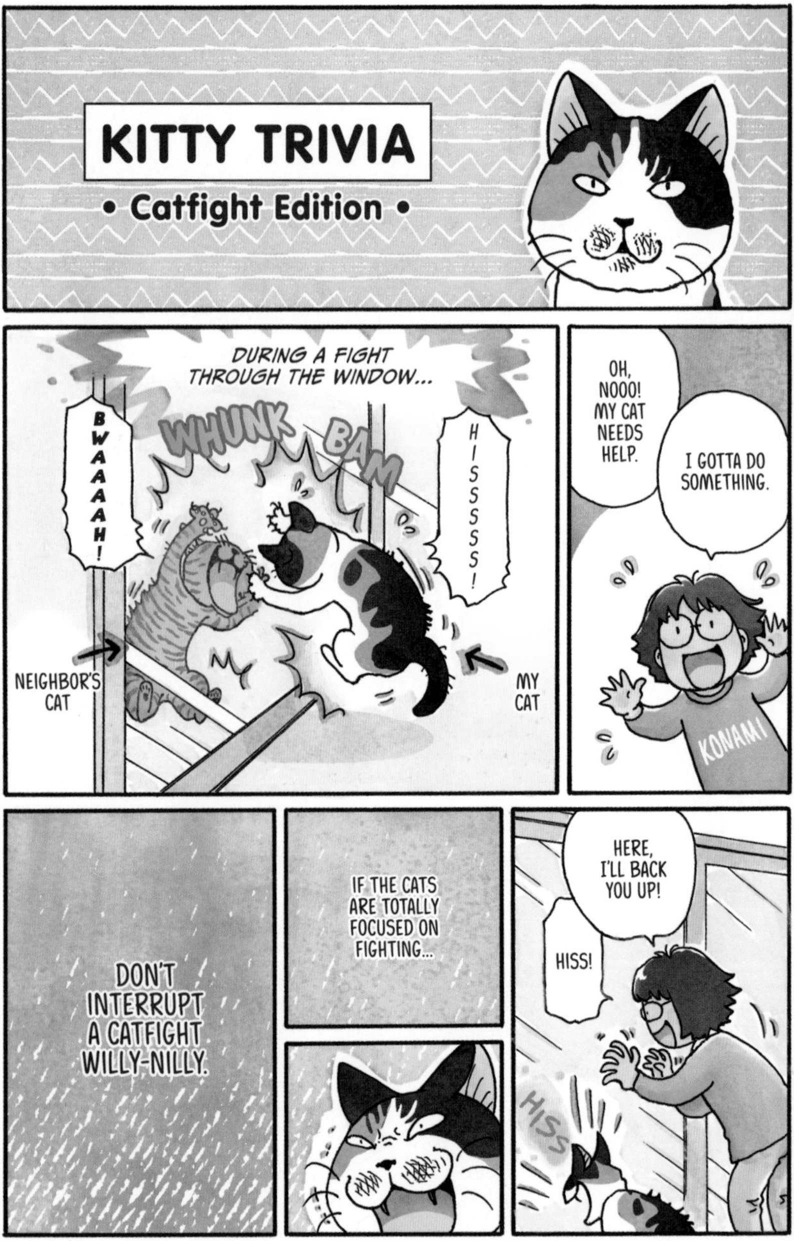
KITTY TRIVIA
• Catfight Edition •
DURING A FIGHT THROUGH THE WINDOW...
WHUNK
BAM
BWAAAAAH!
HISSSSS!
NEIGHBOR'S CAT
MY CAT
OH, NOOO! MY CAT NEEDS HELP.
I GOTTA DO SOMETHING.
KONAMI
DON'T INTERRUPT A CATFIGHT WILLY-NILLY.
IF THE CATS ARE TOTALLY FOCUSED ON FIGHTING...
HERE, I'LL BACK YOU UP!
HISS!
HISS

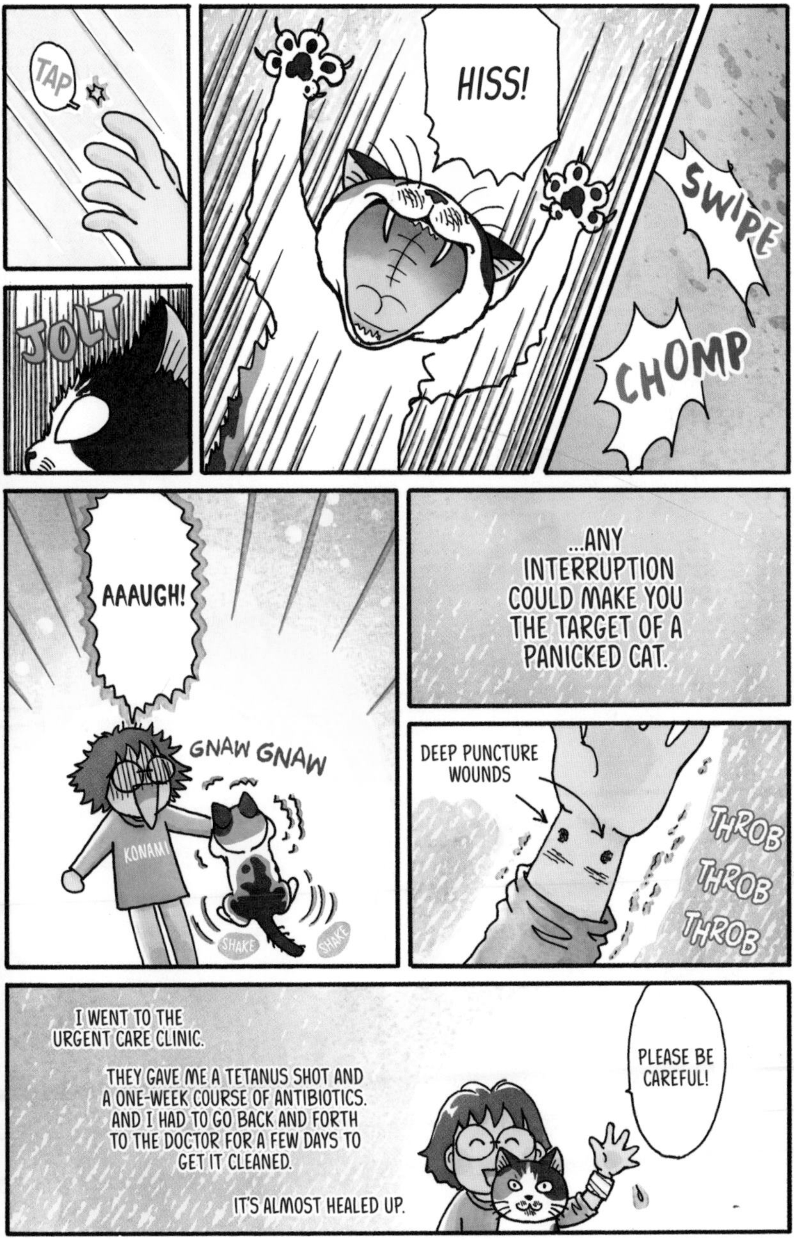
TAP
HISS!
SWIPE
JOLT
CHOMP
AAAUGH!
GNAW GNAW
SHAKE
SHAKE
...ANY INTERRUPTION COULD MAKE YOU THE TARGET OF A PANICKED CAT.
DEEP PUNCTURE WOUNDS
THROB
THROB
THROB
I WENT TO THE URGENT CARE CLINIC.
THEY GAVE ME A TETANUS SHOT AND A ONE-WEEK COURSE OF ANTIBIOTICS. AND I HAD TO GO BACK AND FORTH TO THE DOCTOR FOR A FEW DAYS TO GET IT CLEANED.
IT'S ALMOST HEALED UP.
PLEASE BE CAREFUL!

WHAT'S THAT?

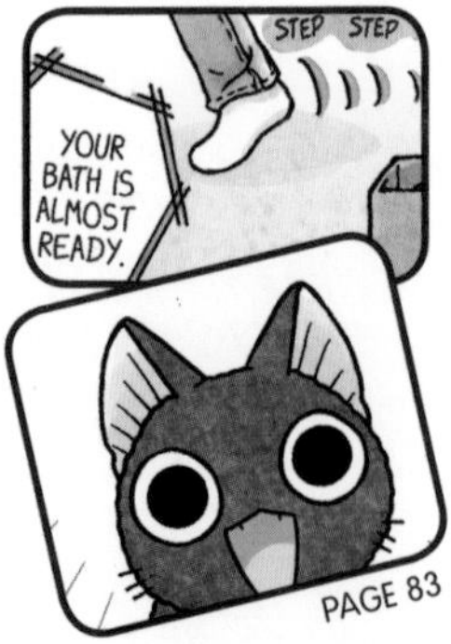
STEP STEP
YOUR BATH IS ALMOST READY.
PAGE 83

This voice is coming from **Natsuki's bathtub**!

Taking baths is very common in Japan, and technology has evolved to make the process of heating one a snap. With Natsuki's type of tub, you just fill it up and set the temperature, and a computer tells you when it's warmed up.

These lacquered trays contain **osechi,** traditional Japanese cuisine prepared specially for New Year's Day.

The feast features a luxurious array of colorful foods, each symbolizing a well-wish for the coming year—not exactly kitty chow!

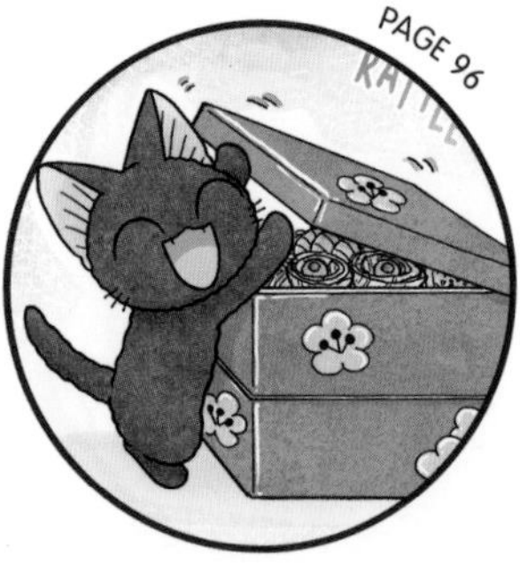
PAGE 96
RATTLE

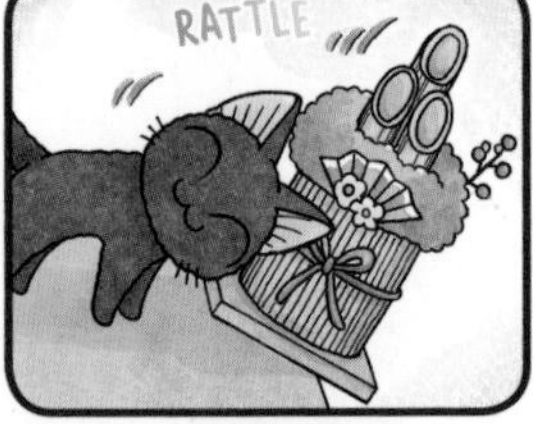
RATTLE

PAGE 97

This New Year decoration is called **kadomatsu,** or "gate pine." It serves to welcome spirits of ancestors and gods.

With pine foliage and bamboo stems, it can be quite heavy...

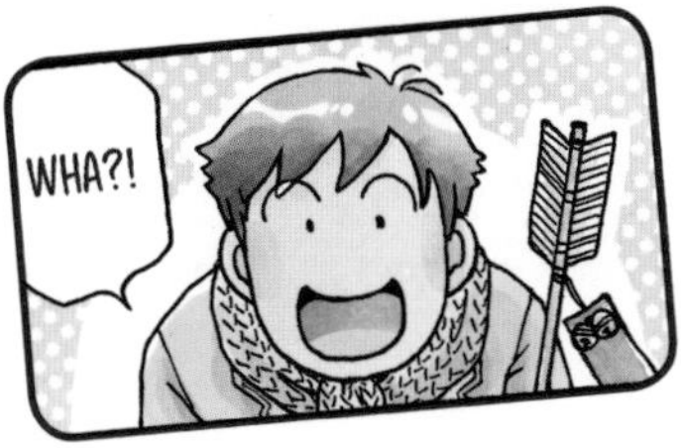
WHA?!

PAGE 100

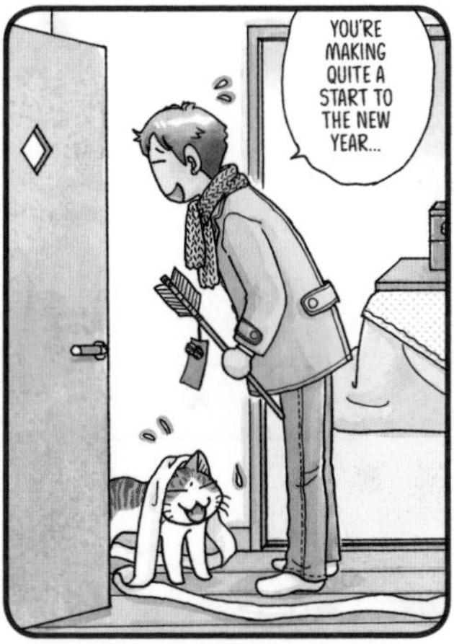
YOU'RE MAKING QUITE A START TO THE NEW YEAR...

Natsuki is holding a **hamaya,** literally "demon-breaking arrow." It is customary for people in Japan to visit a Shinto shrine on New Year's Day to offer prayers for good fortune in the new year.

Shrines often provide or sell hamaya as good-luck charms to ward off evil.

Honorifics Review

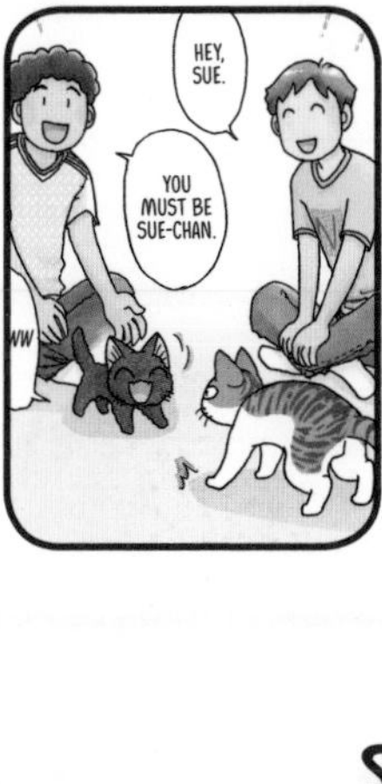
HEY, SUE.
YOU MUST BE SUE-CHAN.

-chan is a cutesy honorific for showing affection, like saying "Little Tai."

-san is a polite honorific for showing respect, like "Mr.", "Ms.", or "Mx."

Not using an honorific means you must be *very* close to someone!

Next Volume

The kitten who was peeking in… returns!

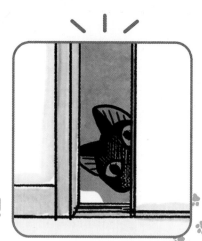

And this time—

What happens when Tai-chan tries to catch the culprit—?

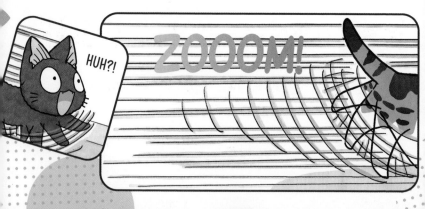

Playful Tai-chan...

...is about to get played!

One more friend joins the fun—

Demon?!

THWAP!

Angel?!

POSE!

It's cuteness cubed!!!

An old cat and a young cat—the oddest but cutest pair!

Sue & Tai-chan 4

A Kodansha Comics Trade Paperback Original
Sue & Tai-chan 3 copyright © 2019 Konami Kanata
English translation copyright © 2021 Konami Kanata

Published in the United States by Kodansha Comics, an imprint of Kodansha USA Publishing, LLC, New York.

Publication rights for this English edition arranged through Kodansha Ltd., Tokyo.

First published in Japan in 2019 by Kodansha Ltd., Tokyo.

ISBN 978-1-64651-071-9

Original cover design by Kohei Nawata Design Office

Printed in China.

www.kodanshacomics.com

9 8 7 6 5 4 3 2 1
Translation: Melissa Tanaka
Lettering: Phil Christie
Editing: Vanessa Tenazas
Kodansha Comics edition cover design by Phil Balsman

Publisher: Kiichiro Sugawara

Director of publishing services: Ben Applegate
Associate director of operations: Stephen Pakula
Publishing services managing editors: Noelle Webster, Alanna Ruse, Madison Salters
Assistant production managers: Emi Lotto, Angela Zurlo
Logo and character art ©Kodansha USA Publishing, LLC